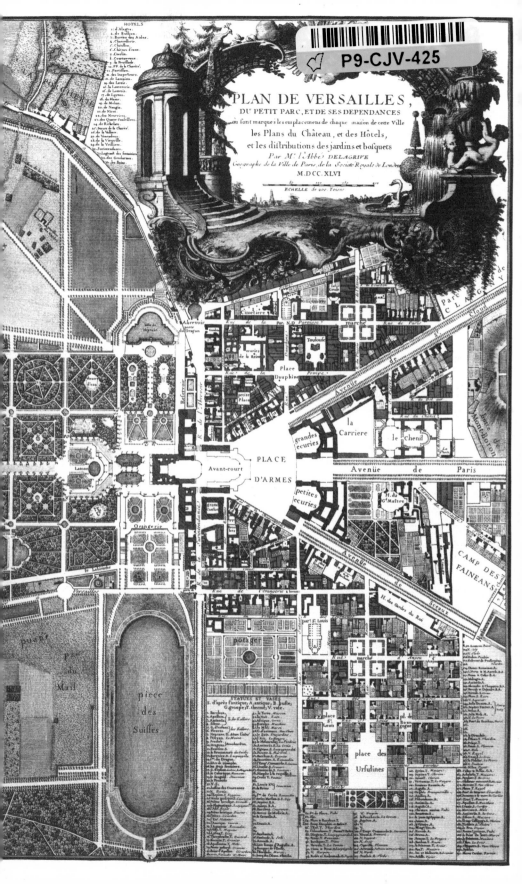

P9-CJV-425

# PLAN DE VERSAILLES,
## DU PETIT PARC, ET DE SES DEPENDANCES
où sont marqués les emplacemens de chaque maison de cette Ville
### les Plans du Château, et des Hôtels,
et les distributions des jardins et bosquets
*Par M. l'Abbé DELAGRIVE*
*Geographe de la Ville de Paris, de la Societé Royale de Londres*
M.DCC.XLVI

ECHELLE de 200. Toises

# VERSAILLES

# *Versailles*

## A BIOGRAPHY OF A PALACE

## *Tony Spawforth*

ST. MARTIN'S PRESS　🙟　NEW YORK

VERSAILLES. Copyright © 2008 by Tony Spawforth. All rights reserved. Printed in the United States of America. For information, address St. Martin's Press, 175 Fifth Avenue, New York, N.Y. 10010.

www.stmartins.com

Book design by Jonathan Bennett

The endpaper map, *Plan de Versailles* (1746) by Jean Delagrive, is used with permission from Historic Urban Plans, Inc., Ithaca, New York, U.S.A.

Library of Congress Cataloging-in-Publication Data

Spawforth, Antony.
    Versailles : a biography of a palace / Tony Spawforth.
        p.   cm.
    Includes bibliographical references.
    ISBN-13:  978-0-312-35785-6
    ISBN-10:  0-312-35785-0
    1.  Château de Versailles (Versailles, France)—History.   2.  Versailles (France)—
Buildings, structures, etc.   3.  Monarchy—France—History.   4.  France—Court and
courtiers—History.   I. Title.
    DC801.V57S67   2008
    944'.3663—dc22                                                          2008024757

First Edition: October 2008

10   9   8   7   6   5   4   3   2   1

IN MEMORY OF

G. G. MEYNELL

# CONTENTS

# PREFACE

THIS BOOK is about the "real" Versailles: the historical reality behind a palace that achieved mythic stature almost as soon as it had been built. Versailles was once *"réal"* in a sense of a French word already antiquated when Versailles was being built: a royal palace, seat of what at the time (the later seventeenth and the eighteenth centuries) was the most charismatic monarchy in Europe. The atmosphere of legend around Versailles draws strength from the tragic ingredients of its royal story. A beautiful palace built by a proud king blazed with glory for a century. Then, abruptly, comeuppance arrived with a revolutionary mob that burst in and led off the king's hapless descendants to a gory death.

There are many books about the palace of Versailles written, like this one, for the general reader. Most belong on the architectural or horticultural shelves of a bookshop. *Versailles: A Biography of a Palace* aims at the gap left by the absence of an up-to-date account of the human and the historical story.

Versailles belonged to a particular moment in French history. It was conceived by the French monarchy as a solution to its political problems. In the end, the palace and what it represented added to those problems. This book is by no means a political history. But ponderings on the causes of the French Revolution are bound to lurk in the background.

Building-history, it is sometimes said, is boring history. To animate royal Versailles, this book draws on the writings—worldly, funny, sharp-eyed, and occasionally moving—of a handful of figures who knew the palace intimately. These accounts preserve the authentic voices of royal Versailles. They are mainly royalty and aristocrats because these were the people for whom Versailles was built. An upper servant is occasionally heard, such as Madame Campan, Marie-Antoinette's "first woman of the bedchamber." They all wrote in the idiom of a courtly civilization that the Revolution swept away so comprehensively that when the survivors returned from exile, they found not only French customs but also the French language transformed. We should not expect these voices to speak as we do. But we can still relish their ear for a good story.

Scribing courtiers like the duc de Saint-Simon or the duc de Luynes took for granted an in-depth knowledge of the palace. Versailles has since changed so much that most of its layout as a working palace remains a mystery to the visitor, who sees nothing of kitchens, stables, storerooms, nursery, lodgings for courtiers, quarters for servants, or ministries. This book places eyewitness anecdotes and reminiscences as precisely as possible. These bring to life for the reader, not only the famous spaces like the Hall of Mirrors or Louis XIV's bedchamber, but the byways of a complex once likened to a small town.

Versailles is an archaeological site. Today's visitor can walk once more on the winding paths in Marie-Antoinette's garden, which the spade has rescued from long oblivion. Another kind of excavator works with the original manuscripts from the archives of the vanished department of state known as the King's Buildings. The French monarchy built and maintained Versailles on strict bureaucratic principles. Original inventories, estimates, orders, invoices, correspondence with palace officials and lodgers, and architectural plans, all survive, most of them in France's Bibliothèque Nationale.

This Aladdin's cave offsets the fact that most of royal Versailles was destroyed in the nineteenth century. Versailles has had a longer life since its drastic conversion into a museum than as a palace. The documents allow vanished royal rooms to be reconstructed not just on paper but in reality. Down to the tiniest detail of daily life, they offer glimpses of how the palace functioned as a residence and seat of government. They shed light on royal secrets.

Consulting these papers, specialists painstakingly piece together the history of the building, the ceaseless repairs and alterations, and, in recent years, the history of the individual lodgings in what was once a vast apartment block. A general book on Versailles is based on this edifice of learning, one that continually grows. But "there still remains, as there will for a long time, much work to do . . ."[1] All books about Versailles, including this one, are perforce provisional.

One of the pleasures of writing about the palace is exploring Versailles itself. The town is a historical gem that most visitors to the palace ignore. Strolling its peaceful eighteenth-century streets at night, the crowds gone, past carriage gateways and street fountains dating back to royal times, is an atmospheric experience. I am hugely indebted to the expert tours and lectures organized by the Société des Amis de Versailles. These provide a uniquely informative way of exploring the town. Above all, they open doors in the palace that normally remain closed to the public.

This book rests on the labors of others. My huge debt to the specialist scholars who write about Versailles is clear from the citations. *Versailles: A Biography of a Palace* could not possibly have been written without the chain of learned books and articles that reaches back to Pierre de Nolhac, nineteenth-century founder of the French school of Versailles scholarship.

Other debts are also gratefully acknowledged here. At the Musée National des Châteaux de Versailles et du Trianon, I am obliged to M. Pierre Arizzoli-Clémentel, Directeur Général, along with M. Roland Bossard, for responding helpfully to my queries.

For help and support of various kinds, including many conversations from which I alone came away the wiser, I would like to thank Richard Archer, Simon Burrows, Jim Crow, Erica Davies, Christine Donougher, Dominique Florentin, Xavier Guégan, Rachel Hammersley, Marie-Christine Keith, Philip Mansel, Alex Martin, Cathy McClive, Elinor Meynell, the Estate of the late G. G. Meynell, Munro Price, François-Joseph Ruggiu, Rowland Smith, Lee Stannard, John Wakefield, and Imogen Walford.

I thank Yaniv Soha and his team at St. Martin's Press for their efficiency and exactitude, and Sheila C. Severn Newton for drawing the map and plan.

Finally, I owe particular debts to Roderick Conway Morris, who generously put time aside to read the book in draft, and to my agent, Andrew Lownie, who has given unwavering support to the project since its earliest stages.

TONY SPAWFORTH
*London, September 2007*

# PALACE OF VERSAILLES

### (FIRST FLOOR OF THE CENTRAL BLOCK UNDER LOUIS XVI)

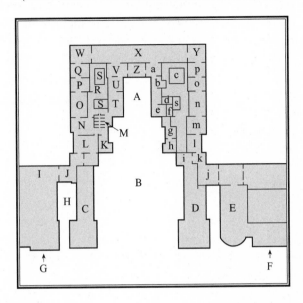

A. Marble Court
B. Royal Court
C. Old Wing
D. Gabriel Wing (formerly Government Wing)
E. Chapel
F. North Wing
G. South Wing
H. Princes' Court
I. Princes' Staircase
J. Comedy Room (ground floor)
K. Madame de Maintenon's corner study
L. Grand Guardroom
M. Queen's Staircase
N. Queen's guardroom
O. Queen's first antechamber
P. Room of the Nobles
Q. Queen's bedchamber
R. Queen's private rooms
S. Courtyard
T. King's guardroom
U. King's first antechamber

V. Antechamber of the Bull's Eye
W. Salon of Peace
X. Hall of Mirrors
Y. Salon of War
Z. Louis XIV's bedchamber
a. Official study or council room
b. Louis XV's bedchamber
c. Stag Court
d. King's private staircase
e. Louis XV's corner study
f. Louis XV's "back study"
g. Louis XVI's library
h. Dining room ("of the new rooms")
i. Louis XVI's gaming room
j. Salon of Hercules
k. Salon of Abundance
l. Salon of Venus
m. Salon of Diana
n. Salon of Mars
o. Salon of Apollo
p. Salon of Mercury

# The Palace and Its Dependencies in the Town

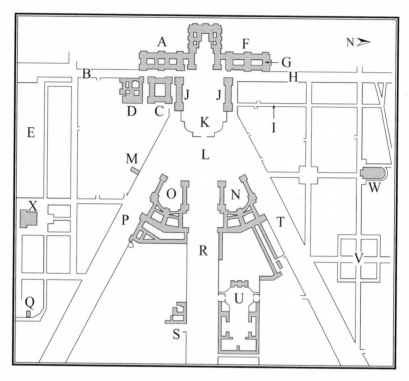

A. South Wing
B. Rue de la Surintendance
C. Grand Commons
D. Ministries of War and Foreign Affairs
E. Potager
F. North Wing
G. Opera
H. Rue des Réservoirs
I. Rue des Bons Enfants
J. Ministers' wings
K. Ministers' Court
L. Place d'Armes

M. Chancellery
N. Grand Stable
O. Small Stable
P. Avenue de Sceaux
Q. No. 4, Rue Mériadec
R. Avenue de Paris
S. Hôtel of the Grand Master
T. Avenue de Saint Cloud
U. Kennel
V. Town market
W. Parish church of Nôtre Dame
X. Parish church of Saint Louis

# VERSAILLES

# I.

# Builders of the Labyrinth

O N L Y  A N aerial viewpoint starts to do justice to the size of Versailles. Even then, it takes one of the delicate eighteenth-century plans of Versailles, with the royal domain delineated in a faded pink, to grasp that the palace, with its multiple wings and hidden courts, was the focus of a much larger complex scattered around the town of Versailles.

Inmates likened royal Versailles to a labyrinth: a maze of galleries, corridors, staircases, and apartments.[1] In 1838 William Talmadge, a visitor from England, confessed: "The place is vast beyond all English imagination: one can hardly conceive it according to its purpose as a place of residence."[2]

A confusing number of French kings called Louis had a hand in the building we see today. This chapter tells the chronological story of the creation of Versailles from Louis XIII's first house on the site in 1623 to Louis XVI's ambitious rebuilding plans on the eve of the French Revolution, which broke out in 1789, when Versailles ceased to be a royal residence.

When Louis XIII succeeded as French king in 1610, Versailles was a prosperous hamlet set in an upland valley as yet only partially cleared for cultivation. The name of the place, formed on the Latin word *vertere*, meaning to turn the soil, immortalizes the hard grind of the medieval farmers who first won a way of life here from primal woodland. In the years around 1600 a windmill topped the knoll on which the palace later rose. Two hundred or so souls made up the population.

As the crow flies, Versailles is twelve miles west of Paris. When Louis XIV moved the seat of the monarchy to Versailles in 1682, the Paris-Versailles road became one of the busiest arteries in Europe, even during the night, when, by the late eighteenth century, streetlights lit the paved surface all the way from the palace to the Paris tollgate. But, in the first instance, the sleepy village of the early seventeenth century owed its new destiny not to the nearby capital, but to the royal residence of Saint-Germain-en-Laye, six miles due north. This redbrick Renaissance château, sited on high ground above the River Seine, commands sensational views of the Paris basin—much better ones, critics would later say, than those of Louis XIV's Versailles.

Henri IV, Louis XIV's grandfather and first king of the Bourbon line of the French royal house, liked this old royal residence, updating it with new royal quarters and terraced gardens running down to the river. Saint-Germain remained a favorite residence of the new dynasty for most of the seventeenth century. In 1638 Louis XIII's queen, Anne of Austria, gave birth there to the future Louis XIV.

Like all French royalty, the Bourbon kings had hunting in their blood. The chief attraction of Saint-Germain, apart from the view, was the stag. The virility and sheer beauty of this monarch of the French forests had made it a badge of royalty since time immemorial. An indefatigable animal, it was the stag that first led Henri IV from Saint-Germain to Versailles. His son and successor, Louis XIII, was only ten when he too first found himself at Versailles in pursuit of his quarry.

No one knows precisely why, but the young Louis XIII took a fancy to the spot. He started to buy up land here for a game reserve. This kind of human intervention was needed because hunting on the Bourbon scale upset the balance of nature. In the sixteen years from 1775 to 1791, Louis XIII's descendant, Louis XVI, killed 1,274 stags. Sustaining this level of slaughter were the gamekeepers whose animal husbandry kept the royal forests well stocked. At Versailles, Louis XIII's reserve is remembered in the quarter of the modern town still called *Parc-aux-Cerfs* (Stag Park).

In 1623, when he was twenty-two, Louis XIII decided to commission a simple country house on the site of the future palace. He intended it for short stays with a small entourage only. He began buying up more local land, including in due course the seigneury, or feudal estate, of Versailles, acquired from the noble family of the Gondi. As lord of Versailles, Louis now enjoyed rights of high and low justice over the local peasantry. No less important, he could now hunt at will over the seigneurial land.

Seven years passed before the king, now aged thirty, plucked up enough nerve to exile his politically overbearing mother, Marie de' Medici. Sharing the reins of power with the formidable Richelieu, his chief minister, he now felt confident enough to rebuild his house as a medium-sized country château in the French style of the day. Walls of creamy stone rose, framing decorative panels of red bricks—in fact, simulated in painted plaster—and roofs tiled with blue slate; the color scheme echoed, deliberately one supposes, the red, white, and blue livery of the king's household. Philibert Le Roy, the architect, added the seigneurial touch of a dry moat. This was not just symbolic; in what was then countryside, the house and its contents needed protection when the monarch was absent.

Louis XIII's rooms are now known mainly from inventories of their contents. As was customary, they were on the first, or noble, floor. They included accommodations for his queen on the south side, with his on the north. This basic disposition of the royal quarters was preserved throughout the history of Versailles as a royal residence. It is ironic, then, that Anne of Austria never stayed the night. Not only was the marriage troubled, but Louis XIII was far from gregarious. He preferred mainly male cronies and disliked the prospect of an invasion of his retreat by the "great number of women" forming Anne's household: they would "spoil everything," as he once told Richelieu. In this respect as in others, his son could not have been more different.

Louis XIII went on buying up local land. By the time he died, he had laid out a modest park to the west of his château. The estate now included the stag park, outbuildings for kitchens, stables, and kennels, and a covered tennis court. Everything was inherited by his elder son and successor, the four-year-old Louis XIV.[3]

The future Louis XIV was first brought to Versailles at the age of three.[4] Once he was old enough to hunt from Saint-Germain, he came to know the place better. But he took no special interest in his father's retreat until 1661, when he was in his twenty-third year and had been king for eighteen years. Then he began to plough funds into what, in hindsight, became a never-ending series of costly transformations continuing until his death.

This sudden change of attitude toward Versailles is often linked with his amorous needs. At the time he was embarked on an adulterous affair with Louise de La Vallière, a young noblewoman of the court. The memoirist Saint-Simon records how Louis used to bring her to Versailles from Saint-Germain for discreet trysts out of sight of the queen and queen mother. But France and Europe were beginning to learn that Louis XIV was a king to his fingertips. At Versailles, reasons of state quickly weighed in as well.

In his twenties Louis redecorated the interior of his father's château and rearranged the approach on the Paris side. He built new kitchens and stables. But his great passion at this time was the park. In concert with the gardener and designer André Le Nôtre, he began to invest large sums in an extremely ambitious redesign and enlargement of the old grounds, gradually extending them with more land purchases until they reached the western horizon.

Le Nôtre's achievement is difficult to appreciate because we can no longer see the terrain as it was when he set to work. He was a landscape gardener on a grand scale. He turned ponds and streams into ornamental sheets of water. He shifted vast amounts of soil to create a terrace in front of the château, where the ground naturally slopes. He imported mature trees and relocated the villages that blocked his new vistas.

In the taste of the day, he regimented nature. Trees and shrubs were clipped and sheared. He divided the terrain into bosquets or groves with geometric shapes. With the help of artists, architects, and fountain makers he decorated these like outdoor rooms. Astonishing waterworks and kinked paths revealing hidden surprises were a feature of this young king's garden. In the royal idiom of the age, Louis and his artists used sculpture, water, and orientation to liken the nature of his rule to the daily passage of the life-giving sun.

The general aim was to impress, and Louis XIV succeeded. By 1668 the modest country house was incongruously married to the most talked-about grounds in France. Called a "theater king" by contemporaries, Louis was aided in this purpose by his innate showman's flair.

He spread word of his works at Versailles by means of a series of nocturnal fêtes in the grounds, the first in 1664, a second in 1668, and a third in 1674. He invited the nobility, bourgeois Parisians, provincial notables, and ambassadors and other distinguished foreigners, like the duke of Monmouth, a bastard of Charles II of England.

He relied on a team of specialists—from actors, playwrights, musicians, artists, and set builders to dressmakers, flower arrangers, and pyrotechnists—all under the general direction of a gifted impresario. Carlo Vigarani hailed from the country of origin of this kind of court spectacular, imported to France along with Medici queens from sixteenth-century Italy.

The young king sought to entertain his entourage and to charm his mistresses. But—and this is true of Louis XIV and Versailles in general—he always had politics in view. He used the fêtes to raise his profile both in France and abroad by showing off his comely person (he took part in fancy dress), his good taste, and his resources. His vehicle for this rather modern attitude to self-promotion was a publicity machine that made liberal use of the engraver's skill.

Its director in all but name was Jean-Baptiste Colbert, the key organizer of "project Versailles" behind the scenes. Thanks to his industry, loyalty, and talents, this older man had been promoted by the young Louis XIV from clerk to the most powerful positions in the government. He ended up combining the finance ministry, which provided the funds, with oversight of the "Buildings, Arts, Tapestries, and Manufactories of France": in effect, an arts minister.

Colbert hired the best artists to engrave the highlights of the royal fêtes—the theatricals, fireworks, balls, and banquets. At a leisurely pace, in a world that moved more slowly than today's, he had these engravings made up into collections bound in calf or morocco. In the 1670s he gave these away by the hundreds to the ambassadors, who were encouraged in turn to show them around in their home capitals. As word spread, overseas sightseers were drawn to Versailles, like the English architect Christopher Wren, an early visitor in 1665. Louis had succeeded in using the arts to get himself talked about.

By 1668, when he had just turned thirty, Louis had won his first war, wresting Lille from his wife's family, the Spanish Habsburgs. Flushed with success, he decided to turn his attention from the gardens of Versailles to the house. This was too small to be much more than a backdrop to outdoor activities. But the ephemeral theaters and ballrooms repeatedly erected for the garden fêtes were wasteful, and these festivities always ran the risk of bad weather. Louis now wanted to build a permanent theater and ballroom at Versailles. Not for the last time in the history of the extravagant palace, expensive new buildings could be claimed as an economy.

At first Louis planned to preserve the original château at the center of his enlargements. But in June 1669, with work already under way, he decided on a far more ambitious upgrade of Versailles into a center of government. He now envisaged the ministers working with him at Versailles, just as they already followed him from Paris to Saint-Germain and to Fontainebleau, the other big royal palace in the vicinity of the capital.

Inspired by this vision, Louis announced his intention to demolish his father's château. He wanted to build huge wings to the north and south to house a ballroom, theater, and lodgings for the courtiers of the household: those with a right to board and lodging under the royal roof. Attracting these great nobles into his permanent entourage was already a key concern for the young Louis. As early as 1663, he was nagging Colbert about their accommodations. Stories of bad-tempered grandees dining in "holes"—a reference to the inns of Versailles—and sleeping in their coaches during the fêtes of 1664 and 1668 were not the best way of tempting French nobles out to Versailles.

A tussle now ensued between Colbert and his master. Each had his own ideas for how France's king should be housed. The powerful arts minister would have preferred to see the king finish his improvements to the Louvre, the Parisian palace that all Frenchmen thought of as the traditional seat of the monarchy. The two men eventually compromised. For the time being the king dropped his talk of demolition and of wings. But he had his way in building something grand and majestic at Versailles.

The architect Louis Le Vau drew up new plans for what became known as the Envelope. His new extension literally enveloped the old château on three sides; the gaps between the new and old buildings created inner courtyards for use by servants. The new façades were built of bright, creamy stone and decorated with Ionic columns in the Italian manner. The second, or attic, story was topped by a balustrade masking a flat roof.

This upper story would go some way to satisfy the king's wish to house his courtiers. Traces remain of the original décor of the attic rooms. They had painted ceilings—a prestigious feature in this period—and sculptured cornices. This richness shows that Louis intended them as lodgings for persons of unusual eminence, probably his cousins, the princes of the blood.

On the Paris side, too, there was a transformation. The detached service wings dating from the 1660s were converted into more lodgings for courtiers and joined up with the side wings of the Louis XIII château. The effect, more chance than design, was to create two elongated wings that progressively narrow as they recede toward the old château. This is still a distinctive aspect of the palace today. At the same time, a huge new forecourt was created. This was flanked by four pavilions, one for each of the four ministers of state, their families, and their bureaux.

In contrast to Le Vau's Italianate façades overlooking the garden, on the Paris side Louis XIV's aesthetic choices were constrained by the older work in the Louis XIII style. Louis and Colbert were troubled by this jarring divorce of styles and materials between the garden and Paris sides. At first they tried to offset it by giving the rebuilt wings on the Paris side flat roofs to harmonize with those of the Envelope. But the need for more accommodations prevailed. Only a year or so later these roofs were drastically raised to provide two superposed attics filled with lodgings.

With massive wings to east or west shelved for the time being, Louis still needed more lodgings for courtiers. At Saint-Germain or Fontainebleau most of the court lodged, not in the palace, but in the town. A senior court official, the grand marshal of lodgings, had the job of requisitioning the billets and chalking up names on townsfolk's doors.

At Versailles the courtiers were now to build their own accommodations. In 1671 Louis XIV announced that he was giving away plots of land on the Paris side and that houses built on them would be exempt from seizure for debt—an enticement for France's great nobles, many of them cash-strapped and in debt. A rush of grandees took advantage.

Louis required the new houses to be built in a uniform style. They also had to defer in both height (no more than two stories) and building materials (the same cream stone, redbrick effect, and blue slates) to the Paris façades of the royal residence on the low hill above them. An English visitor in 1677, John Locke, likened the effect to that of an English manor house and its surrounding cottages.

The new houses lined two of the three tree-lined avenues that fanned out from the trapezoidal plaza in front of the château. Le Nôtre had planned this impressive approach in the 1660s by broadening two avenues that already existed under Louis XIII and, for the sake of symmetry, adding a third to the south, the future avenue de Sceaux, in fact a decorative cul-de-sac. On paper, the total effect resembles a goose's webbed foot.

Behind the northernmost avenue (today's avenue de Saint-Cloud), François d'Orbay, the architect who took over after Le Vau's death in 1670, laid out a new town on a rectilinear grid organized around two reserved spaces: one, further from the château, for a market, the other for a residential *place* along the lines of similar squares seen in Paris by this date. To safeguard the spiritual needs of the enlarged château community, Louis himself laid the foundation stone for a convent of Franciscan friars.

Inside the Envelope, along the north and south sides, Louis created new first-floor state apartments for himself and his queen, Maria Theresa of Spain. Originally, each comprised a symmetrical series of seven lavishly decorated rooms linked by doors lined up with each other in the manner of the time to create a long and imposing vista when all were open simultaneously.

The king's suite of rooms followed the standard pattern of a royal apartment in France at this time, beginning with a vestibule, then a guardroom, an antechamber where the throne was set up, a state bedchamber, a large *cabinet* (study), and two smaller, more private rooms.

Respectively a study and a bedchamber, these led out to a central terrace shared with the queen and overlooking Le Nôtre's garden.

For the first time, these rooms allowed the sovereigns to receive in state at Versailles. In 1674 work began on a monumental marble staircase to serve the king's new apartment. With its magnificent murals and painted ceilings, it was one of the most admired features of Versailles until Louis XV demolished it to provide more accommodations for his large family. Its later name, the Ambassadors' Staircase, underlines Louis XIV's constant preoccupation with impressing rival European powers.

Throughout the 1670s Louis XIV was still only an occasional resident. He came in the summer months, when the garden looked and smelled its best. The chief royal seat remained Saint-Germain. On average, Louis stayed there at least ten months a year in the 1670s, when not at war. For most of this time Versailles was a building site. In the Envelope, work on the king's bath apartment and the new staircase dragged on for most of the decade. So it did in the gardens, where the transformations had been almost continuous since 1661. Fascinated by architecture, Louis was a hands-on client, the true director of works, annotating plans, inspecting maquettes, meeting with his architects on Thursdays, and conducting a detailed correspondence from the front with Colbert.

Louis paid constant visits of inspection. In 1672 an organ of court news and gossip, the *Mercure galant,* informed its readers that "not a month goes by without the King going [to Versailles], only to find that it looks completely different when he returns, the great changes arising from the beautiful things being endlessly added." Between the lines the pressure placed on the contractors can be sensed.[5]

In 1678 a more mature Louis, aged forty, was in the course of concluding a successful war against the Dutch. He now felt ready, politically and financially, to take his plans for Versailles to their logical conclusion. Ideas that Louis had taken up and then dropped in 1669, including the massive wings, were no longer to be deferred. Le Vau being dead, the work was entrusted to Jules Hardouin Mansart, the king's chief architect.

No master plan survives. But an official medal minted in 1680, inscribed with the Latin words REGIA VERSALIUM (Palace of Versailles), shows all the important additions of this largest of all building campaigns at Versailles. By 1677 Louis, Colbert, and Mansart must have been agreed on the scale, if not the detail, of the new works, which were staggered to spread the cost. The plan was to turn Versailles into the main royal residence, the aim that Louis must have had in mind since at least 1669.

In the first step, begun in spring 1678, Mansart filled in Le Vau's garden terrace in the Envelope to create a "grand gallery" on the first floor: today's Hall of Mirrors, with its flanking Salons of War and Peace. The next year he began a huge new wing to the south, two monumental stable blocks opposite the château on the Paris side, and a major remodeling of the forecourts.

On the Paris side, he joined together Le Vau's ministerial pavilions to form two large wings for the ministers set in a vast "Ministers' Court." Beneath its sloping cobbles were underground barracks for the companies of royal troops who guarded it. A second set of gates gave access to an inner courtyard. This Royal Court (Cour Royale) was the entrance to the palace proper and was guarded at night by the king's personal bodyguard.

The slope of the hill meant that a short flight of steps was needed to connect this second courtyard with a third, the Marble Court (Cour de Marbre). This innermost courtyard was bounded on three sides by the Paris façades of Louis XIII's château. By now these had been altered almost out of recognition: windows had been enlarged, balconies and sculptured figures added, and in the center, a false third story had been added to create a pedimental frontal, crowned with an ornamental clock.

With a length of 176 yards (161 meters), Mansart's new south wing was over half as long again as the garden façade of the Envelope. "Wing" is something of a misnomer: the building is a rectangle originally divided into three internal courtyards by two cross wings. It was built to house members of the royal family in the rooms overlooking the gardens, and for this reason was often called the Princes' Wing (Aile des Princes). The inner courts, the attics, and the town side were destined for courtiers, kitchens, and workshops. Much of the life of the royal palace was to be found here and in the wing soon to be built to the north.

The two stable buildings begun by Mansart in this same year face the Paris side of the palace from across the place d'Armes. Identical from the outside, the Grand Stables *(Grande Écurie)* to the north housed the king's saddle horses, the Small Stables *(Petite Écurie)* to the south his carriages. Their monumentality was highly unusual for the time and is a good example of the magnificence for which Louis XIV strove at Versailles. Stone façades and the elaborate central portals topped by sculptured horses spoke the architectural language of a noble or princely residence, not mere service buildings. The large forecourts had no particular function but to add to this aura of stateliness. The real work of an army of ostlers, grooms, coachmen, saddlers, blacksmiths, and horse doctors was conducted out of sight, in a sprawl of low buildings and courtyards behind the imposing façades.

In 1682 Mansart opened up two new building sites. One was the Kennel *(Chenil)*, which housed the hounds, horses, and personnel of the king's hunt—a major court service. Its two-story buildings occupied a sprawling site behind the Grand Stables. The other, the Grand Commons *(Grand Commun)*, occupied the site of the old parish church, which now went the way of the rest of the old village of Versailles, the last traces of which Louis had demolished in 1674.

In scale, the Grand Commons was fit for a king in itself. It formed a huge quadrangle organized around an inner courtyard, with a central fountain delivering the water supply. It was built to house kitchens and refectories on the ground floor. On the five upper floors there were yet more accommodations for courtiers and servants. The main entrance faced another across the street in the town façade of Mansart's south wing. Inside this wing, the Commons Staircase, an imposing sweep of open-air steps, allowed servants, courtiers, and victuals to reach the palace's system of indoor galleries.

In 1684 Mansart began to build a north wing to balance the south. Again, the wing is really a hollow rectangle, divided this time by a single cross wing into two internal courts. As with the south wing, Mansart harmonized the garden façade with Le Vau's Italianate Envelope. Like its counterpart, this wing too was destined to house courtiers. But the king and his architect also had plans to include a palace chapel and the theater that Louis had first envisaged back in 1668.

Louis XIV had to address the challenge of feeding a large court stationed permanently at Versailles. His father had created a small kitchen garden, or *potager,* for his limited requirements. Louis XIV now needed something much larger. As early as 1677, Mansart had chosen a new site southeast of the château, a site that the king could reach conveniently on his walks. Swiss Guards were used to fill in a deep pond with the earth that they were simultaneously excavating for a nearby sheet of ornamental water, known ever since as the Lake of the Swiss Guards.

Covering nearly nine and a half hectares, this walled space was where Louis XIV's head gardener, La Quintinie, produced vegetables and fruit for the royal tables, despite complaining of the mediocre soil, a deficiency that he offset with a ready supply of manure from the stables. Espaliers on sheltered walls allowed him to grow figs, a passion of the king. In 1708 Mansart would die from stomach pains supposedly brought on by a dish of baby peas, one of the novelties from the king's kitchen garden.

Since the royal kitchens were destroyed in the nineteenth century, it is this potager that best conveys visually the challenge of feeding Louis XIV's court. The palace icehouses do the same, but are much harder to visit today. Just one of them, now in a private garden in the town of Versailles, could hold nearly 40,000 cubic feet (1,120 cubic meters) of ice. Workers brought the ice from the frozen Lake of the Swiss Guards on the coldest nights. They then crushed it with iron picks and packed it into the brick-lined pit, which would be covered with wood and thatch. Guarded night and day, the ice was used for summer ices and drinks.

In 1683 Colbert died, but not before seeing the transformation of Versailles into the "architectural monster" he had once feared: "a little man with big arms and a large head." This is an apt description of the effect created by the huge lateral wings, spindly forewings, and bulky central block. As Colbert had pointed out to Louis XIV during their disagreement in 1669, the basic problem was the hilltop site. This was adequate for Louis XIII's modest château, but offered small scope for enlargement. Inside, unexpected changes of level point to the expansion of Versailles over this uneven terrain. Louis XIV's second wife, Madame de Maintenon, had to use a flight of five steps to go from her living room to her reception room because her lodging straddled one of these joins.[6]

In tripling the size of the old château by the addition of new residential wings, Louis and Mansart no doubt gave thought to the circulation of people within this huge complex. As early as 1678, Louis had decided to move out of his magnificent new apartment in the Envelope. These state rooms, including the bedchamber, were now to be used mainly as a magnificent setting for court receptions. At other times they served as a passageway.

Louis needed a new apartment for his personal use. He decided to convert the central rooms on the first floor of his father's old château, close to the queen's rooms. Payments to the workers began in 1679, but the king's new bedchamber was not finished until 1684.[7] As a result of this move, the Ambassadors' Staircase no longer led directly into the king's living quarters. Public access to the new apartment was from the opposite, or south, side of the Royal Court. Here, Mansart converted an old staircase leading to the queen's rooms into a suitably stately approach to the king's new antechambers.

A disadvantage of this new approach was that ambassadors and solemn deputations arrived in the king's antechambers without being shown the splendors of the state rooms and the Hall of Mirrors. But there were benefits in terms of royal security, a concern of Louis XIV, who was the most heavily guarded monarch in Europe. The new layout meant that the guardrooms barring the approaches to the apartments of both the king and the queen were close together. At the foot of the Queen's Staircase—as it was known—the Hundred Swiss *(Cent Suisses)* had their guardroom. On the first-floor landing, visitors then had to pass through either the queen's or the king's guardroom to reach their respective antechambers. In addition, the bodyguards who took turns standing guard in these rooms were based in the largest guardroom of all, known indeed as the Grand Guardroom *(Grande Salle des Gardes),* entered from the same landing. From this guardroom the *Cent Suisses* policed the approach to the apartments of the sovereigns from the public staircases in the new south wing.

The scale of the enlargements begun in 1678 presupposes a firm plan to make Versailles the main royal seat. The momentous transfer is always dated to May 6, 1682, when Louis arrived from Saint-Cloud at the head of a procession of the whole court. The townsfolk turned out to applaud in larger numbers than usual, as if aware of the special significance of this royal entry. But Louis made no public declaration of the move. An organ of court propaganda, the *Gazette de France,* carried the simple announcement: "On the sixth of this month, the Court left Saint-Cloud to go to Versailles, where Madame la Dauphine was carried in a sedan-chair because of her pregnancy, which is far advanced."[8]

This low-key approach shows that Louis was proceeding cautiously. The attitudes of the high nobility to Versailles varied. The inventory of the possessions of the duc de Chaulnes shows that he had a painting of Versailles in his home. Other loyal courtiers doubtless did the same. But some certainly disliked Versailles, which took them away from the pleasures of the capital, where most had houses. The maréchal de Créqui, an old soldier, told Louis to his face that Versailles was a "mistress without merit." The memoirist Saint-Simon, who was a generation younger than Louis XIV, fumed against a court "forever in the countryside." After Louis XIV's death, the duc de Noailles, one of the old king's inner circle, proposed outright demolition.[9]

It is likely that Louis presented the move to Versailles in 1682 as a provisional change of residence, until the new works at Saint-Germain were finished. Coincidentally, these had begun the previous year. By 1689 Louis was sufficiently settled at Versailles to hand over Saint-Germain to his first cousin, the exiled James II of England. Thirteen years later his sister-in-law, Elisabeth Charlotte of the Palatinate, duchesse d'Orléans (known simply as Madame), took for granted that Versailles was "considered as *the* residence."[10]

By 1687 it was noticed that Louis spent his entire time at Versailles on "business." As the new seat of power, Versailles was no longer the pleasure house of the king's youth. For recreation, Louis began to make regular use of two small houses nearby. "I made Versailles for the Court, Marly for my friends, and Trianon for myself," he is supposed to have said.[11]

Louis purchased Marly, a property halfway between Versailles and Saint-Germain, in 1676. As one contemporary put it, he decided "to build a small château in a place where he could sometimes enjoy some repose and privacy with a few of his most favored courtiers . . . where there were woods, water and a view."[12] Marly is nowadays a delightful park, unknown to tourists, the haunt of joggers and dog walkers amid the skeletal remains—foundations, terraces, a sheet of ornamental water—of Louis XIV's vanished house and gardens.

What can still be appreciated is the location, a narrow, sloping valley in the hills west of Paris, commanding a superb view over the basin of the River Seine. Here, in 1679, Louis commissioned a small mansion from Mansart, just as the enlargements at Versailles were beginning in earnest. By 1686 it was ready to receive the king for short stays.

Another small château, now known as the Grand Trianon, stands in the grounds of Versailles, one and a quarter miles (two kilometers) west of the palace. It takes its name from one of the three villages that Louis demolished while building Versailles. His personal fondness for this corner of the park went back to 1668, when he erected a summerhouse there with an interior of porcelain tiles and surrounded it with a garden of exotic and heavily scented flowers of the kind he loved.

After the move in 1682, Louis made increasing use of Trianon for walks, musical entertainments, and al fresco meals. In 1687 he commissioned Mansart to build a house in stone and marble to replace the porcelain Trianon; it was to be substantial enough to permit short stays for himself, his immediate family, and a few courtiers.

Most of the new building was one story only, built around the existing garden. It was self-sufficient, with its own kitchen and a small theater. Part of the charm was the leafy location, with trees just outside the windows, and also the flowers and their scent. In Louis XIV's time these were one of the wonders of Versailles: gardeners changed the beds continually, sometimes even daily, by digging hundreds of thousands of stoneware flowerpots directly into the soil.[13]

With most of Louis XIV's garden altered over time, the wondrous quality that contemporaries ascribed to it in his day is now mainly recalled in plans and paintings. Without them, there would be no visual record of the extraordinary Water Bower, an arch of water that strollers could walk under without getting wet, or the Labyrinth, with its fountains sporting literally hundreds of gilt-lead figures of the animals in *Aesop's Fables,* or the Marsh *(Marais),* with its painted metal tree and reeds spouting water.

From the outset Louis attached a supreme importance to these water effects. Their virtuosity formed the star turn of a tour of the gardens. Until the fall of the monarchy the fountains were always played in honor of visiting deputations and ambassadors. In Louis XIV's time the technological achievement of jets of pressurized water thrown high into the sky had an almost supernatural quality. The effects were the work of engineers whose machines made Versailles a hydraulic as much as an artistic wonder.

In 1674 Primo Visconti, an Italian at Louis XIV's court, made the sarcastic comment that Versailles was the largest lead mine in the world. He meant the vast network of underground pipes that fed the waterworks. But the real challenge was bringing the water to Versailles in the first place. One problem was that Versailles is on high ground—the garden terrace is over 490 feet (150 meters) above sea level. To feed the jets and basins at this level, both Louis XIII and Louis XIV had to raise the water by artifice. In the 1670s, according to Visconti, 150 horses were needed just to feed the small fountain on the first-floor terrace of the Envelope.

The other problem is that Versailles is not blessed with a plentiful local water supply. In the search for a solution Francini, Louis' *fontainier,* tried more or less everything over the years. But neither he nor the other engineers ever solved the problem. Throughout the eighteenth century the waterworks were turned on only for special occasions and sometimes, when the supply failed, not even then.

In the 1660s the engineers had begun by channeling local streams and ponds into reservoirs. In the 1670s they dug ditches for collecting rainwater from the heights to the southwest. With Versailles in mind as his permanent residence, Louis commissioned two far more ambitious schemes.

The first, begun in 1681, was a giant pumping station. It used existing technology but on a previously unknown scale: no fewer than 259 pumps collected water from the River Seine and pushed it up the south bank to an aqueduct at 530 feet (162 meters) above sea level, carried on masonry arches. Gravity sent the water first to a collecting reservoir at Marly, then by pipe to the palace.

But the gardens and the palace needed still more water. Begun before this "Marly machine" was completed in 1685, the second scheme was vastly more ambitious: no less than an attempt to "canalize" a whole river. Engineers had been discussing a final solution along these lines for some time. In the end they chose the River Eure. Its waters were to be diverted into an artificial bed at a point high enough to flow the fifty-two miles northeast to Versailles by gravity. Masonry aqueducts would be needed to span two valleys on the way, the largest on three rows of arches, carrying the water at a height of 240 feet. Work began in spring 1685.[14]

In 1682 Louis was in his mid-forties. The 1680s were the real glory years of the reign, before the setbacks of later years. Now, if ever, was the time for him to address the unfinished business of the clashing styles of the palace façades. In 1699 Madame would write revealingly that Louis privately admitted faults in the architecture of Versailles, the result of not "having the old château entirely demolished," as he had briefly planned in 1669.[15]

Undated plans by Mansart exist for rebuilding the façades on the Paris side. He envisaged a majestic stone frontage in a classical style more in keeping with the garden front. It is difficult to imagine him working on this project except in the 1680s, at the height of the Versailles building boom.[16]

The outbreak of a costly war in 1688 shelved this plan. By 1693 Charles Perrault, a senior official in the Royal Buildings Office, was claiming that Louis had preserved his father's château out of filial piety.

In the eighteenth century, this face-saving version of events formed an integral part of the myth of Versailles, repeated in the guidebooks of the time.[17]

The international crisis that France faced in 1688 was the most serious in all the years of Louis XIV's personal rule to date. Workers on the Eure project downed tools that autumn. The next year all building at Versailles ground to a halt. The north wing, including the palace chapel and the theater, was left unfinished.[18]

The tempo of work at Versailles had always kept time with Louis XIV's wars. The works begun in 1678 coincided with the Treaties of Nimwegen ending the so-called Dutch War. In the peaceful decade that followed, Louis used the troops released from fighting as laborers at Versailles. But in 1688 he found himself reaping what he had sown a decade earlier. He confronted a powerful European coalition that eventually included Spain, England, Holland, and the Holy Roman Empire.

The situation quickly became so bad that in December 1689 Louis felt compelled to send to the mint all the silver furnishings and fittings in the state rooms at Versailles. He never resumed work on the theater, once abandoned. A temporary chapel on the site of today's Salon of Hercules remained in use by the court for twenty-six years. Louis XIV never fully realized his youthful vision for Versailles.

The so-called Ten Years' War ended in 1697 with a victory for a war-weary France. Now nearing sixty, the indefatigable Louis restarted building operations at Versailles. His major new project was to resume work on the permanent chapel. But the project proceeded slowly because Louis was struggling to find the funds.

In July 1701, Louis gave orders for a new round of alterations to his personal quarters. He wanted to enlarge his second, or inner, antechamber by combining it with his bedchamber next door. The enlarged room took its usual name *(Antichambre de l'Oeil de Boeuf)* from its "bull's eye," the large oval window that Louis installed to let in more light.[19] He now transferred his bedchamber to the next room along, hitherto a salon.

It was only now, well over thirty years after he first began to alter his father's château, that Louis XIV came to sleep in a bedchamber that precisely straddled Le Nôtre's great east-west axis running through the gardens and palace. This move is sometimes seen as the last piece in a jigsaw of solar imagery going back to the 1660s. But Louis seems to have lost interest in this form of glorification as he aged. In 1685, to make way for the north wing, he had no qualms about demolishing the Grotto of Tethys, a fountain house that formed part of this solar landscape.

These alterations had more to do with the ceremonial life of Versailles. Over the years Louis had made the daily ceremonies in his bedchamber key moments in the life of the court. Better arrangements were needed to cope with the courtiers who massed here at the start and close of the royal day.

The sheer richness of the new antechamber suggests the importance that Louis attached to these royal rituals. The décor included mirrors (in this period a great luxury), paintings by the Italian master Veronese, and a superb frieze of gilded stucco showing children at play. As well as providing more space, the Bull's Eye improved circulation. Previously, the room had been accessed by a door from the outer antechamber and by a second from the Hall of Mirrors. The new Bull's Eye had two doors into the antechamber and four into the gallery. Understandably it became the hub of the whole palace.[20]

In 1700 Louis XIV had accepted the vast possessions of the Spanish crown, which the last Habsburg king of Spain had bequeathed to Louis' grandson, the duc d'Anjou. This latest French aggrandizement prompted the War of the Spanish Succession, the most crippling for France of all Louis XIV's wars. When an enemy army threatened to march on Paris in 1712, Louis received advice to abandon Versailles. In his seventy-fifth year, the imperturbable king instead contemplated a last stand at the head of his remaining troops: they would "perish together or save the State."[21]

A last-minute French victory pulled France back from the brink. Peace followed. Louis offered thanksgiving in the new palace chapel at Versailles, finally completed in 1710.[22] Driven by piety, Louis had made sure that the project was never entirely starved of funds, even in wartime. Others no less devout murmured their disapproval of such "prodigious magnificence" in a time of national disaster.[23]

In August 1715 Louis contracted gangrene. After three agonizing weeks, stoically borne under the eyes of his courtiers, he died in his new bedchamber, four days before his seventy-eighth birthday, after a reign of seventy-two years.

Before he died Louis gave orders for his five-year-old great-grandson and automatic successor, now known as Louis XV, to be taken to the medieval castle of Vincennes just east of Paris, where the air was better for the health of a young king whose elder brother and parents had all been taken prematurely by illness. This was done on the same day as the departure of the royal hearse.

The Regent and heir-presumptive was Philippe d'Orléans, Louis XIV's only nephew. A clever but freethinking prince, he had rarely been in favor with the late king. He rebelled against the proprieties of Versailles, where he once was seen reading Rabelais, a French author banned by the Catholic church, a few feet from Louis XIV at mass.[24] His personal memories of Versailles were not happy ones. Louis XIV's reign, moreover, had left France heavily in debt, and the prospect of achieving economies in the running costs of the court by closing down the palace may well have appealed to the new régime.[25] The Regent himself, finally, had a well-known penchant for the fleshpots of Paris, where he was doing much to improve the Orléans residence, the Palais Royal. A variety of reasons, then, prompted him to install his ward, not in Versailles, but in the Parisian palace of the Tuileries. The young king was transferred there from Vincennes in December 1715.

Versailles remained uninhabited for seven years. The superintendent of the king's buildings, the duc d'Antin, kept the domain fully maintained, as if awaiting the return of the king.[26] On June 15, 1722, the Regent brought the twelve-year-old Louis XV back to Versailles. The boy was keen to be back in time for his first communion "in the parish church of my birthplace."[27] Royal nostalgia found an ally in political expediency: the popularity of the Regent with the Parisians had waned since the disastrous collapse of a short-lived state bank in 1720. As in the previous reign, Versailles came into its own when the monarchy had reason to distance itself from the capital.[28]

Louis XV and his grandson and successor, Louis XVI, both lived in the political shadow of their ancestor. Both consented to certain refurbishments that destroyed décors which had survived from the 1670s. But in the main they kept the palace and grounds as they had inherited them.

It was natural, therefore, that the young Louis XV should finish Louis XIV's last major project. On the site of the temporary chapel of 1682, redundant since 1710, Louis XIV had started to create a huge first-floor salon. He began to decorate it with musical trophies. This shows that in the last years of his reign he still clung tenaciously to the plan for a ball-room first mooted in 1669. The twenty-year-old Louis XV approved the completion of the work in 1730. To match the other state apartments, the ceiling was painted by the artist François Le Moyne with the classical myth that gave the room its name: the Salon of Hercules.[29]

Because Louis XIV never finished the theater begun in the north wing, Louis XV's Versailles continued to lack an auditorium equipped with the "machines" needed to mount serious opera. Since Louis XV was not a great music lover, this deficiency was mainly felt in the essentially political context of staging royal weddings, when magnificent court operas played a vital part in projecting the prestige of the dynasty. As early as 1743 Louis XV was considering updated plans for the permanent theater.

As in the previous reign, the cycle of war and peace shaped the pace of building at Versailles. In 1748, after the War of the Austrian Succession, construction began. But the outbreak of the Seven Years' War, in 1756, put work on hold. This war, a disaster for the French, left the royal government with a colossal state debt. Even so, in 1768 the king gave the order for the theater to go ahead. The result was the Opéra, as it is called today, one of the jewels of Versailles.

The logic behind this costly decision emerges from the private journal of one of the key figures involved, Papillon de La Ferté, the intendant of the King's Entertainments Office, or *Menus Plaisirs,* the court department responsible, among other things, for palace theatricals. In a memoir to the finance minister recommending completion of the theater in time for the marriages of Louis XV's three grandsons, Papillon de La Ferté pointed out "that the different provisional constructions and repairs which would have to be made could cost more than the building of a solid and permanent auditorium."[30] This spirit of attempted economy was reflected in the triple function of the auditorium as theater, ballroom, and banqueting hall. Conversion to either of these last two was effected by means of a mechanical device creating a continuous floor space from the edge of the stalls (where by tradition the sovereign sat), over the orchestra pit, and joining up with the stage.

Even so, the new opera house was so costly to run that Louis XV's successor reverted to temporary theaters. In an age when auditoria were illuminated throughout performances, no one seems to have foreseen the prohibitive cost of the lighting—three thousand candles were burned on the opening night. It is a measure of the shakiness of crown finances in the later eighteenth century that the opera house was used only thirty-four times in the nearly twenty years down to 1789—an average of less than twice a year.[31]

In his middle age, Louis XV resurrected Louis XIV's dream of rebuilding the Paris façades. The immediate problem was that the northernmost of the two wings framing the Royal Court, known as the Government Wing, was falling down. In 1771 bulging façades, rotten timbers, and a shaky terminal colonnade finally prompted the king to opt for demolition. Marigny, director of royal buildings at the time, admitted that the wing had been "very badly built."[32]

Louis XV approved plans put forward by his chief architect, Jacques-Ange Gabriel, for rebuilding the wing. Stylistically the Gabriel wing, as it became known, broke drastically with the Louis XIII façades around it, being built entirely in stone and in a severely classical style. Louis XV was launching nothing less than the first step in the long-contemplated rebuilding of the Paris side of the palace. Gabriel drew heavily on Mansart's unrealized plans in presenting Louis XV with his own version of the "Grand Project." The new wing formed only one element in a larger neoclassical ensemble, to be crowned by a central cupola.

Louis and his architect were no doubt aware of eighteenth-century critics of the architectural split personality of Louis XIV's palace. In the fourth volume of his *Architecture française,* published in 1756, the influential Jacques-François Blondel had condemned "this alliance of modern architecture with the semi-gothic of former times." Louis XV's compulsion to correct these "faults" shows how much the French monarchy now relied on Louis XIV's palace as a prop to its power.[33]

An impressive reconstruction of Versailles was particularly attractive at this juncture. In the years around 1770 Louis XV faced the worst challenge to royal authority in France since the civil wars of his great-grandfather's childhood. The moment was not propitious financially, but Louis was eager to start. Since the royal treasury was so short of money, he surreptitiously accepted funds for the new wing from a surprising quarter: Madame du Barry, his mistress and a former courtesan.[34]

The Gabriel wing was still unfinished when Louis XV died in 1774. His grandson Louis XVI succeeded him at the age of nineteen. The new king's respect for Louis XIV emerges clearly in his treatment of Le Nôtre's decaying garden. He at once recognized the need to cut down the old trees, many of them dying, and replace them with young ones from the royal nurseries. But taste had changed since Louis XIV's day. The formal gardens of Versailles now offended the fashionable eye, evoking "man-made effort more than the simplicity of nature." Despite the new thinking, eagerly embraced by his queen, Marie-Antoinette, in her garden at the Petit Trianon, Louis XVI, after listening to the experts, opted for a simplified version of Le Nôtre's geometric layout.[35]

In the early years of the new reign, financial economies halted work on the Gabriel wing once it reached the roof. But in 1779, at the height of the Franco-American War of Independence against England, the Royal Buildings Office invited architects to submit new plans for the Grand Project. Their vision was nothing if not ambitious. One architect noted that "of the old Château only the façade and the Grand Apartments on the garden side ought to be kept, along with the new wing built under Louis XV."[36]

The successful conclusion of the American war fostered a celebratory mood at the royal court. Madame Campan, one of Marie-Antoinette's "first women of the bedchamber," remembered hearing conversations in which Louis planned for the implementation of the Grand Project, which was thought to need a decade. To avoid ruining the townspeople, most of them reliant economically on the presence of the court, Louis would leave the government bureaucracy behind in Versailles. The royal family would move into the château of Saint-Cloud, halfway between Versailles and Paris. In 1784 it was bought by Louis XVI for this purpose.[37]

But money had to be spent on redecorating Saint-Cloud. Louis had also started to rebuild the château of Compiègne, to the northeast of Paris. He was personally fond of Compiègne, with its country-house atmosphere and excellent hunting. In 1781 he raised loans to begin work on a new garden façade, with new apartments behind it for himself and Marie-Antoinette. Work dragged on throughout the decade.

In 1787 the monarchy faced its most severe financial crisis since Louis XIV had moved to Versailles over a century earlier. There could be no more talk of the Grand Project for the time being. The architects who submitted plans were now paid off. Two years later the Revolution broke out. In October 1789, Versailles was invaded by a mob from Paris. Louis XVI and his family were forcibly transferred to the Tuileries palace in Paris, never to return. The days of Versailles as a royal residence had come to an abrupt and final end.

## 2.

# *"Rome in one palace"*

POSTERITY HAS thrown the psychological book at Louis XIV. Megalomania, narcissism, and an inferiority complex have all been attributed to him by way of explaining Versailles. Louis certainly had faults of character: at eighteenth-century Versailles, courtiers remembered him as "the vainest man ever." But magnificence is not always a sign of personality disorder. For monarchs it is also a rational choice.[1]

In ancient China the Han emperor Kao-tsu, a man of simple tastes, is said to have flown into a rage when he discovered that his supporters had built him a palace. Then they explained: "Without great and elegant buildings, you will not be able to display your authority and your majesty." The emperor accepted this political logic and moved into the palace.[2]

When the boy Louis XIV succeeded his father in 1643, the French monarchy had been buffeted by civil struggle for nearly a century. The early years of the reign of Louis XIII were plagued by the continuing conflict between the Catholic crown and the twelfth part of the French nation comprising reformed Christians ("Huguenots"). The king faced armed revolts led by the duc de Bouillon and the duc de Rohan, Huguenot grandees. At Versailles he kept a painting showing the royal siege of La Rochelle, a rebel bastion that Louis XIII had personally helped to reduce.[3]

One source of tension was the increasing power of the state in seventeenth-century Europe. In France great nobles saw their feudal power bases reduced by royal force. Landowners of every hue were expected to pay the taxes to fund the monarch's armies. A state bureaucracy—headed by the four "king's secretaries," as they were known in France—had emerged.

This concentration of power did not go unchallenged by subjects. As a child, Louis XIV lived through a wave of anti-monarchical upheavals in Europe. In neighboring England a civil war climaxed in the beheading of Charles I, Louis XIV's uncle. In France the boy-king experienced firsthand the civil war known as the Fronde. Led by the Queen Regent and Cardinal Mazarin, the crown struggled against an alliance of the high nobility and the legal aristocracy, whose seat of power was the supreme court of French law, the Parlement of Paris. Once again, France's grandees plotted and fought against their king: the roll call of blue-blooded families included those of Condé, Bouillon, Lorraine, La Rochefoucauld, Retz, and La Trémoille.

At the height of the troubles, on January 6, 1649, the Queen Regent and Louis XIV were forced to flee their Paris palace for Saint-Germain, where almost everyone had to sleep on straw. The crown jewels were pawned. It was only in 1659 that a treaty with Spain, ally of the rebels, restored real peace to France. Louis XIV never forgot what he later called these "terrible disturbances throughout the kingdom."[4]

With the Fronde a recent memory, the young Louis XIV sat on an unstable throne. In a single-minded way he decided to make the projection of royal power a keystone of policy. In 1661, at the age of twenty-two, he announced that he would rule France in person. He was determined to be seen as a strong and capable king in full control of his state.

In the eighteenth century the new ideas of the Enlightenment encouraged French people to criticize Louis XIV's regal style. "A prince who, in spite of the same great achievements, were to remain simple and modest, would be the first of kings, and Louis XIV the second." But Louis had seen things differently. Raised in a more deferential age, he believed passionately that glory and magnificence constituted the greatness of kings and that France needed a great king to rebuild respect for the monarchy.[5]

The young Louis XIV had conventional views as to what constituted royal glory. Military success beckoned first and foremost. France was at war for half the fifty-four years of his personal rule, and Louis campaigned in person until well into his fifties. Like most monarchs of his age, he also believed in the power of architecture. André Félibien was made royal historian in 1666 so as to record the embellishments that Louis was making to his palaces for—as the warrant of appointment puts it—"the glory of his reign and the honor of the State."[6]

Since the Renaissance, great princes had sought prestige in patronage of the arts. Louis personally loved music, painting, dancing, houses and gardens, theatricals, and objets d'art. As a young man, he had a political agenda that included making the crown the dominant patron of the French arts. The so-called Fouquet affair reveals how ruthless he could be in pursuit of this ambition.

Nicolas Fouquet was the king's super-rich minister of finance, one of a team of clever officials bequeathed to him by Mazarin, his mother's chief minister. At his new château, Vaux-le-Vicomte, south of Paris, Fouquet had displayed a taste and stylishness that put the royal residences in the shade. In August 1661, at the height of his influence, he gave a splendid fête at Vaux to show it off to the king. Within weeks of this extravaganza, Louis had his erstwhile host thrown into prison, where he remained without trial until his death.

Royal mortification at Vaux's brilliance was certainly a factor in Fouquet's shocking fall. Within a year Louis XIV had hired Fouquet's architect, Le Vau, and his garden-designer, Le Nôtre, to work for him at Versailles. The painter of Vaux's ceilings, Charles Le Brun, would go on to mastermind the painted décors of Versailles.

The Renaissance had opened Europe's eyes to the glories of the ancient world. In seventeenth-century France, Roman antiquity was a huge source of cultural authority. Imperial Rome remained a political reality in the Europe of the day in the venerable form of the Holy Roman Empire, a loose confederation of German states under the authority of an elective emperor. In this period the emperor was usually a member of the Austrian Habsburg dynasty, chief rival of the Bourbon monarchy on the European stage. Since the sixteenth century, French kings—including Louis XIV—had toyed with the idea of wresting this imperial title from the Habsburgs. For all these reasons, Louis saw antiquity as an irresistible source of inspiration for royal image-making.

In 1663 the efficient Colbert formed the Little Academy, ancestor of one of modern France's most august institutions of learning, the Academy of Inscriptions and Belles-Lettres. In its earliest form under Colbert, this was a committee of paid intellectuals and artists hired by the crown for their expertise in "all the magnificence of Greece and Rome." Their job was to devise how to glorify the king in architecture and décors. When Colbert took them to meet the king, Louis made clear the momentousness of their work. "You can judge, gentlemen, my esteem for you, since I am confiding in you the most precious thing in the world to me, my glory."[7]

This steering group played a major part in the creation of Versailles. At their twice-weekly meetings in Colbert's house, the five members were consulted on "all the proposed decorations for the apartments and for the embellishment of the gardens." They approached their job in the spirit of their times. They took for granted that the viewer of an artwork would be alert for, and would understand, its hidden cultural meanings, in much the same way as modern advertisers assume that their audience will recognize veiled references to, say, contemporary cinema.

In the seventeenth century, the Europe-wide technique for praising a living monarch was comparison. When Henri IV, Louis XIV's grandfather, entered Lyon in triumph, a huge painted canvas showed him side by side with Julius Caesar, each in the act of forgiving his enemies. The viewer was expected to know that Caesar too was famous for his clemency. In the classically saturated culture of seventeenth-century France, educated people understood this language. It was familiar from classical plots on the stage and from French translations of classical works such as Suetonius's *Lives of the Twelve Caesars,* published in multiple editions in this period.

Artists and writers of the time also used astrology to highlight a prince's qualities. This pseudoscience was not only popular in seventeenth-century France, but respectable, at any rate until 1679, when horoscopes, black magic, and some of France's greatest names were all mixed up in the scandal known as the Affair of the Poisons.

The sun had long been an irresistible metaphor for a French monarch when the young Louis XIV adopted it as his personal emblem in 1662. As Louis himself explained in his memoirs, the sun did good everywhere; it stood for fairness, because it shone its light equally all over the world, and for authority, by dominating the other heavenly bodies. Just as the sun regulated night and day and the seasons in its daily journey through the sky, so the equable rule of the sovereign guaranteed terrestrial harmony.[8]

In the 1660s, Le Nôtre and the Little Academy started to use water and sculpture and orientation to reflect these unexceptional ideas in an ambitious solar landscape at Versailles. Their core idea was to present the château as the home of a sun king, whom the scholars equated with Apollo, the classical god whose day began and ended—according to one version of this myth—in the waters of the ocean.

At the far end of Le Nôtre's Royal Alley, a group of gilt-bronze statues set in a water basin showed Apollo emerging in his chariot from the "ocean" in the direction of the château. Le Nôtre's main west-east perspective, on which this basin was sited, then represented the god's journey across the heavens. Along this trajectory as it neared the château, a second fountain depicted Apollo with his mother, Latona. Right next to the château, a fountain house represented the Grotto of Tethys, wife of Oceanus. Inside, a marble statue group showed the sun god and his horses at rest.

Louis and his advisers conceived this landscape around 1664. It was created at a leisurely pace over the next decade or so. The resting god was not installed in the grotto until 1676. The viewer was not supposed to be too literal, since the "sun" in this landscape "rose" in the west and "set" in the east. This reversal of reality was necessary in order to orientate the composition toward a viewing point from the first floor of the château.

After Le Vau built the Envelope, for the first time Louis had a state apartment to decorate at Versailles. He and Colbert decided to extend the solar theme of the gardens to the interior. They entrusted supervision of a team of artists to Le Brun, now the king's First Painter. They assigned each room to a planet, represented by the image of the corresponding ancient deity painted in the central compartment of the ceiling.

On the usual principle of comparison, subordinate scenes depicted "the actions of the Heroes of antiquity associated with each of the Planets, and with the actions of His Majesty." In the Salon of Mars, the war god, for instance, the lesser scenes showed Caesar reviewing his legions, the Persian king Cyrus the Great haranguing his men, and so on.[9]

The quote is from Félibien's guide to Versailles, published in 1674. Other guides followed. These explications helped the viewer to recognize the more recondite subject matter, especially in the ceilings of the state rooms on the south side of the Envelope, occupied by the queen. Despite having no political influence, Maria Theresa of Spain was important to Louis dynastically as the mother of his heir—another Louis, known at Versailles as Monseigneur—and as the genealogical conduit of French claims to Spanish territory.

As a result, her rooms received the same planetary treatment. With difficulty the scholars pieced together a gallery of royal heroines from ancient times for her ceilings. They scoured classical authors to produce obscure figures such as Artemisia, commander of the Lycian ships at the battle of Salamis in 480 B.C. To those in the know, the contrast must have been almost comical between these ancient "action women" and the meek and pious queen, of whom Louis said that the only time that she gave him any trouble was by dying.

As the 1670s progressed, Louis XIV's mounting tally of achievements at home and abroad gave him the confidence to abandon metaphor and compare himself explicitly with the great warriors of ancient Rome. On the ceiling of the Ambassadors' Staircase, decorated between 1676 and 1680, Le Brun introduced Louis in person, garbed as a triumphant Roman general in cuirass and laurel crown.

Nearly 240 feet (73 meters) in length, the Hall of Mirrors was the fullest expression of this overt glorifying of the king. Plans for its painted ceiling preoccupied the highest deliberative body of the realm, the council of state, where they were discussed in 1679 under the watchful eyes of the monarch. On the table was Le Brun's initial proposal for a traditional program of comparisons, with Louis idealized as either Apollo or Hercules, along with an alternative: depictions of the king's royal triumphs, including his personal leadership of French armies against European neighbors.

This second option was politically sensitive. Louis XIV was careful to share the final decision with his council of state. Decades later Saint-

Simon, one of Louis XIV's more critical courtiers, observed that the ceilings of Versailles had helped to turn Europe "against the King's person rather than his kingdom." But in 1679 recent victories tipped the scales in favor of triumphalism, and Colbert's prudent reservations were dismissed.[10]

The Hall of Mirrors is a summation in paint of what Louis as king of France aspired to be. Le Brun spread his epic narrative over thirty painted tableaux. He began the story with a literal centerpiece depicting Louis' assumption of personal rule in 1661. The happy results of this decision for the king's subjects are then shown in scenes of the legal and financial reforms in the immediately following years.

Since Louis and Colbert believed passionately that the state could and should intervene to promote the French economy, Le Brun included on the ceiling in the Hall of Mirrors a scene depicting their most spectacular single intervention in this area, the Canal of the Two Seas. Begun in 1666, this canal allowed French vessels to navigate between the Bay of Biscay and Sète on France's south coast. Involving 150 miles of engineered waterway and ten thousand workers, the project nicely captures the huge ambition of the young Louis XIV's vision for France.

The Hall of Mirrors is above all a gallery of battles. Le Brun depicted both of the wars that Louis XIV had fought and won by this date. The tableau of Louis leading the French crossing of the River Rhine in 1672 sums up the bombastic approach. Hair streaming, dressed in Roman style and holding a thunderbolt like a projectile, Louis sits godlike on a silver chariot pushed by Hercules while riding roughshod over female personifications of nearby enemy towns. This was not an image calculated to win the hearts and minds of the Dutch, who had been so alarmed by the Rhine crossing that they opened their sea dikes, turning Amsterdam into an island.

Nowadays it is rare to see tourists with upturned faces studying Le Brun's ceiling with the same fervor as they do, say, the frescoes of the Sistine Chapel. But there is no doubt that Louis fully expected the ceiling to be scrutinized. Viewing was to be helped by the famous wall of mirrors, which diffuses the daylight, except above the windows, where the detail is shadowy.

Le Brun also introduced painted captions in French. Latin, language

of ancient Rome and of the Catholic liturgy, would have endowed the
tableaux with a timeless quality. But Louis wanted to communicate.
Women, generally less well educated than men in this period, were said
to be suitably "ravished by this change, which allows them to read with
admiration the great Actions of His Majesty."[11]

Themes of Louis as arbiter of war and peace echoed throughout the
palace. There are the obvious set pieces: the Hall of Mirrors and its two
salons. In the Salon of War, the sculptor Antoine Coysevox used an
image of royal victory as old as the pharaohs: a giant stucco medallion
above the chimneypiece shows a mounted Louis trampling his foes beneath the hooves of his horse. The martial imagery saturates the lesser
spaces of the palace as well. Trophies of arms nestle in the corners of
the ceilings in the state apartments. In stone they rear up against the
skyline on the garden façade. Sculptured helmets decorate the frames
of the ministers' windows. The sentry boxes flanking the outer gates
support carved groups of winged women personifying Victory doing
more trampling, this time of the Spanish lion and the Austrian eagle.
In the garden, the flotilla of miniature vessels moored on Le Nôtre's
Grand Canal was not just a pleasure fleet of gondolas. It included
replicas of actual French men-of-war, among them the flagship of
France's Mediterranean fleet, an oared galley that went by the splen-
didly archaic name of *La Réale*. These boats advertised France's naval
power, built up systematically by Louis XIV and Colbert.[12]

All this militarism glorified the commander in chief. But Louis could
only fight his land wars thanks to a formidable army machine reorga-
nized by Louvois as war minister and capable, in the 1690s, of mobiliz-
ing more than a quarter of a million men.[13] The high nobility forming
the social core of the court at Versailles was by vocation an officer class.
After the French defeat at Oudenaarde in 1708, the atmosphere of extreme anxiety at Versailles was palpable. Saint-Simon says that noblewomen with husbands in the army scarcely left the churches, and
everyone in the palace was milling around waiting for news.[14]

One of the most familiar sights at Versailles was that of the old soldiers with their wounds and their proudly displayed order of Saint

Louis. A cash-strapped Louis had invented this military order in 1693, at the height of the Ten Years' War, as a "reward of honor." A century later, little had changed. Under Louis XVI large numbers of retired officers would set out daily from Paris to "besiege the bureaux of Versailles, people the antechambers, fill the gallery [the Hall of Mirrors], discuss the news and talk incessantly of past wars."[15]

At Versailles, Louis XIV was constantly petitioned by former servicemen. Once, in 1698, when he replied with his customary "I shall see" to a one-armed officer who had fought in the recent war, he received a franker reply than deferential petitioners were normally wont to give: "But, Sire, if I were to have said to my general, 'I shall see,' when he sent me to where I lost my arm, I would still have it, and would not be asking you for anything." A touched Louis XIV gave him his pension.[16]

The martial image of Louis XIV's Versailles resonated with the concerns of a significant swath of French society. The palace played its part in whipping up an enthusiasm for the king's wars in the country at large. A glimpse into the national mood is provided by the family chronicle of a notary in Nîmes. In 1691 Étienne Borelly recorded his fervent praises of "our great and irresistible king Louis XIV, whom the divine bounty allowed to capture [Nice] as if by miracle."[17]

Louis and his ministers intended Versailles to showcase French taste and its luxury industries: a forerunner of the national pavilions at the international trade fairs of more recent times. For an eighteenth-century Frenchman, the rich fabrics of the royal bedchamber advertised "the progress and superiority of our manufactories in France over those of all Europe."[18]

In the 1670s, French mirror-glass and marble were both novelties. The former had been a monopoly of the Venetians until Colbert successfully set up a state-sponsored French manufactory in 1665. The seventeen arcades filled with blown glass in the Hall of Mirrors displayed this new French product on a previously unprecedented scale.

The state apartments of Versailles were the first in a French palace to make copious use of colored marble from French quarries such as Campan (green), Rance (veiny gray), or Languedoc (red). The names of marble workers abound in the accounts. They supplied marble revetment, columns, chimneypieces, door frames, and floors. Public rooms such as the Salons of Venus and Diana, which have kept their original marble décor, resemble showrooms of French marble work.

The tapestries and other wall hangings, the carpets, and the silver objects were made at the state-controlled factory called the Gobelins in Paris, where Colbert directed the output of around 250 craftsmen working to designs by the prolific Le Brun. At Versailles, these products imposed an integrated look on the fixtures and fittings in the state apartments, as if everything had been supplied by the same firm—as indeed was the case.

The dominating note was magnificence. Louis personally loved "rich materials and ingenious craftsmanship." His own taste helped to shape the heavy opulence, the rich materials, and the rigid symmetry of the furnishings. The silverwork at Versailles went far beyond the normal display of plate and objets d'art to be found in princely residences of the time. In the 1670s and 1680s Louis commissioned silver balustrades for the royal bedchambers, silver tubs for the orange trees that perfumed the state rooms, and a spectacular suite of silver benches and stools for the Hall of Mirrors.[19]

Louis and Colbert meant these décors to show the world that the French arts could rival those of Italy, seat of the Renaissance and until now the arbiter of European taste. In 1682 Louis had two huge canvases hung side by side in the Salon of Mars. The French Le Brun's depicted the family of the Persian king Darius III, the Italian Veronese's a religious subject, the pilgrims of Emmaus. This didactic juxtaposition was meant to show that French painters were now as good as Italian ones.

The palace aspired to be a new benchmark of artistic excellence, as ancient Rome had been since the Renaissance. In the gardens Louis amassed a spectacular collection of accurate copies of ancient statues, like the writhing group of Laocoon and his sons entangled among killer snakes, now at the top end of the Royal Alley. Louis and his contemporaries believed that the original, unearthed at Rome in 1506, once stood in the palace of the Caesars. These statues were meant to enhance the Roman aura of Versailles.

Echoes of ancient Rome are clearly audible in the plan to divert the River Eure. This was the brainchild of Louvois, who had succeeded Colbert as superintendent of royal buildings in 1683. Where the "canalized" river had to cross the plain of Maintenon at a challenging height of 210 feet (nearly 65 meters), Louvois turned for advice to one of Louis' new instruments of French cultural endeavor, the Academy of Architecture. The architects in turn looked for inspiration to antiquity. The Pont du Gard outside Nîmes was studied. Evoked, too, were the Byzantine and Ottoman aqueducts outside Constantinople, misunderstood in the seventeenth century as ancient Roman.[20]

On the seventeenth-century principle of analogy, the architects of Versailles could have pressed the comparison with ancient Rome in more literal ways. The palace sits on a hill, evoking the Palatine Hill, seat of the Caesars. There, the palatial buildings were supported by vaulted basements, just like the wings of Versailles. With its three stories, columnar decoration, and flat roof adorned with sculpture, there is even a loose resemblance between the garden façade and Renaissance reconstructions of the Septizonium, the Roman palace of Septimius Severus.[21]

An anonymous French engraving showing the palace as it looked in 1678 makes the Roman ambitions of Versailles explicit. In the sky, hovering over the garden façade, an angel holds a portrait of Louis XIV in one hand and in the other blows a trumpet. To this a banner is attached, inscribed with the boastful quatrain:

*World, come and see what I see,*
*And what the Sun admires;*
*Rome in one palace, in Paris an Empire,*
*And all the Caesars in one King.*

Here is the spirit of Versailles at the high noon of Louis XIV's reign.[22]

The chapel has dominated the skyline of the palace since its completion in 1710. Originally it was even loftier, since the roof as built supported a forty-foot-high lantern, removed in 1765 during repairs. In the eighteenth century the chapel came to be seen as a defect in the over-all appearance of Versailles. The French professor of architecture Jacques-François Blondel criticized the "dissonant" effect on the overall appearance of the Paris side created by its off-center position and its ex-terior of pale stone amid a sea of red brick.[23] But Louis XIV's main concern was to create a powerful symbol of the traditional claim of the French monarchy to rule by divine right.

Louis lived in an age when Europe was bitterly divided by religious differences. The Reformation had given rise to the Catholic Counter-Reformation. The direct descendant of Saint Louis, "eldest Son of Rome" and de facto head of the French wing of the Catholic Church, Louis XIV stood firmly on the side of orthodoxy. He took only too seriously his coronation oath to stamp out heresy. In 1685 he revoked his grandfather's edict of tolerance for the Huguenots, putting some two hundred thousand religious refugees on the roads to France's borders.

Louis, or at least his régime, was capable of manipulating the reli-gious aura surrounding the king's person. At his coronation Louis in-herited the centuries-old healing power supposedly passed down from one French monarch to another and exercised in the ceremony of the royal touch. Louis performed this assiduously throughout his life. But the fact that royal officials under Louis XIV made payments to the poor to encourage them to turn out for these ceremonies shows that his government grasped the political mileage to be gained from advertising his supernatural powers as much as possible.[24]

Because the chapel of Versailles was built late in the reign, there is a tendency to see it—and Versailles as a whole—in personal terms. It is true that Louis became more ostentatiously pious in middle age. In 1695 his sister-in-law complained that the atmosphere at Versailles had changed: all was now "devout." But the history of the Versailles chapels shows that Louis had envisaged a prestigious place of worship in his new palace when he was still a young man.

Since the time of Louis XIII, Versailles had always had a modest chapel for the monarch's personal devotions. As soon as his son decided to turn Versailles into a palace, he felt the need for an edifice symboliz-ing royal piety in a more public way. In 1672, when the king's adultery with Madame de Montespan was in full spate, he commissioned a new and much larger chapel on the south side of Le Vau's Envelope, on the site of what later became the Grand Guardroom and is now the Coronation Room. Its importance in Louis XIV's eyes is shown by the fact that a painted ceiling—always a sign of a prestigious décor in this period—was planned for it by Le Brun, and possibly begun.

The enlargements to Versailles from 1678 on condemned this unfinished chapel after only six years: it obstructed communication with the new south wing. This is another example of the short-term planning at Versailles during the decades of rapid architectural expansion, and its costly consequences. Since Louis now aimed openly at converting Versailles into the chief royal seat, he and Mansart started to plan for an altogether more ambitious edifice.

Half measures were out of the question. In 1682 the *Mercure galant* declared that Louis XIV's intention "has always been that the Chapel of Versailles would be the most magnificent part of this sumptuous and brilliant palace." To allow time for the design and financing of something suitably spectacular, a new temporary chapel was commissioned on the north side of the palace, on the site of the future Salon of Hercules. Despite its impermanence, this chapel was more impressive than its predecessors. The ceiling was unpainted. But the interior received a noble décor in carved and gilded wood, a splendid altar, and framed paintings on religious subjects by eminent artists.[25]

Meanwhile, Mansart was producing designs for the permanent chapel. Work finally began late in 1688, only to be brought to a standstill by the outbreak of war. When work resumed a decade later, Louis and Mansart had rethought the design, opting for a tall, elongated building.

Versailles is often seen as a predominantly secular monument. But this final chapel formed the heart of what was almost a mini monastery within the royal palace. A side door from the aisle led to a sacristy for storing liturgical equipment. Beyond were quarters for the chapel musicians and choristers. Above were dormitory-like accommodations for the group of twenty or so friars to whom Louis XIV had entrusted the running of the chapel.[26]

Like its predecessors at Versailles and, indeed, most royal chapels in France, the new chapel was a two-story structure. The altar and the area for presiding priests were on the ground floor. The king normally took part in the service from a first-floor "tribune" opposite the altar below and on the same level as his living quarters. This internal layout and the overall form—a long, thin building with a high roof—were rooted deep in French history, harking back to the thirteenth-century Sainte-Chapelle in Paris, built by Louis IX, and ultimately to Charlemagne's eighth-century chapel in his palace at Aachen.

Louis used the chapel to emphasize his links with Louis IX, or Saint Louis, as he was universally known in seventeenth-century France. Louis included him among the saints to whom he dedicated the new chapel, and transferred two of the saint's relics there. Louis, like all the Bourbons, was immensely proud of his saintly ancestry. On the eve of the Revolution one of his descendants, the duchesse de Bourbon, was seen going down to the street from her Paris house as a procession of the Holy Sacrament passed by in order to kiss the cover of the communion chalice "from the same side as the priest, prerogative of the race of Saint Louis."[27]

Inside the chapel, the décor made the most of this ancestry, presenting the sainted king as an idealized version of Louis XIV. As usual, scholars worked out the details; their identity is unknown, but the Little Academy has been suspected. An example of their modus operandi can be seen in a relief in the side chapel of Saint Louis, off the north side of the nave. It depicts a victory trophy incorporating Saracen standards, two of them decorated with the crescent moon of Islam. In the middle of the trophy, Saint Louis is shown adoring the Crown of Thorns. These are historical references to the saint-king's crusades in the Holy Land and to the holy relics that he redeemed from Venetian pawnbrokers and brought back to France, building the Sainte-Chapelle in Paris to house them.[28]

To understand the relief fully, it is necessary to know that Louis XIV claimed a place in Christian Europe's continuing struggle against "infidels." In 1686 Le Brun painted a scene on the ceiling of the Salon of Peace depicting a woman personifying Christendom with her foot on an Ottoman helmet, symbolizing the Muslim realm of the caliph-sultan Mehmed IV. It can still be seen above the fireplace. Behind this image was Louis' claim that the peace treaties of Nimwegen had left his erstwhile foe, the Holy Roman Emperor, free to concentrate on the threat from the sultan, whose siege of Vienna a few years later was indeed beaten off by the emperor with last-minute Polish help. In fact, this French claim was disingenuous: France actually encouraged the Turkish invasion of Habsburg lands. But rhetoric, then as now, played its part in international politics.[29]

Overall, Versailles did not present an original image of Louis XIV's kingship. The techniques of comparison and the depiction of battles derived from an Italianate "tool kit" for praising rulers that was in common use at the time. It was no novelty for a French king to claim the succession to imperial Rome in France or to be a new Saint Louis. What was unparalleled was the scale of the glorification of Louis XIV at Versailles—as if a familiar song were being sung at the highest volume.

In the previous century the weaker kings of the Valois dynasty were the ones who made most use of Roman imagery. Perhaps there is something defensive about the relentless projection of royal majesty at Versailles. Louis made no overt reference to the civil war of his childhood in the decorative programs of the palace, probably because the suppression of domestic strife was not seen as particularly glorious, especially in a monarchy that modeled itself on imperial Rome: Augustus, one of Louis XIV's Roman role models, had studiously avoided public crowing over his defeat of Mark Antony.

Revenge could have taken a subtler form. One of the grievances of the rebels—or Frondeurs, as they were known—had been the high taxation inflicted on the king's subjects by the royal government under Mazarin. But Louis did not cut royal expenditure once he assumed personal rule in 1661. Was his extravagant use of taxpayers' money to fund the works at Versailles his way of avenging himself on the Frondeurs?[30]

The overwhelming message of royal omnipotence emitted at Versailles was bolstered by the natural limitations of the site. As Saint-Simon acerbically put it, Louis XIV sought "to ride roughshod over nature and to use his money and ingenuity to subdue it to his will." Others took a patriotic pride in this "victory." In the following century a French writer pointed out that Louis could easily have embellished a locale that nature had already made beautiful. But only a great king could transform a place as thankless as Versailles into the most magnificent spot in the world.[31]

To create Versailles, Louis XIV was prodigal not only with French ingenuity but also with French lives and money. At the height of building activity in the early 1680s, tens of thousands of workers labored day and night without even the basic precaution of safety ropes. Over the years the crown paid out indemnities to an estimated three thousand or so injured workers. The meager compensation for a man no longer capable of work was, at best, the equivalent of two months' subsistence for a family.

Epidemics decimated the workers. In 1678 the corpses were carted away at night to avoid demoralizing the healthy. Ironically, the labors of the workforce exacerbated the health hazards of the building site. The artificial ponds created in the surrounding countryside to collect water encouraged typhoid and marsh fevers, especially when the water level dropped in summer. Contemporaries ignorant of the true causes wrongly blamed the "air" of Versailles.[32]

Cocooned as he was, Louis was rarely confronted with this human cost of Versailles. During preparations for the fête of 1664, five or six workers were crushed by falling stage machinery. A bereaved mother attended one of Louis' public audiences at nearby Saint-Germain. Armed with the courage of grief, she let fly with a volley of colorful insults: Louis was a "king of machines," a tyrant, and a consorter with whores. A startled Louis asked if she was referring to him. When she said yes and continued her tirade, she was arrested and condemned to a rigorous whipping. The embarrassing episode was reported in the foreign gazettes printed in Holland and smuggled into France, but did not appear in the censored prints of seventeenth-century France.[33]

Versailles was a mirage. The investment of huge sums there did not prove Louis XIV's power. As emperor Kao-tsu had grasped in the second century B.C., magnificence helped to create the illusion of power in the first place. The culture of extravagance at Louis XIV's Versailles—a culture inherited by his successors—is clear from the constant demolition and rebuilding. Its tone is caught in a summary of expenditure for the period 1664–90 drawn up by one of Mansart's clerks. It begins with the boast: "No European prince has taken expenditure as far as the King in order to create a residence worthy of his Royal Majesty."[34]

The exact cost of Versailles has been hotly debated since at least the eighteenth century. Under Louis XIV the monarchy did not publish accounts, and Louis was shrewd enough to have his departmental chiefs record expenditure on Versailles under different headings. At the time only he, working with his ministers one by one, had a panoramic view. The accounts kept by the Royal Buildings Office were finally published in the nineteenth century. They produce a total figure of 66.6 million livres for the château of Versailles itself, with almost half as much again spent on the total project, including the garden and waterworks. This yields a grand total of 91.7 million livres. To put this amount in some kind of perspective, work on the château rarely consumed more than one percent of the annual total expenses of the royal government, and even the total cost is dwarfed by Louis XIV's expenditure on his other great passion, the military: in 1692, total war costs amounted to over 114 million livres in one year alone. There is some truth in the claim, made by more than one modern historian, that Versailles was "cheap at the price."

But the impression of boundless resources succeeded only too well. Eventually it came back to haunt Louis XIV's descendants. During the Revolution the popular orator Mirabeau could seriously claim that Versailles had cost twelve hundred million livres, roughly five million English pounds in the money of the time. But this sum did not seem as fantastic then as it does now. It helped to create the persistent myth that the cost of Versailles was itself a cause of the French Revolution.[35]

Louis XIV believed in the principle of an open palace. As he wrote in his memoirs, "If there is anything singular about the French monarchy, it is the free and easy access which subjects have to their prince." The guards opened the gates at six and closed them at midnight. There is plenty of evidence to suggest that once a visitor had gained entry to the palace, the king was, if not exactly accessible, then at least visible.

For instance, a provincial from Douai wrote an account of his visits to Versailles around 1700. He describes gaining access to the state apartments with ease. With an introduction to the ushers from a friendly Swiss Guard, he watched the king's *lever* and supper in his bedchamber. He was shown the ground-floor apartment of Monseigneur after being given slippers, "from fear of spoiling anything."[36]

But it is unlikely that Louis XIV's palace welcomed all comers without distinction. French people believed that Louis used Versailles to withdraw from the sight of the Parisian crowd. Saint-Simon thought as much.[37] Under Louis XVI the Parisian journalist Jean-Sébastien Mercier wrote that the effect of Versailles was to "render the Monarch invisible" and "screen him from the eyes and shouts of the multitude."[38] This was probably a widespread view in Paris, and Louis did not exactly discourage it. In 1685 the courtier Dangeau recorded in his journal that the king had ordered the guards to admit only court people to the garden because he felt overwhelmed by the crowds of Parisian "riffraff" when he went out for walks. The splendors of Versailles did not particularly target the humbler sort of subject.[39]

The dress code for admission to the palace reinforces this impression. It was the job of the guards to ensure that visitors were respectably dressed. A revealing convention decreed that male visitors had to wear swords, even if this meant hiring them from the palace concierge. This custom shows that, in principle, access to Louis XIV's palace was restricted to nobles, whose swords were a badge of their rank.[40]

Louis took major steps to improve access to Versailles. When his father discovered Versailles, communication with Paris was poor, apart from an old drovers' track that passed through Versailles on its way to the Paris cattle markets. By about 1680, at considerable expense of money and labor and much moving of earth, Louis had built an imposing new royal road that left Paris by the Champs-Élysées, crossed the Seine on a new bridge at Sèvres, and made its final approach to the palace in a broad avenue of Roman straightness that became known as the avenue de Paris.

Louis also set up by a system of privately run public transport between palace and capital. Persons of quality could buy a seat in a four-seater carriage that took two hours. In the eighteenth century there was a two-seater version too, humorously known as a "chamber pot." These were the so-called carriages of the court. For twenty-five sols the less well-off could take an early form of horse-drawn omnibus, the much slower *coche,* which left twice a day from near the Tuileries, carrying up to twenty passengers each time.[41]

But at all times the normal means of transport for ordinary Parisians was by ferry to the Sèvres bridge and shank's pony the rest of the way. Even respectable people walked if there were no seats available on the limited public transport. Around 1699 the professor from Douai was forced by the biting wind to walk with his eyes half shut from Viroflay down to the bridge. Another time, the mixture of wind, rain, and dust had turned his black frock coat to gray by the time he reached the palace.

The sort of people whom Louis was really interested in attracting to Versailles is shown by the quality of the invitees to his three early fêtes in the gardens: the high aristocracy; provincial nobles, including ones from the new territories; ambassadors; other distinguished foreigners; and rich burghers, especially Parisians. These were the influential people whom Louis sought to impress by building Versailles. As we shall see next, above all Versailles allowed Louis to put relations with his leading nobles on a new footing.

# 3.

# *A Gilded Cage?*

LOUIS XIV rebuilt Versailles in the years following 1677 mainly to accommodate the vast royal entourage, known to all French people simply as "the court." At the heart of this court community was the royal household *(maison du roi)*. This fossil of an institution had roots as old as the French monarchy—the ancient service of the royal tables, the quaintly named King's Mouth *(Bouche du Roi)*, can be documented as far back as the thirteenth century and was certainly much older. The Mouth was one of over twenty services into which the household was organized by Louis XIV's day. A list hints at the organizational complexity of this institution:

Chapel-Oratory *(Chapelle-Oratoire)*
Chapel-Music *(Chapelle-Musique)*
Commons Chapel *(Chapelle du Commun)*
Provostship of the King's Hotel *(Prévôté de l'Hôtel du roi)*
King's Mouth *(Bouche du roi)*
King's Bedchamber *(Chambre du roi)*
King's Music *(Musique du roi)*
King's Wardrobe *(Garde-robe du roi)*
Faculty *(Faculté)*
King's Cabinet *(Cabinet du roi)*
Ceremonies *(Cérémonies)*
Lodgings *(Logements)*
Buildings *(Bâtiments)*
Furnishings *(Garde-meubles)*

Entertainments *(Menus Plaisirs)*
Grand Stables *(Grande Écurie)*
Small Stables *(Petite Écurie)*
Hunt *(Venerie)*
Grand Falconry *(Grande Fauconnerie)*
Wolf Hunt *(Louveterie)*
Boar Hunt *(Vautrait)*[1]

This multitude of services provided for the sovereign and his family explains why the permanent installation of the court at Versailles required a host of dependencies around the palace: stables, kennels, barracks, a kitchen garden, a furniture depot, an art gallery, a theatrical store, and—always—lodgings and more lodgings for personnel.

To a large extent, the court was self-sufficient. It grew its own vegetables, baked its own bread, and made its own ice. The royal hunt supplied the game consumed at the royal tables. The court made its own music—some of the most sublime in the Europe of the day—and built its own theatrical sets.

The court had its own jurisdiction, headed by a major dignitary known as the grand provost of France. He—or, as was the normal practice at Versailles, his deputies—heard all litigation to do with the king's "hôtel": the community of people and services in permanent attendance on the monarch. At Versailles the guards of the grand provost helped to police the palace, patrolling the interior in their traditional smocks, or *hoquetons*. Their original guardroom at Versailles, with frescoed walls dating from the 1670s, can still be seen on the ground floor of the central block.

The court had its own following of licensed merchants, who were allowed to set up their stalls of books, lace, gloves, fans, and other luxury goods inside the royal palace. For a long time at Versailles these merchants were assigned the upper-floor room of the small building linking the south wing to the central block. Appropriately, today this room is a museum shop.

No one seems to know how many people lived in the palace of Versailles. On official lists the numbers of household personnel always ran into several thousands. In addition, there were the unknown numbers of servitors too humble in status to deserve official listing. As dauphin, the future Louis XVI hired a water carrier and cesspool emptier for his personal service at Versailles. Vital to the royal comfort, these casual servants, paid by the month, were not included among the privileged grouping of the "domestic officers."[2]

Numbers varied anyhow, depending on how large the royal family was at any one time. It was particularly numerous in 1789. In addition to Louis XVI's household of just under nineteen hundred officers, eleven others catered for the needs of his wife, children, siblings, nephews, aunts, and a cousin, the duc d'Orléans. These households added thousands to the roster of court personnel and made the task of Louis' ministers, who sought to implement cutbacks, more difficult.[3]

Any estimate must take account of the household troops. These were divided into the indoor and outdoor guards. The outdoor guards were drawn from two infantry regiments of the line, the red-coated Swiss and the blue-coated French Guards, which sent detachments for weekly tours of duty at Versailles. Each detachment took one-half of the outer courtyard to guard; the French Guards were stationed on the more honorable right, or southern, side of Louis XIV's bedchamber. Off-duty, the men were billeted in barracks beneath the Ministers' Court. Above them the cobblestones rested on an underlay of mastic-coated canvas to contain the smell from their latrines. In 1699 outdoor and indoor guards numbered 2,690 men.[4]

The only exact figure for the population of the palace and its annexes is provided by a police census taken shortly after the return of the boy-king Louis XV in 1722. Narbonne, the police commissioner at Versailles, counted 8,254 heads, including four thousand people said to be residing within the palace proper. But this last figure is so suspiciously round that it is unlikely to have been based on door-to-door visits to the 364 lodgings known to have existed in the palace at the time.[5]

It seems rather high. Inside the palace, a person accorded the privilege of a lodging by the king might be joined by spouse, kin, friends, and certainly servants. In 1754 the marquis and marquise de Durfort resided in their lodging with their household of five to six servants: seven or eight in total. If eight were taken as an average and multiplied by 364, the numbers beneath the king's roof at Versailles would total around three thousand: a rough order of magnitude at best, bearing in mind that some palace lodgings were larger than others, such as those of the four secretaries of state.

The figures of Narbonne can be set beside two unofficial estimates from the eve of the Revolution. In 1782 the marquis de Bombelles described Versailles in his journal as "a palace which lodges more than twelve thousand people." Assuming that by "palace" he meant all the dependencies as well, his figure is not incredible. He certainly knew the court well. The marquise was a lady-in-waiting of Louis XVI's sister. He was a French diplomat, trained to record accurately.[6]

Five years later, an anonymous memoir penned for senior members of the government refers to "the fifteen to sixteen thousand people who form the court." This even larger figure perhaps offers a rough estimate of all the court personnel living in the town at the time, not just the lodgers in the palace and its annexes. It may also have included casual labor. Even so, the impression given is that the real size of the court grew as the eighteenth century progressed.[7]

All in all, these figures for the size of the court at Versailles bear out the impression of Louis XV's father-in-law, the ex-king of Poland, who thought that what made it unusual among its European peers was the great number of royal servants.[8] In an aristocratic age in which a Spanish duke might have as many as six thousand servants, Louis XIV needed a swollen entourage to signal the unique magnificence of the French king.[9]

This entourage explains why Louis XIV required such a huge palace. The north and south wings alone were built to house around 175 lodgings. The Grand Commons was planned to provide a further 103.[10] Mansart's two stables housed not just horses and carriages but hundreds of members of the court, including the school of royal pages. Other dependencies too, such as the Kennel and the kitchen garden, housed lodgings for court servants.

Madame de Boigne, memoirist-daughter of a former lady-in-waiting to one of Louis XVI's aunts, describes the class structure of Versailles. There existed "a line of demarcation, impossible to cross," among the court personnel, depending on whether or not a person took orders from a departmental head with the title of "Grand":

*So the gentleman of the bedchamber in ordinary, since he took his orders*
*from the first gentleman of the bedchamber, was a very subaltern figure,*
*while the first equerry, taking his orders from the grand equerry, was a man*
*of the Court; but the equerries who took their orders from him belonged to*
*the subaltern class. . . . Monsieur de Grailly, a mere equerry, found all the*
*doors of the Court people closed.*[11]

Everyone recognized the primacy of the *grandes charges*. These
were the most important offices in the king's household. The grand
master of France was titular head of the whole household. He had his
own official residence on the avenue de Paris, on the site of today's
town hall.

The grand chamberlain was titular overseer of the service of the
bedchamber. In the Middle Ages his predecessors slept nightly in the
king's bedchamber, or at any rate next to it. But this duty had long
since devolved to others. At Versailles the grand chamberlain was a pan-
jandrum with mainly honorific duties. Among the privileges of the
post, its incumbent by tradition was allowed to place his escutcheon on
the doors of the royal bedroom. In Louis XIV's bedchamber at Versailles, the wooden paneling was carved with little towers. These were
the arms of the Bouillon family, who monopolized the office for most
of the history of Versailles as a royal residence.[12]

The other *grandes charges* at Versailles were the grand almoner, who
headed the ecclesiastical household; the grand equerry, overseer of the
Grand Stables; the grand huntsman, in charge of the Kennel; and the
grand master of the wardrobe. They had all gone down on bended
knee before the monarch to swear the oath of office "between his
hands" in a special ceremony in the royal bedchamber at Versailles.
Thereafter, they all took their orders directly from the sovereign—a
crucial calculus of personal prestige among the courtiers.

The royal household was a conservative institution. Ancient positions became ossified. Long before the reign of Louis XIV, the medieval writ of the grand master had shrunk from total control of the
household to mere oversight of the Mouth. Since the treason of a
sixteenth-century incumbent, the duc de Guise, the grand master no
longer had direct responsibility even for the sovereign's own table.

Notionally he was responsible for some five hundred or so officers employed in the Mouth. Physically this service was divided between the Grand Commons, where the suppliers made their deliveries, and the kitchens and storerooms across the street in the south wing. These were grouped around an inner courtyard known as the Court of the Mouth. A watercolor cross section of this part of the palace dating from 1836 still shows the basement kitchen in which the king's meals used to be cooked, with its high-vaulted roof and vast fireplace. This was the hot and greasy domain of the chefs, soup and pastry makers, spit roasters, scullions, and kitchen boys known from the departmental registers.[13]

From here, processions set off with food for the royal tables. The dishes were carried via the Princes' Staircase to the first-floor antechambers where the sovereigns ate in public. The food was not necessarily cold on arrival: the journey took no more than five minutes, and covers of silver or gold plate slowed the cooling of food on the way.[14] If necessary, the food could be warmed up, as was the dinner of Louis XV's daughters on September 17, 1749. Horace Walpole was among the spectators "almost stifled in the antechamber, where their dishes were heating over the charcoal."[15]

All this complicated machine was routinely overseen, not by the grand master, but by the first maître d'hôtel. This important personage received the king's daily orders for his meals and oversaw their execution. It was he who arranged the hospitality for distinguished visitors such as the foreign ambassadors, who were always welcomed at Versailles with tea, hot chocolate, and pastries on their arrival from Paris for their Tuesday audience. He was aided by the general controller, a commoner who monitored the cost and quality of the provisions and inspected deliveries by the suppliers. They were contracted every six years to deliver fixed amounts of bread, meat, wine, and table linen at agreed prices, in an attempt, not always successful, to contain the budget.

The post of grand master was not a complete sinecure. The grand master passed the monthly accounts and was in charge of staff appointments. The hereditary incumbents—the king's cousins, the Condé—were entitled to take a share from the sale of any new offices and from the resale of old ones. This lucrative trade was a significant source of income for the Condé. Prince Louis Joseph protested furiously, but in vain, when the old perks were swept away in 1780 by the reforming government of Louis XVI.

Other *grandes charges* were more directly involved in the routine life of Versailles. The stables, a core service of the French royal court, had ancient origins: the king and his household had, since time immemorial, relied on horses for fighting and transport. Both Louis XIV and Louis XV rode to war. As for Versailles on the move, it was an awesome sight. In 1699 a party of English travelers ran into the court on its way back from the autumnal "voyage" to Fontainebleau. They counted "above three hundred coaches with six and eight horses," not to mention troops and baggage.[16]

Coaches and horses were housed in the two stables flanking the main road from Paris. The Small Stables, domain of the first equerry, was built to shelter twenty-two royal carriages and nearly five hundred horses.[17] Just as the use of carriages at court was a relatively recent innovation, so was the independence of this service from the domain of the grand equerry. Despite the fact that the two buildings were linked by an underground passage, the junior service was locked in an enduring rivalry with the Grand Stables. In 1715 a full-scale battle erupted in the courtyards between the coachmen and grooms of the two services.

Of the prince de Lambesc, Louis XVI's grand equerry, an eyewitness later remembered: "From five in the morning, even in winter, he was at the riding school which he had had illuminated, mounting or dressing horses and giving riding lessons."[18] His duties required him to be in constant attendance at the monarch's side when he was out on horseback. He oversaw the palace school of pages and maintained the king's stock of saddle horses, which numbered nearly seven hundred in 1715.

Both equerries and their subordinates expended much time, energy, and money on searching Europe and beyond for the finest breeds of horses for royal use. Louis XIV hunted on English steeds and had his carriages drawn by Oldenburg grays from Sweden and Polish "Tigers." In 1731 Lambesc's predecessor but one, his great-uncle the self-styled "Prince Charles" (of Lorraine), wrote to his counterpart at the court of Persia for Arabian stallions.

The Grand Stables was home to two colorful corps of ancient origin.

By the age of Louis XIV, the eleven heralds of arms, led by their king Mountjoy (Montjoie), only appeared at court on state occasions. Their playing-card costume was one of the most quaint of the many archaic survivals in the royal household at Versailles: coat of arms of crimson velvet, doublet and hose of crimson satin, black velvet cloak and feathered cap, with the king's portrait on a medallion round the neck.

Also employed at the Grand Stables was a band of musicians who specialized in playing the sort of loud instruments that carried above the din of open-air processions: trumpet, fife, bassoon, and kettledrum. Heralds and musicians were considered so necessary to royal ceremonies that they survived various eighteenth-century cutbacks in court personnel. They made their last appearance at Versailles in the procession that opened the Estates-General in May 1789.[19]

The Kennel was the preserve of another ancient officer of the crown, the grand huntsman *(grand veneur)*. Like that of grand master, this position was so important in a hunting-mad palace that royalty deigned to fill it. The comte de Toulouse, one of Louis XIV's legitimated children, was succeeded by his son, the duc de Penthièvre, who served both Louis XV and Louis XVI.

The father knew nothing about either dogs or hunting, but was an excellent horseman and blew his old-fashioned hunting horn well. Instead of always asking the king for extra funds, he subsidized the stag hunt from his own pocket, allowing a canny Louis XIV to benefit from the huge fortune that he had allowed Toulouse to accumulate.[20]

That rare bird, a Bourbon prince who disliked hunting, Penthièvre likewise owed his office to birth, not aptitude. But the duke served conscientiously in a fatiguing post that required him to oversee the king's hunting parties, the different packs of hounds and hunting horses, the rambling premises of the Kennel, and a staff of two lieutenants, twenty-nine gentlemen, two pages, four quartermasters, four huntsmen, eight grooms, forty-four dog handlers, including eighteen for the bloodhounds, and a marshal.[21]

Just as the heads of the stables were supported by expert horsemen, in the Kennel the grand huntsman could call on the expertise of the experienced officers under his orders like Monsieur de Nestier, one of the best horsemen in France: "You would think that the man and the horse were but one." The septuagenarian marquis de Dampierre, "all wrinkled, with blotchy red skin," entertained Louis XV with tall stories of the hunt. There was the one about the hare that he would swear he had seen transform into a sheep, then a boar, and so on. At Versailles there was much of this talk of hunting. It was one of the few harmless topics of conversation for a king. Louis XV "led all his conversations round to the day's hunt or the next day's."[22]

The most colorful of all these characters from the hunting world was Monsieur de Landsmath, another aging officer in Louis XV's hunting establishment. He was a former military man of enormous bravery who stood out at Versailles for his habit of speaking his mind. The king liked this quality, and the two developed a camaraderie illustrated by a little episode recorded by Madame Campan, who knew Landsmath in her youth.

Like most people, Landsmath disliked getting old. Once, when Louis XV asked him his age, he avoided replying. In a spirit of raillery, the king secretly sent for Landsmath's baptism certificate. Fifteen days later, he suddenly produced it in front of its subject and read out the details, which revealed that the old soldier had been born back in 1680. An irritated Landsmath did not hesitate to reply: "Put that away at once, Sire; a prince charged with the happiness of twenty-five million men should not torment a single one of them for fun."[23]

The clothes-conscious Louis XIV had sent out a clear signal about the importance of dress at court by creating a new office, grand master of the wardrobe *(grand maître de la garde-robe)*, in 1669. At Versailles the wardrobe was physically housed on the ground floor of the central block in rooms overlooking the Marble Court. Here, the king's clothes were stored in coffers guarded by the wardrobe valets, who slept there at night and during the day assembled the outfits to be taken up to the king's bedchamber. A lace maker was on hand to repair that particularly fine and vulnerable fabric.

Saint-Simon likened François VII, duc de La Rochefoucauld, Louis XIV's grand master of the wardrobe, to a slave. "The *lever*, the *coucher*, the two other changes of clothes each day, the king's daily hunts and walks, he was present at all of them, sometimes spending ten years on end without sleeping away from the court."[24] Under Louis XV his grandson Alexandre de La Rochefoucauld, who had inherited the office, would go in person to Paris to choose the royal suits for each change of season.[25]

The closer their attendance, the more influence with the monarch his household officials stood to wield. The best placed was the troika of first gentleman of the bedchamber in waiting *(premier gentilhomme de la chambre)*; captain of the bodyguard in waiting *(capitaine des gardes du corps)*, who had plentiful opportunities for a word in the royal ear while carrying out his chief duty, which was to walk directly behind the king as soon as he left his rooms and "never lose sight of him or become separated from him"[26]; and first valet in waiting *(premier valet de la chambre)*, who slept each night at the foot of the king's bed, ready to answer his master's needs—the recumbent Louis XV even had a cord at hand, the other end attached to the valet. Under Louis XIV the royal confessor was also a figure to be reckoned with: unlike the two kings who followed him, Louis placed unusual confidence in his successive confessors, especially in the matter of recommendations for lucrative church offices.[27]

The first gentlemen of the bedchamber were among the most important officials at Versailles. Four of them served on an annual rota. Under Louis XIV the posts conferred so much prestige that dukes came to monopolize them, as they continued to do down to the Revolution. An official description of the household from 1699 sums up their job as follows: in the absence of the grand chamberlain, to present the royal shirt at the daily *lever,* to control access to the bedchamber and to wait on Louis when he ate there, to receive the oaths of loyalty from the lesser officers of the bedchamber, and to oversee royal ceremonies and court entertainments. This mix of "real" and ceremonial duties—of paperwork and performance—was typical of most of the higher household posts at Versailles.

A breakdown of *la chambre* gives a better idea of how the household worked in practice. The department included sixteen ushers of the bedchamber and three of the antechamber, who filtered admissions to the king's rooms; thirty-six valets, who made the king's bed and helped him to dress; six *garçons,* or errand boys; nine barbers; thirteen dressers to pass the king his cane, cloak, and gloves; the archaic-sounding arquebus carrier, whose frozen title reflected a time when the sovereign wielded this obsolete firearm, but who now tended the royal hunting rifles and pistols; twelve clock makers to wind the royal timepieces; two bearers of the king's chamber pot; eight furniture arrangers *(tapissiers)* to oversee the two annual changes of the royal furnishings (one for summer, one for winter); eight furniture bearers; and a muleteer for when the court was on the move.

But the numbers of personnel are misleading. Like the first gentlemen from whom they took their orders, most of these subordinate officers served on a rotating basis, usually for three months. At the end they surrendered the official lodgings that went with their service in favor of newly arrived colleagues. One of the animating rhythms of Versailles four times a year was the changing of "quarters" throughout the services of the court. One set of officers packed up and left for home—mostly in nearby Paris or the Île-de-France—and another arrived with their traveling trunks, with all the attendant hustle and bustle.

The main reason for this job sharing was the long-standing royal practice of selling household offices to raise revenue, a practice that intensified in times of war, as under Louis XIV from 1690 on. Quarterly service allowed the crown to sell the same task four times over. The practice provided lucrative rake-offs for the *grandes charges,* but did not make for the highest levels of service in the palace. "What they have learnt in three months they unlearn in the nine others, if they have learnt anything in the first place," complained Madame, Louis XIV's sister-in-law.[28]

At Versailles the market for the sale and resale of household offices prompted the preservation of sinecures, such as the post of master of the queen's wardrobe. The incumbent's only real task—relic of earlier times when the court was constantly on the move—was the occasional one of supervising the loading of the queen's trunks when she traveled.[29] The post of the bearer of the king's chamber pot *(porte-chaise d'affaires du roi)* continued to be bought and sold long after the arrival of an early form of flush toilet in the king's apartment at Versailles in the 1730s had rendered its duties purely honorific. The scope for retrenchment among this luxuriant undergrowth of household offices is shown by the number in the Mouth alone—over four hundred—suppressed in the government economies of 1780.

Many middling and junior posts in the Mouth, the Bedchamber, and the Hunt were bought by commoners as investments. As "king's officers" they were exempt—down to 1766—from the chief land tax; they received modest emoluments paid by the interest that the crown earned from the original investment; they were entitled to board and lodging at court during their quarter, taking their meals at the officers' tables on the ground floor of the Grand Commons, or payment in lieu; and for those whose faces became personally familiar to the sovereign and his family, there was the prospect of a pension at the end.

These practical advantages were enough to make a household office the principal asset of modest families like the Padelin, who swept the royal chimneys, son following the father, for three centuries. Dynasties formed and intermarried, creating a family network "below stairs" at Versailles, a counterpart to the aristocratic clans of the household's upper echelons. The system even offered a precarious form of welfare for the elderly: when Marie-Anne Thierry retired as a tirewoman (lady's maid) to one of Louis XV's daughters, her niece and successor paid her old aunt an annual pension from the revenues of the post.[30]

For aspiring members of the bourgeoisie, an added attraction of royal service was the social cachet. Household offices tenable in absentia, such as the many sinecures in the hunt establishment, were popular with notables from small towns in the surrounding provinces, the sort of people who could afford a couple of servants and were important enough locally to merit burial in a side chapel of the local church.

In pre-Revolutionary France's society of ranks, membership of the royal household conferred marks of outward distinction keenly savored by those who were entitled to them. In 1714 one Marc Quatremer, owner of a post in the royal falconry, launched and won a court case against the wardens of his local church in Paris. He was asserting his right as a king's officer to be served before all the other parish bigwigs when the priest and his acolytes distributed the blessed bread *(pain bénit)* to the congregation at mass.[31]

Under Louis XVI the post of the bearer of the chamber pot was rotated between two incumbents on a biannual basis. "The one was a little tailor, his appearance as burlesque as his charge, bought with the proceeds of a lucky draw on the lottery; the other was the owner of a faience shop on the Rue du Vieux-Versailles." Each now solemnly discharged his duties at the king's *lever* wearing velvet court dress and a sword. Each could proudly sign his daughter's marriage-contract as "king's officer."[32]

Many of these officers of modest origin must have barely registered, if at all, on the royal radar. The first valets, servants of the royal body par excellence, were an important exception. The potential for intimacy between monarch and servitor was obviously great where two men shared a bedroom for days on end. Once in their beds, conversation may well have struck up as "friend to friend, and no longer master to valet."[33]

Louis XIV and his successors were all famously close to their first valets. Louis XIV's favorite first valet, Alexandre Bontemps, was a figure of Jeeves-like loyalty and discretion who was rumored to have been the go-between in his master's extramarital romances. Deploring all forms of social mobility that raised individuals out of the station into which they were born, the duc de Saint-Simon was particularly suspicious of Bontemps and the other first valets, crediting them with the same sort of political influence over their master as the powerful freedmen of the Roman emperor.

These relationships worked because the first valets were of modest origins. The father of Bontemps was a Parisian barber-surgeon who used to administer bleedings to Louis XIII. La Vienne, another of Louis XIV's first valets, was a literal barber, shaving and cutting hair before running a Parisian bathhouse. His hair-dressing skills recommended him to Louis once the king took to wearing wigs in his thirties.[34] From the sovereign's viewpoint, the friendship of valets was unthreatening and their loyalty absolute. Saint-Simon's fears about their political influence may not have been baseless, at least where the eighteenth century was concerned. Binet, one of Louis XV's head valets, is known to have written to his master on political matters.[35] Another head valet, Thierry, was believed to have "contributed greatly" to Louis XVI's appointment of the comte de Vergennes as minister for foreign affairs.[36]

Thanks to royal favor, first valets moved up in the world. The same Binet was rich enough to build an Italianate pavilion on the avenue de Paris, which was later bought by Madame du Barry, the king's mistress; it still exists, housing the local Chamber of Commerce. In the next reign, Louis XVI was said to be shocked when he saw the luxurious house and garden created by Thierry on the estate that his master had given him near Versailles. Head valets aspired to turn themselves into nobles: "the ultimate sign of social success" in pre-Revolutionary France.[37] The son of Thierry, himself the grandson of a peasant from a village near Saint-Germain-en-Laye, went on to style himself marquis de Ville d'Avray, after the name of his father's estate.[38]

Ranged on the other side of that "line of demarcation, impossible to cross" were the few hundred royal servitors recruited from the military nobility. These "persons of the sword" regarded themselves as socially superior to the nobles "of the robe," who derived their nobility from service in the legal courts. At Versailles the youngest servitors from the sword nobility were the royal pages, some of whom arrived in the palace when they were only nine.

In France there was a long tradition of nobles sending their sons to serve in the royal household. Louis XIV was keen to encourage the nobility to serve in the army and developed this tradition. At Versailles he set up a school for the pages. Most were housed in the stables, since horsemanship formed the keystone of their court education. After their years at court, pages were expected to serve as army officers. In 1786 the pages at Versailles numbered 158.

The families of applicants had to submit documents proving at least two hundred years of direct nobility and had to be able to provide their sons with an allowance. "Thereafter, the parents were relieved of all concern: costume, nourishment, teachers, medical care, everything was provided with a truly royal magnificence."[39] Memoirs and letters home give a vivid picture of the pages' way of life and the affectionate nostalgia that these schooldays inspired in later life.

A former page of Louis XVI, Félix d'Hézecques, describes in his memoirs the pages' quarters in the Grand Stables, occupying the whole of the left wing of that huge building, on the avenue de Saint-Cloud:

> *On the ground floor there was a very fine chapel, and a dining room with two billiard tables. This last room, vast and rather gloomy, its vaulted ceiling supported by four pillars, was lit by lamps. . . . We were split between four tables and, for nourishment, lighting and heating by three or four stoves, the king gave to the maître d'hôtel eighty thousand francs a year. On the first floor, in a vast gallery, were arranged, on two equal lines, the chambers where we lodged, all painted in varnished yellow and uniformly furnished. . . . At the end of the gallery a large room, well-heated, served for study. The two under-governors, the preceptor and the almoner had their lodgings in the attics, where the linen-store was as well. The governor occupied the pavilion, on the place d'Armes. There was arranged our library, open two hours daily, to change books and read the public journals.*[40]

The aristocratic pages were not a studious group, and some no doubt were virtual strangers to the library. But they learned to ride in a covered riding school under the eyes of some of the best riding masters in Europe, experts of the caliber of François-Étienne de la Bigne, who once rode his Spanish steed at a light gallop on the place d'Armes for a whole hour, using nothing more than a silk thread as a "rein."

The routine duties of the pages were light. Their most vigorous activity was on royal shoots, where they collected the game. In the palace they were assigned mainly decorative tasks in the service of different members of the royal family. Two handed the king his slippers; others held the trains of royal princesses, not always the gentlest taskmistresses. Hézecques remembered being "sharply scolded by Madame Adélaïde [Louis XVI's redoubtable aunt] for putting my hands in the muff which she gave me to hold while she climbed a staircase."[41]

Away from the palace, the rosy-cheeked youngsters lived much like their counterparts in English public schools of the time. Discipline was lax and rites of passage violent. Fifty years later one ex-page still bore the scar from a branding on the buttock with a red-hot spur. Of his time in the school, Hézecques thought it worthy of note that "no page died."[42]

The older pages were among those most likely to engage in the amorous intrigues for which the court of Versailles has a (somewhat over-rated) reputation. At sixteen years of age Alexandre de Tilly, a handsome page of Marie-Antoinette, could have stepped out the pages of the contemporary novel *Dangerous Liaisons*. Among his conquests was a countess. This widow of thirty-six, "still extremely beautiful," had a post in the household of the king's aunts. Tilly's account of their affair merits pausing over as a vignette of palace life.

The countess knew Tilly's parents. The two lovers first met socially in her lodging, apparently in the attics of the south wing. Here the countess wrote letters, gave small suppers, and received in her salon. Not long after their first meeting, Tilly was handed a note from her while at the play. Presumably he was in the cramped Comedy Room *(Salle de Comédie)*, the usual venue for court dramatics at this time.

In her note the countess suggested a rendezvous around five in the afternoon, when she would be returning via the garden terrace from the aunts' ground-floor apartments, "if the weather continues fine." They met and Tilly escorted her back to her rooms as far as the door of a neighbor, Madame de Saulx-Tavannes, one of the queen's ladies-in-waiting, " 'to whom I owe a visit,' she said."

Once their affair was launched, "we agreed that she would no longer receive me in her lodgings, but in an apartment on the Avenue de Paris." Once, he had terrified her by throwing himself at her knees when they were alone together in her rooms: " 'If one of my people were to come in!' she cried." For persons of rank there was little or no anonymity inside the palace, and clandestine affairs were best conducted off the premises. Royalty had less choice in the matter.[43]

At Versailles fifty or so families monopolized all the highest court positions for both men and women. Most of these families belonged to the highest ranks of the French nobility, the dukes and princes. Two branches of the royal house served respectively as grand masters and grand huntsmen. At the Grand Stables four generations of the princely Lorraine family filled the *charge* of grand equerry.

Theoretically, no post in the royal household was hereditary. But powerful families placed pressure on the sovereign by asking him for the reversion *(survivance)* in favor of another family member, who would take over when his or her relation resigned from office or died in it. Louis XIV and his successors all disliked reversions because they narrowed the room for maneuver in the distribution of court positions. But it was difficult even for the king to deny a request from a father or mother who had been in close attendance on the royal family for years—and his or her forebears before that.

Under Louis XIV the presumption grew up that a family had a claim on a position held by one of its number. This presumption became so entrenched that, in 1776, the young queen Marie-Antoinette caused real offense when she unilaterally conferred the reversion to the post of first equerry in her household on a favorite, the comte de Polignac. The trouble was that Polignac was unrelated to the then incumbent, the comte de Tessé, who had his own kin in mind for the reversion. The Austrian ambassador reported back to Vienna that the powerful court families "were used to passing their places to their children or their relations; the example which the queen has just given menaces everyone with [the imposition of] a reversion-holder against his or her wish."[44]

At all levels of the household, the standard of the service offered to the monarch and his family seems to have been, at best, uneven. The duc de Luynes, who kept a court journal under Louis XV, gives an amusing list of minor failings as an example of that monarch's forbearance. An empty sugar bowl elicits this royal comment: "There was certainly some sugar in it yesterday." Standing naked to don his shirt on a winter's morning, he received no shirt. "Ah, no shirt yet," he merely said as he put his dressing gown back on and went over to the fire. When he was preparing to mount his horse at the hunt, two boots for the same foot were brought up. "Whoever forgot it is more annoyed than I," he said before sitting down patiently to wait.[45]

Things had not always been better in the days of the more formidable Louis XIV. More than once he had to reprimand his grand chamberlain, the nineteen-year-old prince de Turenne, for his rude manners. Matters came to a head one morning in 1684, when the prince omitted to remove his gloves as he handed the king his shirt at the *lever,* hitting the royal nose rather sharply with their fringing. Louis was irritated enough to exile this member of the Bouillon family, onetime rulers of a small principality now straddling France's frontier with Belgium.

The incident underscores the importance to Louis XIV of good manners at the court. The general air of politesse at Versailles is captured in a semiofficial engraving that shows Louis in 1710 presiding over a royal marriage feast in his bedchamber. The table is laid with knives and the newfangled fork, which Louis was too old-fashioned to use, and both princes and princesses daintily extend their little fingers as they hold cups or morsels of food in their hand.[46]

For Louis, the maladroitness of Turenne was probably more than a personal irritation. The French books on good manners of the time suggest the anxiety that decent people felt about table manners (no licking the cutlery), personal cleanliness (nails should be cut and teeth cleaned), or behavior toward a grandee (one's hat should be removed even to his footman). People looked to Louis XIV's court to set the benchmark for courteous behavior. In the seventeenth century it was widely believed that ancient Rome had given civility to the barbarians of Europe. How could Louis XIV's Versailles, the new Rome, be less than exemplary on this score?

At Versailles the service of the princesses and royal offspring suffered from the same negligent attitudes. In 1712 the duchess of Burgundy, briefly dauphine, was served by a mistress of the wardrobe *(dame d'atours)*—the comtesse de Mailly—who, according to Saint-Simon, was too lazy to do her job. She was by no means the first or last royal servitor at Versailles to delegate her duties to an underling, one who, in this case, enriched herself at the expense of the duchess, who was reduced to borrowing ribbons and muffs from her own ladies.

Eventually the aged Louis XIV had to intervene, the countess screaming dishonor as she was relieved of her duties. Even so, sixteen years later, her powerful connections—she was a cousin of Madame de Maintenon—ensured her reappointment in the same post to Louis XV's young queen, Marie Leczinska.

In 1782 a piece of glass was found in the gruel being fed to the baby dauphin in the royal nursery at Versailles. It was shown at once to the person in overall charge, the princesse de Guéméné, governess of the "children of France" *(gouvernante des enfants de France)* and a friend of the mother, Marie-Antoinette. According to the well-informed Bombelles, the princess, member of one of France's grandest families, the Rohan, seemed less than overwhelmed by "the frightful danger which had menaced the heir to the throne."

On investigation, it turned out that Madame du Parc, a junior governess responsible for the baby's nourishment, had considered herself too good for the gruel making that was one of her express duties. She delegated the task to a kitchen servant, who had carelessly employed the base of a damaged bottle to pound the bread. Despite this serious dereliction of duty, Madame du Parc kept her job, being protected by none other than the princess, whose tirewoman, or lady's maid, she used to be. Marie-Antoinette herself felt powerless to protest. She only rid herself of Madame du Parc once the princess herself resigned not long after, for unrelated reasons.[47]

Surrounded by servants themselves, great aristocrats were not self-evidently cut out to wait on others. It must obviously be asked next why a grande dame like the princesse de Guéméné sought court employment in the first place. The wages paid to many household officials, even senior ones, were too modest to be the answer. Another would be the perks, such as the rake-offs from the sale of subaltern offices—a significant source of income for the grand master or the grand equerry.

By ancient custom, some household officials also inherited the monarch's personal possessions at his death. When Louis XIV died in 1715, the grand equerry claimed all his equestrian effects, horses, and their trappings. In the same way, the first gentleman in office at the king's death had the right to the furnishings of his bedchamber. This is how the superb chest of drawers by the cabinetmaker A.-R. Goudreaux, which stood for thirty-five years in Louis XV's bedchamber at Versailles, fell into the hands of the duc d'Aumont, first gentleman in waiting when the monarch died in this room in May 1774. By a circuitous route it found its way into London's Wallace Collection, where it can be seen today.

Lower down the food chain, the ushers had the right to the night's candles once they had extinguished them, the valets of the bedchamber expected a handsome tip—six thousand francs in 1782—for "the rights of the hassock," that is, for placing before the king's armchair the hassock on which new marshals knelt to receive their baton from the monarch; and so it went on.[48] Those who were entitled to them hung on for dear life to these ancient perquisites.

Like Madame de Guémené, senior officials at court could give positions in their departments or in other ways help the people whom one minister of Louis XVI called "their creatures." This was an important factor for great aristocrats, whose success as patrons of large networks of dependents of one sort or another was vital to maintaining their status and satisfying their sense of noblesse oblige.[49]

Above all, the plunder of court office included the favors that a court official obtained for her or his family. The princesse de Lamballe, Marie-Antoinette's friend, is often portrayed as featherbrained. But on her appointment as the superintendent of the queen's household *(surintendante de la maison de la reine)*, she moved rapidly to lever favors for her family, a junior branch of the royal house of Sardinia: a generous pension of forty thousand livres for her brother, along with fourteen thousand livres' worth of appointments for his colonelcy in the French army, "although the appointments of colonels are only four thousand livres."[50]

Under Louis XIV, the reaction of the prince de Turenne's family to his disgrace is documented in an extant letter from his uncle, the powerful cardinal de Bouillon, to the prince's father, the duc de Bouillon. The cardinal's overriding concern was to stop the king from taking away from the family the prince's post of grand chamberlain.

The cardinal suggested that Louis XIV should be asked if the *charge* could be transferred to one of Turenne's brothers—not to the next in age, as would be normal, but to the youngest, because "as a result he will have more time in a position to do whatever will be required." Bouillon had in mind the true gold to be mined from a senior court office, namely, the daily chances given to the incumbent for a word in the king's ear on behalf, above all, of himself, his family, and kin.[51]

In his memoirs Saint-Simon offers his analysis of why Louis XIV decided to move the seat of the monarchy from Paris to Versailles. One reason, he claims, was that Louis had taken a dislike to Paris since the civil wars of his childhood. He never forgot the traumatic moment when rebels invaded the royal bedchamber. It is true that, from 1661, he preferred Saint-Germain-en-Laye to Paris. After the permanent move to Versailles, he visited the capital only eight times in thirty-three years.[52] In the annals of the French monarchy, this royal withdrawal from a troublesome capital was by no means without precedent: the medieval fortress of Vincennes, to the east of Paris—towered, moated, and self-sufficient in water—had repeatedly served this purpose in the thirteenth and fourteenth centuries. In more recent times, Louis XIII was lodged at Vincennes after his father's assassination; Louis XIV himself stayed here frequently in the 1650s.

Saint-Simon gives as another reason the fact that Louis, an absolute monarch, felt fettered in his freedom of action by the Parisian crowds, who surrounded him whenever he left his palace. "The awkward situation with his mistresses and the dangers involved in conducting such scandalous affairs in a busy capital, crowded with people of every kind of mentality, played no small part in deciding him to leave." One result of the relocation to Versailles was that Louis and his successors became dangerously cushioned from the impact of their actions on public, especially Parisian, opinion.[53]

Saint-Simon was a disappointed courtier under Louis XIV, who never offered him a position. As one of Philippe d'Orléans' friends, he briefly tasted power under the Regency. In retirement he wrote memoirs: "the only revenge, the only compensation, to which he could pretend once he knew that his hour had passed."[54] The duke disapproved of what he perceived as Louis XIV's deliberate distancing of the high nobility from the levers of political power. Even so, his intelligence and his long residence at court under Louis XIV make him a very serious witness to the meaning and purpose of Versailles.

Looking back on Louis XIV's reign in the eighteenth century, the aging Saint-Simon presents Versailles as a gilded cage in which the king held captive the formerly troublesome high nobility. Louis moved to Versailles because the rural location would make absenteeism from court more noticeable and plotting in Paris harder. He made known that he expected the grandees of France to court him on a more or less permanent basis. After attracting a large entourage, he encouraged his courtiers to impoverish themselves through lavish spending on clothes, gambling, and carriages. This reinforced their dependence on royal favor and handouts.

This picture is not just a figment of Saint-Simon's imagination. Other contemporaries saw court entertainments as a calculated way of "spoiling" the great nobles and making them more "submissive."[55] The marquis de Flamarens, a young man at Versailles in the last decade or so of Louis XIV's reign, remembered how the old king expected his entourage to be in permanent attendance on him: "The ministers never left Louis XIV without leave. Neither did the great officers of the crown absent themselves without permission. Those with [household] posts stayed in continuous residence at the Court. Versailles was their homeland [*pays*]: Paris was foreign to them."[56]

Louis XIV's memoirs show that, at the start of his personal rule, the young king was well aware of the political need to do something about his courtiers: "in my Court, very little loyalty without self-interest, so that my most ostensibly submissive subjects in fact were as much on the attack and as great a threat to me as the most rebellious."[57] In the 1660s, when he was still in his twenties, he seems to have broadly decided on the new direction that the court was to take.

Accommodating his courtiers was one of his constant preoccupations from the start of his personal rule. Eventually Louis solved this problem by building a palace big enough to house the royal family and the nobles of the household under one roof. Here Versailles had the great advantage of being a "green field" site. No previous French king had been particularly worried about whether his courtiers lodged within his palace. In the 1670s Saint-Germain-en-Laye contained only sixty-three lodgings, and most courtiers had to stay in the town, as indeed they did in Paris. Versailles was a new kind of palace for a new type of court. After the permanent move, Louis always oversaw the allocation of lodgings inside the palace and made clear his concern for the comfort of individual lodgers.

Louis used the allure of the royal person to attract nobles to his new palace. In his memoirs, he wrote that the "shared pleasures [of court entertainments], which give the members of the court an honest familiarity with us, touch and charm them more than one can say." The reaction of the marquise de Sévigné after a visit to Versailles in 1683 shows how well Louis XIV understood his target group. "I have seen these beautiful apartments, I am charmed by them. . . . Everything is grand and magnificent, and the music and dancing are perfect. . . . But what pleases me above all is to spend four whole hours with the sovereign, to share in his pleasures and he in ours."[58]

That Louis was successful in attracting the grandees into his entourage is shown by the rising rank of the nobles seeking posts in the royal household. Madame de Sévigné again: "Formerly the queen's ladies of honor were marquises, and all the great offices of the king's household were mere lords: now they are all held by dukes or marshals of France, and everything has gone up."[59] That was in 1680, two years before the permanent move to Versailles.

Louis used his court to provide families of former rebels with a means to reinstate themselves in his graces. François VI, duc de La Rochefoucauld, was never forgiven by the king for his part in the civil war, when he raised a feudal army against the crown from his own estates. His son François VII redeemed the family by a life of devoted service in the king's household, obtaining the post of grand master of the wardrobe in 1672, then becoming grand huntsman in 1679. Scions of other distinguished but disloyal lineages—the Condé, the Lorraine, the Bouillon, the Soubise—likewise atoned by deferential service in Louis XIV's household at Versailles.

Louis did indeed keep his court under close observation. His lifelong surveillance of the upper nobility is shown by an episode in Saint-Simon's youth. After the duke made a journey on personal business to Rouen, "the king wrote to me through his ministers enquiring about my reasons."[60] At Versailles the king's first valets ran what in effect was a spy network. They used Swiss Guards "to frequent the corridors and passages, courts and gardens by day and night, morning and evening, to hide, observe people, follow them, see where they went and when they returned, overhear their conversation and report exactly on everything."[61]

But the grandees who benefited from Louis XIV's generosity with pensions and other royal graces did not necessarily see Versailles in the same gloomy light as Saint-Simon. The duc d'Antin, a successful courtier of Louis XIV who was still a youth when the court moved to Versailles, recalled in his memoirs how, from childhood, he had been encouraged to dream of "the king, the court, and great possessions."[62]

The duke's relations, the Noailles family, are an example of nobles who played the system at Versailles to their own great profit. The total value of the favors that the Noailles obtained from successive monarchs down to the Revolution was estimated by an ex-courtier at two million livres. This works out at roughly £83,000 in English money of the time: a colossal sum.[63]

At a still higher level socially were the Condé family, cousins of Louis XIV. Louis II de Bourbon, the "Grand Condé," born in 1621, was a military genius whose generalship saved France from defeat by Spain by his victory at Rocroi in 1643. In the civil wars he was a prominent rebel against the crown, and endured imprisonment and exile before Louis XIV eventually pardoned him in 1659. After his return to France, the prince turned himself into a courtier to recoup his family's fortunes.

The king's sister-in-law, the princesse Palatine ("Madame"), remembered the Grand Condé's slavishness in pursuit of royal favor: "If he had not been able to walk he would have crawled."[64] Of the prince's son, Henri-Jules, Saint-Simon reports: "He would doze more often than not on a stool in the corner by the door [of Louis XIV's bedchamber at Versailles], where I often saw him thus, waiting with the rest of the courtiers for the king to come and undress."[65] The son used his rooms in the palace to entertain the court, as did his son, Louis III.

The king was pleased with the family's submission, and Louis III made a most advantageous marriage to one of Louis XIV's illegitimate daughters. Meanwhile, the Condé exploited this favor with the king to protect and extend their own interests and those of their extended family and clients, using their credit with the king to bring influence to bear on his ministers. They succeeded at Versailles on their own terms, not just the king's.[66]

Leading nobles, once they grasped the role of Versailles, adapted their behavior accordingly. From 1661 Louis XIV made clear that it was he alone who was "running the show." Nobles were now in no doubt that their king, not a powerful minister or a favorite, was at the helm of state. They knew when and where to find the monarch. Saint-Simon writes: "Those who showed themselves never or hardly ever incurred his full displeasure. If one of these desired something the king said proudly: 'I do not know him,' and such a judgment was irrevocable."[67] His courtiers lived in hope that the converse was also true.

# 4.

# "How right to insist on ceremony..."

IN SEVENTEENTH-CENTURY France there was a long tradition of royal pageantry. Louis XIV inherited this tradition. But his increasing reluctance to go to Paris meant that Versailles, after the move of the court, was now the routine site for royal ceremonies. Many of these took place inside the palace; others placed the monarch in the forecourts or brought him out into the streets of the town for religious processions. To an eighteenth-century Parisian, the king at Versailles sometimes seemed invisible. But ordinary Parisians thought nothing of walking out to Versailles to watch colorful festivals like the processions of the Holy Ghost. In ceremonial terms, the move to Versailles was not a complete break with the capital.

Spectacles are entertainment. But a royal procession also offers the viewer a panorama of who is who in society. The sequence in which people pass by becomes a snapshot, and a reminder, of their place in the social order. In seventeenth-century Europe, order was associated in people's minds with hierarchy. In Catholic France there was a widespread belief in the Great Chain of Being, a set of divinely ordained hierarchies into which the whole world was organized, from God down to the meanest animals. In human society this idea was realized in the existence of ranks. Seventeenth-century France assigned everyone their due place based on occupation and, above all, birth.

Saint-Simon's writings show how completely his social outlook was saturated with this ethos of hierarchy. "Without gradation, inequality, and difference, order is impossible."[1] French history would prove the duke wrong within forty years of his death in 1755. But under Louis

XIV, the dominance of this principle in men's thinking explains why ceremonies at Versailles, which displayed the precise cadences of hierarchy, united in mentality both the monarch and his noble entourage.

The famous etiquette of Versailles was a theatrical system for showing respect. By means of words or actions, individuals formally acknowledged each other's place, and asserted their own, on the tiered pyramid of French society. Performing this etiquette at Versailles hour after hour, day after day, courtiers absorbed, as if into their lifeblood, both the minutiae of the rules and the underlying assumptions. In a royal palace, this etiquette above all was meant to pay respect to the unassailable place of the sovereign, followed by his consort, at the social summit.

Marie-Antoinette shivered naked one winter's morning in her chilly state bedchamber because each time she was about to be handed her chemise by one courtier, another of higher rank entered the room. The chemise had to pass from the head tirewoman to the lady of honor, from her to a princess of the blood, and from her to the queen's sister-in-law, before it finally reached Marie-Antoinette. Under her breath the queen could be heard muttering, "This is odious! What importunity!" Reporting this incident, Madame Campan noted that at Versailles the royal dignity required everyone to be servants, "beginning even with the brothers and sisters of the monarch."[2]

Etiquette at Versailles exalted the French royal dynasty above other sovereign houses. Foreign princes preferred to visit incognito, if they came at all, because they were treated no better at Versailles than French noblemen beneath the rank of duke. Their carriages would not be admitted to the Royal Court, the guards in the guardrooms would not salute them, and there would be no stool for their wives. The king of France's ministers never addressed rulers of Germany's little principalities as "Highness."[3]

For French aristocrats, etiquette was a matter of honor, a precious, intangible commodity that went to the heart of their sense of self. The "honor" a personage was accorded on entering royalty's rooms and the seating arrangements in the presence of royalty: these were burning questions. Aristocrats constantly sought to gain more honor by challenging the rules. At Versailles these were mainly policed by the royal ushers. It was their job—not always an agreeable one, given the tempers that etiquette aroused—to know whom to admit and when.

The ushers were responsible for seating arrangements. Today, few visitors who pass the variety of stools displayed in the royal apartments have any idea what passions, what ambitions, once swirled around this uncomfortable form of seat, which came in two forms. One, the folding stool *(pliant),* was the more ancient type, reflecting the itinerant origins of the royal court. The other, seemingly a seventeenth-century invention, was a rigid square with four legs known as a *tabouret.* These antiquated types of furniture survived at Versailles long after they had gone out of fashion in polite society.

Ushers arranged stools around the walls or in semicircles with a royal armchair in the middle, depending on the occasion. To sit on a stool in the royal presence was a stratospheric privilege confined to duchesses and nonroyal princesses, known as "seated ladies" or simply as "stools." The pages of Saint-Simon are full of incidents that hinged, as it were, on doors or stools. Today they seem funny or simply baffling, like a report by an anthropologist from a faraway land. But for Saint-Simon these episodes were no laughing matter.

In 1699 several women of one particular court family, the Lorraine, tried to sit "above" the duchesses at a formal reception presided over by the young duchess of Burgundy, at the time the "first lady" of Versailles. They carried out this concerted and premeditated maneuver by arriving early in a group in order to occupy the stools arranged on the more "honorable" right side of the duchess's armchair.

Finding one duchess already seated there, the strongest and most aggressive of these women, the princesse d'Harcourt, wrestled her off her seat and sat down on it herself. When Saint-Simon's duchess arrived, feeling unwell, she was reproved by one of the Lorraine women for sitting "above" her. Saint-Simon was so outraged when he heard that he risked the dangerous step of complaining to Louis XIV.[4]

Unless securely placed on the throne itself, even lesser royalty was vulnerable to the wounds that the travails of etiquette inflicted on self-esteem. In 1711, "from carelessness or inexperience," an usher whose domain was the portal to the bedchamber of the imperious duchesse de Berri, wife of Louis XIV's youngest grandson, made the mistake of opening both doors—an honor reserved for the king's legitimate children—to the duchess's mother, the duchesse d'Orléans, a royal bastard Weeping with rage, the duchesse de Berri demanded that the usher be sacked, because he had shown her own mother "too much honor."[5]

This passion for the fetishes of rank among the French high nobility was not a new phenomenon at Versailles. The rebel duc de La Rochefoucauld had taken up arms against the crown when Louis XIV was a boy mainly because the Queen Regent had refused his daughter-in-law, the princesse de Marcillac, the right to a stool in the royal presence.[6]

Louis XIV recognized the force of this social compulsion and set out to manipulate a worldview that lent such strong ideological support to the monarchy. He was a master of the particular form of politeness that characterized the society of Versailles right down to the Revolution. This consisted of displaying different degrees of courtesy to people according to their rank. Louis XIV would doff his hat for a prince of the blood, lift it for a nobleman, and merely touch it for a gentleman.

Louis learned to love ceremonies once he realized their usefulness. According to his mother, as a teenager he had disliked them.[7] His youthful passion for ballet allowed him to develop poise and physical presence. This in turn allowed him to refashion himself into the "theater king" of history. "His smallest gesture, his walk, bearing and expression were all perfectly becoming, modest, noble, and stately, yet at the same time he always seemed perfectly natural."[8]

Etiquette and ceremonies flattered nobles who were inordinately touchy about their rank, like François VI. As the antics of the Lorraine family show, the formalities of court life at Versailles provided endless opportunities to bend the rules in attempts to acquire more honor. Saint-Simon captured the ceremonial ethos of Louis XIV's Versailles when he agreed with the king's grandson and heir to the throne: " 'How right to insist on ceremony, for when it is neglected nothing else is honored!' "[9]

The return to Versailles in 1722 (after a seven-year absence following the death of Louis XIV, in 1715) saw a reconstitution of most of the etiquette of Louis XIV's court. A combination of factors—including the lapse of time, a new generation, and the generally more relaxed atmosphere of the Regency—resulted in a certain loosening of old forms on which sticklers commented. After Louis XV's marriage to Marie

Leczinska, for instance, gentlemen in the queen's sight at performances in the Comedy Room no longer stood up from respect during the intervals, as courtiers had done in the time of the king's mother, the duchess of Burgundy.[10]

But the hierarchical mind-set of which etiquette and ceremony were a luxuriant offshoot maintained its grip on court nobles down to the Revolution. Under Louis XV, the duc de Luynes kept a court journal. Two incidents, typical of any number described by Luynes, show how the courtiers of Louis XV's Versailles breathed etiquette and ceremony as they did oxygen, just as in the days of Louis XIV.

In 1735 the new duchesse de Châtillon had gone to the young Louis XV's rooms to thank him, as was the custom, for elevating her husband to the rank of duke and peer. The king's chief minister, the cardinal de Fleury, advised the monarch not to ask her to sit in the sovereign's presence, as was a new duchess's right, because he thought—mistakenly according to Luynes—that this right could be exercised only after the customary registration of the new duchy-peerage with the Parlement of Paris.

Etiquette required that the duchess next call to thank the queen. Inadvertently gainsaying her husband, Marie Leczinska sat down so as to allow the new duchess to enjoy her right to be seated. In order of rank the duchess then called on the other members of the royal family in their rooms at Versailles, ending up in the rooms of Mademoiselle, the elder sister of the head of the Condé branch of the royal family.

She was about to take a seat, when this princess upbraided her: "Madame, the Queen can do as she sees fit in her rooms, but it is the King who confers ranks in France, and Madame de Châtillon has not taken her stool in his rooms; the Queen cannot confer rank, even if she be regent."[11] Who was in the right? This crux of etiquette could only be savored by those in the know, of whom Luynes was one.

He relished the maneuver of Madame de Léon in 1745. With no right to be seated at Versailles, she was encouraged by the men of her husband's family, Messieurs de Rohan-Chabot, to claim the same rank as their cousins of the Rohan-Soubise branch, whom the monarchy had recognized as "foreign princes" so as to secure their loyalty in the civil wars of Louis XIV's childhood.

The plan was for her to pay a courtesy call on one of Louis XV's daughters, accompanied by two "seated" ladies. When, as etiquette required, the princess rose for these two, she would seem to rise also for Madame de Léon. But a vigilant usher foiled her game by making the three women enter individually. When the turn of Madame de Léon came, Louis XV's daughter remained firmly in her seat.[12]

A generation later, the love of etiquette was alive and well in the circle of Marie-Antoinette. It was of this epoch that Hézecques, a onetime page of Louis XVI, commented: "The women have always been more difficult than the men on matters of etiquette."[13] The queen's sometime best friend, the princesse de Lamballe, suffered from an "attachment to ceremony" compelling enough to obstruct her duties as superintendent of the queen's household. As a princess of the blood, she was entitled to deploy an etiquette that ignored the normal courtesies of Parisian high society. Instead of inviting ladies individually to the balls that she was expected (and paid) to host on the queen's behalf at Versailles, she insisted on her royal prerogative of merely announcing that she was "at home" for the occasion. Parisian ladies took offense and stayed away from Versailles.[14]

Marie-Antoinette is often held up as an example, or even a proponent, of the growing taste for informality in the second half of the century. Away from the Petit Trianon, where she sought to live as a private individual, this was true only up to a point. At Versailles the stool in both its forms remained a staple of the furnishings of her state rooms down to the Revolution. It was the same in the other royal residences. In 1786 fifty-two new stools were ordered for her gaming room at Compiègne.[15]

Nor was she unaware of etiquette's underlying significance as a mainstay of hierarchy. As dauphine she quickly mastered the art of royal greeting at Versailles, from a salutation delivered "with the respect owed to rank" via an inclination of the head to a mere smile accompanied by "an expression of benevolence" in the royal eyes.[16] In 1789, when the revolutionary mayor of Paris failed to kneel before the queen in an audience at Versailles, as was the rule, but merely gave a low bow, she showed her displeasure "by a nod of the head which was not very cordial."[17]

When the Estates-General met at Versailles in May of the same year, all France was fired up by this momentous political event. Watching the opening procession, a courtier like Bombelles could not help but be struck by an oddity in its order: the ducal peers were walking immediately after the princes of the blood, "despite the pretensions of the House of Lorraine." This was because, as he noted, one of the two Lorraine brothers, the prince de Lambesc, was absent with his regiment and the other was standing in for him as grand equerry in another part of the procession. The observation is pure Saint-Simon, who devoted some of his most splenetic pages to "the origins, endeavours and successes of the House of Lorraine, in their attempt to gain precedence in France."[18]

For Louis XIV's plans for his court to work, his movements needed to be predictable. By 1673, when the king was thirty-five, an Italian habitué of his court noted: "He has divided the hours of the day and night between his affairs, his pleasures, his devotions and his duties, in such a way that one knows from his courtiers what he is doing and where one can pay him one's court."[19] Saint-Simon comments on the enormous convenience of his punctuality for his courtiers.

Long before the mid-1690s, when Saint-Simon settled at Versailles, Louis XIV had stylized the royal day into a series of ceremonial set pieces performed before an audience of courtiers and public: the *lever* (rising) and *coucher* (going to bed), the public meals, the putting on and taking off of the king's hunting boots, the afternoon walk, and so on. These ceremonies were reinstated when Louis XV returned to Versailles in 1722 and survived right down to the Revolution.

Their longevity is explained by the importance of such ceremonies in the business of paying court to the king. "Most of the people who come to the Court are persuaded that, to make their way there, they must show themselves everywhere, be absent as little as possible at the king's *lever*, removal of the boots, and *coucher*, show themselves assiduously at the dinners of the royal family . . . in short, must ceaselessly work at having themselves noticed." A courtier wrote these words, not under Louis XIV, but in 1784.[20]

These domestic ceremonies were older than Louis XIV's reign. But Louis invested them with a new significance and stateliness as part of his plan to attract courtiers and reassert the charisma of monarchy. The chaotic scenes at the *levers* of his youth show that this change was gradual: "Throw yourself into the crowd," "elbow your way," "give no quarter," the playwright Molière had comically advised in 1663.[21]

The construction of Le Vau's Envelope was probably a turning point. In 1676 Madame de Sévigné praised its spacious interiors, in implicit contrast to the older royal residences: "You pass from one place to another with no crush anywhere."[22] Louis was always responsive to the requirements of paying court; he enlarged his antechamber in 1701 to create more room for the courtiers.

At Versailles the atmosphere of these daily ceremonies developed an almost religious solemnity. Louis had fashioned himself into such an awe-inspiring figure that whenever he appeared the same silence engulfed his courtiers as used to fall on the entourage of Alexander the Great. His actions and those of his officials acquired a ritual quality: they were performed in a set sequence, like a liturgy. At the *lever,* the first valet always intoned the same words as he opened the velvet curtains of the royal four-poster: "Sire, it is time." At the *coucher,* the master of the wardrobe always took the right-hand sleeve of the king's frock coat, and a valet of the wardrobe, the left.

Indeed, the order of events at these daily ceremonies was so predictable that it could be, and was, described in print. Louis permitted a member of his household, the almoner Nicolas Besongne, to publish a semiofficial list of household officers and their ceremonial duties called "The State of France," which was updated every one to three years. Here is a typical extract:

> *When the ushers of the bedchamber have taken control of the door, one of them murmurs into the ear of the first gentleman the names of the people of quality waiting outside. . . . Then the first gentleman passes these names to the King. His Majesty at once indicates that they are to enter, sometimes simply by saying nothing to the contrary; this same usher passes on this order to his comrade who mans the door.*[23]

Under Louis XIV there was a reading public for the "States," extending from France into neighboring countries like England and Holland.

The last printed "State of France" was published in 1749—a sign, perhaps, that public interest in royal ceremonial was flagging by the middle years of Louis XV's reign.[24]

Louis XIV improved the inherited script for these daily ceremonies so as to provide opportunities to flatter individuals. One of his innovations, the ritual of holding the candle at the *coucher,* acquired notoriety. The king would single out a high-ranking courtier, to whom the first valet presented the candlestick. The favored individual removed his glove, took a step forward, and held the light for the duration of the ceremony.

Saint-Simon claimed that Louis used this rite to conceal his annoyance with an individual, which may well be true; the duke was in a good position to know, being himself in disgrace at Versailles from time to time. Befitting his analysis of Louis XIV's court, the duke was generally cynical about the king's talent for using "trifles" to manipulate his courtiers. But he himself was pleased when Louis named him for the honor, which he often did. With a pinch of dry humor, so was the prince de Croÿ under Louis XV: it "made a courtier's day."[25]

The ceremony enjoyed its huge success because the gentlemanly Louis XIV, followed by his successors, always asked the courtier concerned to hold the candle as a favor. Honor was upheld. "Far from being felt as an act of servility, it was envied and desired, because people only saw in it an honorable choice and a flattering preference."[26]

A spectacle more or less guaranteed to visitors to Versailles when the court was in residence was that of royalty dining in public. Food had played a central part in royal display at Versailles since the magnificent collations that Louis XIV had laid on for guests in the garden fêtes of his youth. These feasts certainly had an ideological component, proffering a carefully controlled image of Olympian abundance, superlative elegance, and matchless generosity.

After 1682 Louis XIV transferred to Versailles the ritual of dining in public to which French kings had submitted themselves since medieval times. These royal mealtimes humanized the monarch and his family by showing them fulfilling a universal need. At the same time, the awesome opulence and deference surrounding the royal table served to emphasize the unbridgeable abyss between diners and spectators. Ushers admitted all who had a recommendation and were decently dressed, and the resultant crowd horrified a Russian princess in 1768, since it comprised "certainly anything but *le beau monde*."[27]

In the eighteenth century, when public dining fell out of fashion in other European courts, the custom was so entrenched that it was maintained at Versailles. Madame Campan describes mealtimes at Versailles in the late 1760s: "At the dinner hour [one P.M.] the staircases were full of the brave souls who, after watching the dauphine [the widowed Marie-Josèphe of Saxony] eat her soup, went to watch the princes [her sons] down their boiled beef, and then ran breathless to see Mesdames [Louis XV's spinster daughters] eat their pudding."

Louis XIV, a prodigious trencherman, always put on a good show. "At the first spoonful of soup his appetite came, as I have many times heard him say," recalled Saint-Simon, "and he ate prodigiously of solid meals, each morning and evening, and so steadily that one never grew accustomed to watching him."[28] Louis XVI inherited his ancestor's appetite. "His healthy and vigorous temper, sustained by continuous exercise [i.e., hunting], gave him an appetite which he satisfied with a good humor which was a pleasure to watch."[29] By contrast, Marie-Antoinette, like Louis XV, performed out of duty, not pleasure: she "did not take off her gloves or unfold her serviette, which was a great mistake on her part," according to Madame de La Tour du Pin. This judgment, although ludicrous, suggests how much the public still liked to scrutinize royal appetites on the eve of the Revolution.[30]

After the death of his queen, Maria Theresa, in 1683, Louis XIV, officially a widower, gradually settled into a routine of each day eating his evening meal ("supper," taken at ten) in public. This was called the "grand supper setting" *(souper au grand couvert)*. The venue was usually his outer antechamber, where the party wall with the guardroom next door concealed a service staircase and a cupboard for storing the trestles and boards of the royal table. The king sat with his back to the fire and admitted to his table only his immediate family—brother and sister-in-law, legitimate son, and grandchildren. Protocol firmly excluded Madame de Maintenon, his secret second wife, who had to stay shut up in her apartment a few rooms away. In front of the table, at a respectful distance, sat or stood the courtiers and the curious, with more people crammed into the outer rooms. Royal conversation in these circumstances was limited to banalities, including as ever that fail-safe topic at Versailles, hunting.

Part of the spectacle was the ritualized pomp of these occasions. The sovereign ate and drank from silver and gold plate. On a side table stood his *nef,* a mastless ship in gold enamel, symbol of royalty at this date no less than the crown. Courtiers stood as "the king's meat" *(la viande du roi)* made its way to the antechamber in a procession of some twenty servitors escorted by bodyguards and led by the head maître d'hôtel in waiting, holding his baton of office. The act of presenting the monarch with his napkin was an honor to be performed by a prince of the blood if one was present; all victuals were ceremoniously tasted by the king's officers at a special "preparation table"; and the gentlemen who served the food and drink did so with low bows, or *révérences.* Another moment to relish was the traditional cry of "A drink for the king!" *("A boire pour le roi!"),* shouted by the gentleman butler. No wonder that the spectacle "made the happiness of the provincials."[31]

An annual calendar of royal processions drew the crowds from Paris to Versailles. The most popular were the pageants marking the three annual chapters of France's highest order of chivalry, the Holy Ghost. This had been founded by Henri III in 1578, a time of religious conflict, with the aim of fostering the bonds between the monarchy and the leading Catholic gentlemen of the realm.

The monarch was the grand master, holding periodic promotions to maintain the full complement of the order at a hundred knights. The great families counted the blue sash *(cordon bleu),* which knights were entitled to wear over their court dress, as one of the most honorable means of "illustrating" their rank. There was a waiting list for vacancies. Courtiers competed to have their names inscribed. The eminence of the participants was one of the attractions of the occasion.

Another was the spectacular "Tudor" costume of the knights: white hose and slashed doublet, black hat with white feather, the effect crowned by a velvet mantle about thirteen feet (four meters) long, woven with the tongues of fire that descended on the Apostles at the first Pentecost. One of these cloaks now displayed in the Louvre—a heavy, trailing mass of glittering embroidery on a black background—shows how impressive the sight of all the knights in their finery must have been.[32] Novice members had their own costume based on court dress under Louis XIII. As one middle-aged novice wryly observed, it "sits very well on young, well-made persons, but unfortunately one only serves at an advanced age."

At the reception of new knights there was a procession in which the whole order, holding tapers, walked in pairs with the king at the rear, passing between two lines of Swiss Guards in parade dress, beating their drums, under the eyes of a huge crowd that included ambassadors, come from Paris for the occasion. The route took them through the Hall of Mirrors, the queen's apartment, down the Queen's Staircase and out into the Royal Court, before arriving in the chapel. Here the novices swore their oath on bended knee, and the king placed the dazzling collar of the order around their shoulders.

These were honorific, but also burdensome, occasions for the members: financially, because they had to pay for their own costumes, and literally, given the weight of their mantles. These were so heavy that Louis XVI's complaints about his own prompted the designing of a lighter version just before the Revolution.

In the chapel on these occasions, knights had to kneel directly on the marble: a quarrel between dukes and foreign princes over the right to use hassocks caused Louis XIV to have these removed for everyone in 1688. For aging knights, aching knees and the below-zero temperature of the chapel made the New Year and Candlemas chapters a physical ordeal.

Knights also worried about their place in the order of procession. The processions of the Holy Ghost were among the few spectacles at Versailles at which courtiers walked in order of formal rank. The predicament of Emmanuel de Croÿ at the Candlemas chapter of 1759 shows one of the reasons why formal rank mattered so much to courtiers in practical terms.

By birth, he was a prince of the Holy Roman Empire. But foreign ranks and titles were not recognized at Versailles. In formal processions at the French court, only the noble cream who counted as "having a rank" walked in order of precedence: princes of the blood in order of genealogical seniority, and French dukes by the date of creation of their titles. Others followed in no particular order. To his embarrassment, Croÿ found himself at the back of the procession, bringing up this undifferentiated mass of gentlemen-knights, a position that "did not flatter me at all." Croÿ was prompted to redouble his efforts to court Louis XV in the hopes of a French dukedom, which he eventually obtained.[33]

The religious atmosphere of Versailles is peculiarly hard to grasp. The assertive worldliness of the place is shown by the traditional ban on prelates and monks, who were not allowed to enter the state apartments unless they were on duty in the chapel, in which case the guards let them pass.[34] It is easy to find episodes in the annals of Versailles to support a picture of godlessness.

Saint-Simon tells the story of the guards' officer, Brissac, who tricked the ladies of the court into absenting themselves from evening prayers—this was in the old chapel, finished in 1682—by dismissing the waiting bodyguard with the words "The King will not come to Benediction." Of course, the king did come, only to find that the usual throng of ladies had vanished once word went round that the monarch would not be a witness to their show of piety. Given the ostentatious devotion that he acquired in middle age, it says something for Louis XIV's sense of humor that he was much amused.[35]

But these anecdotes can be misleading. In 1788 a British spectator was struck by the conduct of Louis XVI at mass. He and his two brothers passed the service "laughing and talking together the whole time without so much as opening their prayer books."[36] Yet the king's brother, the comte de Provence, was punctilious on matters of correct ritual, just like his grandfather Louis XV, whose fondness for discussing the ceremonies of the church disarmed even the pious duc de Luynes.[37] As for Louis XVI, a recent biographer has called him, with justice, a "profound believer."[38]

It could be argued that a seemingly casual approach to devotion is possible only when religion is taken for granted as part of the fabric of human existence. The sources for Versailles are also full of examples of pious courtiers, not least among the noblewomen, most of them the product of convent educations. Four palace ladies of Marie Leczinska, Louis XV's Polish queen, were so ardent in their Lenten devotions that the courtiers nicknamed their shared week of service the "holy week."[39] Almost always the fundaments of belief were there, to fortify courtiers in old ages spent in good works or renunciation of the world, or to be called upon in crisis, as when the princesse de Lamballe resolved in her Revolutionary prison "to return to her religious principles, which she had rather neglected."[40]

Placed under the authority of the grand almoner of France, the royal chapel was the religious hub of the palace. Every day at his *lever* the monarch prearranged with this personage the hour of the royal mass, normally around ten in the morning. Down to the Revolution this public ceremony endured with few changes to the routine established by Louis XIV.

The monarch left his rooms escorted by bodyguards at the head of a procession made up of the royal ladies in order of rank, followed by the courtiers. After walking through the Hall of Mirrors and the king's state apartments, he entered the first-floor royal tribune between rows of Swiss Guards who played their fifes and drums until the moment when the monarch knelt at his prayer stool.

On Sundays and holy days the king heard a solemn mass, chanted rather than recited by the priest. For this the king descended to the ground floor. His prayer stool stood on the royal carpet in the middle of the nave. Behind were rows of velvet hassocks for the royal family and princes of the blood to kneel on in strict order of rank. Further back, the courtiers who followed the king into the chapel had to kneel directly on the marble. At routine services only the courtiers "with a rank" were entitled to hassocks, and they had to be careful to position them correctly. Louis XIV and his successor were extremely vigilant in these matters. In 1738, during vespers, the twenty-eight-year-old Louis XV detailed a bodyguard to order a surprised Luynes to move his hassock because he was too near the king.[41]

When the king heard mass from the tribune, the celebrants below made deep bows to him at the beginning and end of the service. When he joined them down in the nave, the priest included him in the liturgy as if the king were a fellow priest. After the reading, he carried over the Gospel for the monarch to kiss. At the end of the service, he offered the corporal cloth for the same purpose. This was the sacred square of altar linen on which the sacramental chalice and dish rested. When the king took communion, he alone was entitled to drink the wine from a special chalicelike gold cup.

The sacred aura of the king of France was advertised in two other ceremonies at Versailles. One was the *cène* (from *cena*, Latin for dinner), an old ceremony that Louis XIV transferred to Versailles. Annually on Maundy Thursday, just before Easter, the king of France mimicked the action of Jesus, who washed the feet of the twelve disciples at the Last Supper. The day before Maundy Thursday, the king's first doctor selected thirteen of the best-looking boys from the poor of the parish, inspecting their feet for ulcers and other blemishes. The next morning they were given fresh clothes after they had had their hair and toenails cut and their legs and feet soaked in warm, scented water, "lest His Majesty receive any bad smells from them."

The ceremony itself took place around nine in the morning in the Grand Guardroom on the first floor. As further protection for the royal nose, the royal gardeners provided bouquets of hyacinths, roses, lilies, and other scented flowers. The boys sat on a long bench and awaited the arrival of the royal procession. This included rare appearances by otherwise obsolete court functionaries like the Grand Baker, the Grand Butler, and the Grand Slicer.[42] After the king had sat down in his armchair, the preacher was allowed by custom to inveigh against the vices of the court. In 1774, in the presence of Louis XV, at the time deeply embroiled with Madame du Barry, the bishop of Senez repeated the biblical prophecy *"Adhuc quadraginta dies, et Ninive subvertetur"* (In forty days from now, Nineveh shall be destroyed). As it happened, forty days later the king died from smallpox.[43]

Then the ceremony proper began. The king knelt before each boy in turn, washing, drying, and kissing the right foot. A procession of princes then brought relays of wooden platters of meat, fish, and other dishes, twelve in all. The king ceremoniously served these dishes one by one to each boy. The boys in fact ate nothing: their parents or friends removed the food as soon as it appeared on the table.

The other ceremony that Louis XIV brought to Versailles, one that made far greater claims for the sovereign's sanctity, was the king's touch. The royal touch was widely believed to cure scrofula, a common tubercular disease that caused disfiguring sores on the neck and face. Traditionally the monarch touched on the five great feasts of the holy year after he had confessed, communed, and been absolved of his sins. Leaving the chapel in this state of grace, Louis XIV would find as many as three thousand sick, usually marshaled for his arrival in the ground-floor galleries or loggias of the two great wings. Given the sometimes putrid smell of the scrofulous sores, these loggias had the advantage of being open to the air (they were only glassed in during the nineteenth century).

Before the monarch approached, his doctors had examined the sick and sent away the malingerers attracted by the distribution of money on these occasions. The genuinely ill then awaited the king on their knees in one of the galleries, their hands together in the praying position. Imposingly costumed in a mantle carried by two trainbearers, and surrounded by guards, priests, and princes, the king touched each sufferer on the brow, made the sign of the cross, and uttered the formulaic words "The king touches you, God cures you." These contain the "theology" of the ritual: the anointed monarch acted as a sort of conductor for God's healing power. Such was the renown of the French royal miracle that even foreigners traveled to Versailles. On All Saints Day, 1712, Louis XIV touched ten Spaniards specially come for the ceremony.

Both Louis XIV and his successor were too pious to take communion during their adulteries. As a result, the ceremony was subject to scandalous cancellations. Louis XIV resumed touching after 1680, when his affair with Madame de Montespan had run its course. Louis XV stopped touching in 1739, when his adultery with the comtesse de Mailly became known beyond the court. He or his advisers had already responded to the more doubting climate of the eighteenth century by subtly modifying the formula to "The king touches you; *may* God heal you." Louis XV never resumed the ceremony, and this prop to the sanctity of the monarchy disappeared from Versailles for good.[44]

These echoes of divine right in the religious ceremonies of Versailles were far from being lost on contemporaries. When the Revolutionary artist David sought to capture the momentous end of an era, he showed lightning striking the roof of the palace chapel on the same day—June 20, 1789—that rebel deputies from the Estates-General founded France's first National Assembly.[45]

The envoys of foreign powers were key targets for the magnificence of Versailles. Louis XIV built the palace just as it was becoming normal for the European powers to exchange permanent ambassadors. After 1682, the official reception and leave-taking of ambassadors formed part of the ceremonial rhythm of the palace; in the eighteenth century, they arrived every Tuesday to pay their respects and see the ministers.

The court officials who oversaw diplomatic ceremonies and kept written records of their finer points were the grand master of ceremonies *(grand maître des cérémonies)* and the introducer of the ambassadors *(introducteur des ambassadeurs)*. This last post was one of those that could be bought and sold. Purchasers had to keep in mind the costly extras, such as new liveries for servants and horse trappings. These made the post ruinously expensive for Dufort de Cheverny, an introducer for thirteen years under Louis XV.[46]

The extras were needed because the ambassadorial processions were occasions of great pomp. The introducer's carriage led the procession of carriages escorting a newly arrived envoy from Paris to Versailles. The public turned out to watch these events. They had a competitive edge to them, since national honor was involved. In Paris, new ambassadors hired the best-looking liverymen they could find, and the French public appraised their coaches with a critical eye. In 1743 those of the new Venetian ambassador did not find favor.[47] But in 1738 the duc de Luynes, watching the arrival of the Austrian ambassador's procession in the forecourts of Versailles, was impressed by his "extraordinarily rich" carriage drawn by "eight horses of great height."[48]

These occasions gave a ceremonial prominence to the Lorraine princes. They had the right to escort the ambassador up the stairs into the king's presence. The inclusion in the royal entourage of scions of a sovereign house added to the impressiveness of the occasion. At Versailles the monarch received the ambassador in his state bedchamber, sitting on an armchair behind the balustrade of the royal bed, his hat on, surrounded by the grand officers of the crown. There was plenty of scope for adjusting the warmth of the welcome according to the politics of the moment, for instance, by standing or remaining seated, or by inviting some, but not others, to enter behind the balustrade.

All this was for envoys from European states. For powers beyond European Christendom, Louis XIV and his successors used the ceremonial of Versailles to stress France's superiority. For emissaries from the sultan-caliph or the kings of Morocco and Siam, France's monarch elevated himself on a throne surmounting a high dais, something never done by European rulers greeting each other's ambassadors.

On rare occasions, such as the reception of the Persian ambassador in 1715, Louis XIV and his successors offered a spectacle to non-Christian envoys best described as the ceremonial equivalent of "shock and awe." Artisans employed by the Entertainments Office transformed the Hall of Mirrors, setting up the throne on an eight-stepped dais under a plumed canopy at the south end, nearest the queen's rooms.

After climbing the Ambassadors' Staircase and crossing the packed state apartments, the envoy turned left into the Hall of Mirrors to see, at the far end of two lengthwise grandstands filled with up to fifteen hundred magnificently dressed courtiers, France's monarch raised up in majesty and sparkling with crown jewels. Saint-Simon, an eyewitness in 1715, saw the ambassador visibly disconcerted in the face of this carefully staged splendor.

After Louis XV returned to Versailles, the palace saw just two more of these spectaculars, one for the sultan's envoy in 1742, and another in 1788 for the ambassadors of Tippoo Sultan. They continued to attract a large public: in 1742 the carpenters were told to nail banquettes to the parquet in the state apartments in order to contain the anticipated crush.

In 1788 the need for economy compelled Louis XVI to have his throne set up in the Salon of Hercules, a less imposing space than the

Hall of Mirrors. With the Ambassadors' Staircase destroyed in the previous reign, the traditional order of procession had to be reversed. The ambassador now entered the palace by the Princes' Staircase in the south wing and walked successively through the queen's official apartment, the Hall of Mirrors, and the king's state rooms. According to the *Mercure galant,* the three envoys—with diplomatic tact—asked the king's permission to pause at the door of the Salon of Hercules "to enjoy for a moment the brilliant and majestic spectacle."[49]

After 1682, Versailles was the habitual seat of the French government. Louis XIV continued to migrate for the autumn hunting to his other governmental residence at Fontainebleau, south of Paris. In the eighteenth century Louis XV favored Compiègne. The ministers followed him there too, the chancellor taking up residence in his own chancellery, just as he did at Versailles and Fontainebleau.

In the royal council, everyone apart from the king sat on folding stools to symbolize this wandering tradition. Right down to the Revolution the royal "voyages," as they were called, continued to disrupt government business. In 1783 a courtier noted the inconvenience caused when the ministers and their head clerks dispersed for days on end within an hour of the king's departure from Versailles.[50]

Since medieval times the king of France had ruled the kingdom from his residence. The chief council of state was known as the Council Upstairs *(conseil d'En-haut)* because it always met in the king's rooms on the first, or "noble," floor of a royal palace. At Versailles Louis XIV convened his council in his official study, or council room *(cabinet de conseil)*: a narrow room with two windows overlooking the Marble Court, next to his bedchamber. An inventory of 1708 describes the council table, over seven feet long and covered in green velvet, and the seats—an armchair for the king and stools for the rest—which a bedroom valet arranged before each meeting. Outside each door an usher of the cabinet stood guard to prevent any eavesdropping on the secret discussions inside.

Under Louis XIV's successors, the official bedchamber and next-door study continued to constitute the bridge of the ship of state.

Louis XV and Louis XVI both held their public audiences in the bed-chamber. Deputies from the most august corporations of the realm, the clergy of France, the royal courts of justice, or the city of Paris, tra-ditionally delivered their harangues before the monarch on bended knee. At Versailles they found themselves doing so before a sovereign seated in his armchair before the fireplace in a bedchamber, his hat on, surrounded by an entourage of domestic officials in full court dress. In the eighteenth century this was not necessarily a tactful image of royal rule with which to confront proud lawyers from the French courts.[51]

Louis XIV had denied the magistrates of France's *parlements* or courts of justice their traditional right to lay remonstrances at the foot of the throne. After the Regent restored this prerogative and Louis XV returned to Versailles, the palace became a destination for these legal deputations. As relations between crown and *parlements* entered a diffi-cult phase in the course of the reign, these audiences ceased to be mere formalities. On August 16, 1751, Louis XV called on his not inconsid-erable reserves of majesty to adopt "the tone of a master who is not happy." Rebuking a mass deputation of forty-one magistrates from the Parlement of Paris, he told them: "Submission is the first duty of my subjects, and my Parlement ought to provide the example of this fun-damental law."[52]

Louis XV received deputations of remonstrating magistrates in the official study. His increasingly bitter quarrels with the law courts help to explain his decision in 1755 to make this room more imposing. He now enlarged it by knocking through a next-door room used by Louis XIV to house the big periwigs for which he was famous. These were a key constituent of the royal image: he never showed himself bare-headed, removing his wig only once his bed curtains were drawn; he apparently felt that the sight of a wrinkled bald head would detract from his majesty.[53]

Now extended by some eight or nine feet, the new study was given paneling carved with scenes symbolizing the work of the king's coun-cil. A rampart and cannon stood for war, a sailing ship for the navy, the hand of justice from the royal regalia for the monarch's position as supreme judge. At this time, the magistrates were claiming by virtue of their ancient prerogatives to be the only true counselors of the crown.

The new décor asserted the crown's counterclaim that the royal council was the sole forum for legitimate debate on the great affairs of state.[54]

This increasing militancy of the courts of justice sometimes forced Louis XV and Louis XVI to stage the ceremony of the *lit de justice*. The archaic name of this venerable ceremony derived from the fact that the French word for bed (*lit*) once also denoted the canopy under which the monarch sat. The *lit de justice* was an exceptional convocation of the Parlement of Paris, the body that gave binding force to royal laws by agreeing to enter them on its registers. If its magistrates disputed royal legislation, as increasingly they chose to in the eighteenth century, as a last resort the monarch would stage a *lit de justice* to impose his will on the magistrates in person.

By staging this ceremony at Versailles, Louis XV and XVI forced the magistrates to attend on the monarch, rather than paying them the compliment of visiting them in their Parisian seat, the Palace of Justice. At Versailles the venue chosen was, once more, the Grand Guardroom, one of the biggest rooms in the palace, roomy enough to accommodate the four hundred or so people present on these occasions.

The Entertainments Office now transformed the guardroom into a ceremonial set piece. The walls were decorated with the finest royal tapestries. Above them were suspended hangings of violet velvet seeded with the royal lilies, or fleurs-de-lys. A stepped dais and a canopy were set up in one corner of the room for the royal seat. Louis XV sat on a modern armchair at these ceremonies. Louis XVI preferred the traditional throne formed from five large cushions.

On either side of the dais rose tiered seats for the lay and ecclesiastical peers of the realm, the marshals of France, and other dignitaries. Below it were the benches for the magistrates, who took their seats first. They arrived from Paris in a procession of carriages. They found their seats after being offered hot refreshments in the Ambassadors' Room. This was the ground-floor room on the south side of the Royal Court used for receiving ambassadors. To the martial sounds of drums and trumpets from a next-door room, the monarch next arrived in an imposing procession including bodyguards, princes of the blood, ushers with ornamental batons, and the royal heralds.

While the heralds knelt, the great officers of crown and household took up their positions on the lower steps of the throne. They included the grand equerry holding the royal sword and the chancellor of France, wearing a magnificent robe of violet velvet doubled with crimson silk. Seated on the throne, the king uttered the formula "Messieurs, I have sent for you to have made known to you my intentions and my wishes; my chancellor will explain them." He then turned to the chancellor, who read a short paper on the disputed legislation before going through the formality of inviting the assembly for its views. He then declared the law registered.

Under Louis XVI, the extreme rebelliousness of the magistrates on the eve of the Revolution turned the last *lit de justice* held at Versailles, on August 6, 1788, into something more than a foregone conclusion. During the chancellor's speech Louis seemed to doze and even to snore. But after the magistrates became vocal in their resistance to the proposed measures, the king "arose from his throne and shouted in a strong voice filled with indignation: 'You have heard my wishes; I mean them to be executed.' " But the crowds in the palace courtyards were already revolutionary in spirit, cheering the magistrates as they mounted their carriages to return to Paris.[55]

Louis XVI was not destined to die at Versailles. His grandfather did, in his new bedchamber after falling ill at Trianon. It was easier to administer the bleedings and other treatments of the time at Versailles, and Louis XV's doctor insisted on an immediate return to the palace. Driven flat out, the royal coach covered the distance in three minutes. Croÿ was one of those whose entrées allowed him to be admitted to the royal sickroom. "Finding myself next to the console table, I had a good look at his blood, there on the table in three dishes, and to me it seemed of good quality."

But Louis turned out to have smallpox, an incurable disease. The doctors first saw the red spots that evening on his face, but were too scared to tell the patient, who found out only after the marks spread to his hands. He kept pointing them out to his entourage, but received no reply. This wall of tongue-tied courtiers finally confirmed the king's fears.[56] After his death the bloated royal corpse was deemed so infectious that it was embalmed without the customary opening and hurried off to Paris within forty-eight hours.

Death was a constant and close presence in seventeenth- and eighteenth-century France. Mourning too was pervasive, with long periods the norm—six and a half months for grandparents, eighteen months for husbands. Mourning customs were particularly elaborate at Versailles thanks to the high status of royalty, the political uses of mourning to show solidarity with foreign courts, and the extended ramifications of the royal lineage.

In 1755 Louis XV went into a week's mourning for the princess of Baden-Baden. By today's standards they were not closely related. The princess was the aunt by marriage of the wife of the king's second cousin once removed (the third duc d'Orléans). Her husband, a German prince, was (as Luynes punctiliously records) Louis XV's "kinsman in the fourth or fifth degree by his [the prince's] Soissons grandmother."[57]

Even a minor period of mourning such as Louis XV's for the princess had to be followed by the whole court, with all the expense that this entailed. The monarch controlled all the details, which were published in public gazettes with dates and sartorial instructions. Saint-Simon claims that Louis XIV had "detested any sign of mourning."[58] This was not true of Louis XV, who was well known for his morbid temperament.

In 1752, when Louis XV put the court into what was called "grand mourning" for his daughter, Madame Henriette, the prescriptions were specific. Male mourning included the customary fringed shirt cuffs. The obligatory black was extended to black steel for buckles, buttons, and swords. The princess's entire household went into mourning. Her ladies were required to "drape," that is, to hang black crepe on the walls of their antechambers and also their carriages and sedan chairs. They also had to put their own households into mourning clothes, including tirewomen and liveried manservants.[59]

The monarch himself wore violet mourning, and his drapes were the same color. When the duchess of Lorraine, Louis XV's mother-in-law, died in 1747, his first gentleman was responsible for putting up violet drapes in the king's antechambers, including the Bull's Eye. The draping included not only walls but also the ceiling, floor, and shutters. The effect must have been striking.[60]

At Versailles mourning etiquette was one of the classic ways in which rank was displayed. After the death of her mother in 1778, the princesse de Lamballe was one of the last before the Revolution to observe to the letter the rigorous etiquette prescribed for a princess of the blood on such an occasion. She drove out to Versailles with relations and ladies in waiting, all in full mourning. By ancient custom her rank entitled her to receive the condolences of the king, queen, and royal family in person while lying on her bed in her apartment. As soon as her last royal visitor had departed, the etiquette required her to get up and go from apartment to apartment in order to repay the royal visits one by one, all the time followed by her own entourage.[61]

Despite his aversion to mourning, the only French monarch to die at Versailles with all the due pomp and circumstance was Louis XIV himself. From self-importance perhaps, Saint-Simon claims in his memoirs that he persuaded his friend the duc d'Orléans, who became Regent, to economize by staging a simple funeral. But an extant description by the royal master of ceremonies shows that in fact the obsequies at Versailles were prolonged and imposing.

For the first twenty-four hours the king's body was exposed on his deathbed. This was an ancient custom that was meant to defuse any suspicion of poison, traditionally believed to leave telltale black marks on the victim's face.[62] All day courtiers, members of the household, and the public filed past the corpse to the sound of prayers chanted by nuns.

The next day the king's surgeons performed the customary opening of the body on an operating table set up in the Bull's Eye. This was done with ceremony in the presence of a Lorraine prince (the duc d'Elboeuf), a senior military figure (the maréchal de Montesquiou), and various members of the household. The French tradition of treating royal corpses with a quasi-religious reverence meant that the heart and intestines were now removed, embalmed, and sent in procession to Paris like holy relics. The intestines were received at Notre Dame by the archbishop of Paris. Enclosed in its golden urn, the heart sat on the lap of a French cardinal in a coach escorted by thirty bodyguards to another Parisian church, Saint-Antoine.

In the palace, the embalmed corpse in its coffin lay in state for eight days on the official bed behind the balustrade in the Salon of Mercury, the bedcover acting as a pall. The room had been converted into a funerary chapel, with four altars in the window embrasures. From these the clerics addressed their nonstop daily masses for the royal soul to the king's empty armchair and praying stool, according to the abbé Besongne, an eyewitness, "as if the king full of life was still there." Only on the ninth day was the coffin carried out of the palace on the shoulders of twelve bodyguards by means of the Ambassadors' Staircase.

The final cortège went straight from Versailles to the Abbey of Saint-Denis, north of Paris, where royal funerals traditionally took place. The twelve-hour journey occurred at night, not because the king was unpopular but to suit the abbey chapter, for prayers had to start as soon as the corpse arrived.

In bypassing the capital, the cortège denied Parisians the old tradition of a royal procession including the monarch's death mask borne aloft through the streets. The Parisian funeral of Louis XIII in 1642 turned out to be the last to strengthen the emotional bonds between the dynasty and the capital in this way.[63]

Louis XIV's vision of Versailles as a stage for ceremonies presumed that the king had what nowadays would be called "star quality." Louis XIV did. Not only had he held center stage as a dancer in court ballets in his youth, but he was famously polite and affable. These qualities were especially necessary at Versailles to offset the unnerving etiquette governing all intercourse with the sovereign.

It was not done to spit in the monarch's vicinity (a hint of what went on elsewhere in the palace). If the king approached a courtier, say, in the Hall of Mirrors, it was incorrect to bow, let alone speak. People were supposed to retreat in silence, as far back as the wall if necessary, where "they continued to paw the ground with their feet in the hope of being blest with a word from the sovereign."

Only the few on terms of the greatest familiarity would speak to him first; even then, this had to be in the third person: "Has the king still got a cold?" Under Louis XVI even "modern" courtiers, the sort who no longer observed the custom of bowing to the king's empty bed, or who lounged against its balustrade when the monarch was not present, observed these rules. It was an art on the monarch's part to put the other party at some sort of ease amid this atmosphere of extreme deference.[64]

Louis XIV's successors did not manage this art as well as their forebear. Louis XV had a noble appearance: at the age of forty-two he could be praised for his "beauty."[65] But his "lazy, timid eyes" spoke of a crippling shyness.[66] Luynes, who spent years at Versailles studying him, thought that "sometimes he seems to want to speak; timidity holds him back, and the expressions seem to refuse to come." This social awkwardness meant that Louis XV rarely could find the right words to say to the courtiers or ambassadors: "The bows and curtsies at presentations, leave-taking and arrivals require some obliging words: unfortunately they are very rare."[67]

Contemporaries portrayed his grandson Louis XVI as cutting a much poorer figure in public. The most that his loyal ex-page Hézecques could find to say in his favor was that, "seated on his throne, he did not make a bad show." But even he conceded that Louis' walk was ungainly and that his uneven teeth made his smile "rather ungracious."[68]

In her post-Revolutionary memoirs the marquise de La Tour du Pin, wife of one of Louis XVI's ministers, was much blunter. Time and subsequent events could have affected her memory, but probably not that much. Of Louis XVI at the time of the Revolution she recalled: "He was so short-sighted that he could not recognize anyone at three paces. He was a fat man of medium height, with high shoulders and the worst form that you could imagine. He had the air of a peasant, and there was nothing lofty or royal in his mien. He was always embarrassed by his sword and did not know what to do with his hat."[69]

Along with this unimpressive exterior, Louis had shocked his court early on by an apparent lack of concern for his regal dignity. The year after his accession he arrived at a carnival ball in the Salon of Hercules unannounced and without bodyguards. As a result, he had great difficulty making his way through the crowds, failed to find his armchair, and had to share a noblewoman's stool. This happened in front of eight hundred spectators seated in the special grandstands put up on these occasions. The crowd included many strangers as well as Parisian high society and the foreign envoys, said to be "scandalized."[70]

In public Louis XVI could seem disobliging even with the best will in the world. "He would bear down on someone to the point of forcing him to back against the wall; if he couldn't think of anything to say, as often happened, he let out a loud clap of laughter, turned on his heels and walked away. The victim of this public scene was always pained, and, unless a habitué of the Court, left furious and convinced that the King had wanted to deliver a kind of insult."[71]

This apparent rudeness stemmed from more than just shyness. In 1783 the elderly Croÿ at last obtained the coveted baton of a marshal of France. Louis XVI presented this in his official study. According to Croÿ, "the King rushed past, someone pushed me to show me that he was already sitting in his armchair and that a hassock had been set down for me. I knelt. . . . Monsieur de Ségur [the war minister] took the baton, the King handed it to me, pushed back his armchair, got up and disappeared. This all happened so quickly that I was still kneeling. I rose with difficulty, the baton in my hand, and there was hardly any-one left in the study!" Croÿ observed that ceremonies bored Louis XVI. He had the fairness to add that, "in private, he is altogether differ-ent."[72]

Louis XVI's disdain for ceremonies influenced other participants. At the ceremony of the *cène,* the duc d'Enghien, a young prince of the blood, once "killed himself laughing" after playfully putting a handful of crayfish in a royal page's hat, at the time on its owner's head. No prince would have dared to conduct himself in this way under the eye of Louis XIV.[73] In a constitutional monarchy, a lack of formality can be a virtue: it was a trait for which England's Princess Diana was much admired. Not at Versailles: "The people respect their sovereign less for his virtues and his rank than for the gold which covers him and the pomp which surrounds him."[74] After the incident of the ball in 1775 Maurepas, Louis XVI's principal minister, felt obliged to take his young master aside: "We are not accustomed to seeing our king count for so little in public."[75]

Versailles was all about surfaces. Louis XIV was always "as he should be" in the ceremonies that put the royal person on display. Whatever their other strengths and weaknesses, his successors lacked this gift, espe-cially Louis XVI. The ceremonies of Versailles emphasized their personal shortcomings rather than playing to their strengths. In such a stage-managed monarchy, this was an unfortunate "own goal."

It might be said that Louis XVI was in touch with his times. By the late eighteenth century the whole baroque edifice of hierarchy was going out of fashion in France. In 1710 the order of precedence among the royal princesses was an affair of state: Louis XIV opened a meeting of the council with his ruling on the matter.[76] In 1774 Maurepas advised Louis XVI that court etiquette was a matter of complete indifference to the nation.[77]

Away from Versailles, high society in late-eighteenth-century France no longer troubled much with etiquette. The well born "were all brought up in the idea of the equality of mankind and disdain for vain distinctions."[78] The duc de Lévis remembered the social pleasures of Paris before the Revolution. "Ease with all the graces reigned in the salons; a respectable familiarity, tempered by good taste, gave to conversation that free and playful tone which was its chief charm."[79] In Paris, ducal town houses still had a formal room for the ducal dais and canopy.[80] But it was never used. In the salons, a financier's wife would no more dream of offering her seat to a duchess than a duchess would dream of accepting it if offered.[81]

Marie-Antoinette fostered these fashionable new ways at Versailles. She considered herself no longer queen at her country house at Trianon. When she entered a room at the Petit Trianon, her guests did not have to rise as they would at Versailles, but were allowed to continue their games or tapestry work.[82] This was not new behavior for a queen: Marie Leczinska had liked to say that she was no longer queen when she visited the palace lodging of her friends the duc and duchesse de Luynes.

But Marie Leczinska upheld the traditional etiquette in public. At Versailles she received "with much grace and dignity," even if she tended to repeat herself in small talk.[83] But Marie-Antoinette, despite her intuitive respect for hierarchy, brought her informal ways into Louis XIV's palace. For instance, she imposed a loosening in her presence of the draconian dress code. In 1783 men at Versailles still wore the peacock finery of full court dress to call on the ministers or on Madame Adélaïde, Louis XVI's conservative aunt. But the queen now permitted them to appear before her in the plain *frac,* or frock coat.

This was a dark monochrome coat of English origin now taken up by fashionable Frenchmen in the spirit of Anglomania and in affectation of a kind of "constitutional" simplicity. Bombelles, for one, regretted the introduction into the palace of this "tone of liberty."[84] The innovation highlights the web of contradictions in which Versailles was snared on the eve of the Revolution. The palace that Louis XIV built for royal ceremonies was now presided over by a king who disdained these performances and a queen who preferred informality and simplicity.

## 5.

# Follow the King!

AFTER 1670 Versailles was less a pleasure palace than a seat of government—after 1682, the habitual seat. This function changed the atmosphere. By the late 1680s Louis XIV sought relief from the cares of kingship in smaller residences like the Grand Trianon and Marly. With the return of Louis XV in 1722, the preoccupations summed up by the words *duty, affair,* and *solicitation* once more became the order of the day for courtiers at Versailles. The king's chief minister in all but name, the duc de Choiseul, claimed that, in his early career, when he went to court for pleasure he presented himself only at Marly and Fontainebleau, avoiding Versailles.[1]

In an age of plodding communications, Versailles itself played its part in concentrating power in the hands of the monarchy. "Haste and efficiency were essential to seventeenth-century government."[2] The physical proximity of king, ministers, and clerks under the one roof streamlined communications at the topmost echelons of government. Louis XIV had made it easier than ever before to summon ministers at any time of day or night for policy discussions and instructions given by word of mouth, there and then.

How far Louis and his ministers anticipated these efficiency gains from the move to Versailles is unknown. But the courtiers were quick to appreciate the convenience of the palace as the new hub of French networks of power, influence, and information. According to Saint-Simon, someone going to Versailles on business "could see everyone he needed in the space of an hour; whereas in Paris, one might go ten times to the same house and cover any number of different districts."[3]

In 1785 the French diplomat Bombelles thought much the same: by walking down a few galleries, people could be found at Versailles who in Paris lived several leagues apart.[4] In the topography of power, Versailles was vastly more convenient than the capital.

In the absolute monarchy all important decisions ultimately rested with the king, counseled by his ministers. For many nobles whose birth made them eligible to pay their court, the ultimate point of doing so was to compete successfully for the monarch's "graces." The French king's patronage was huge. As well as the award of titles and honors, it included military promotions, diplomatic posts, church benefices, and economic concessions such as mining rights, as well as court offices and honors, pensions, and cash handouts. In practice, the king made many of these decisions in consultation with the responsible minister during the one-to-one working session known as the *travail*.

For leading families, a quasi-hereditary hold on one of the *grandes charges,* maintained from one generation to the next by the right of reversion, gave them a weapon they could activate when they wanted something from the monarch. Louis XVI's cousin, the prince de Condé, a fourth-generation grand master of France, was notorious for soliciting favors.[5] Dufort de Cheverny's years at Louis XV's court prompted him to characterize the "assiduous courtier" as essentially a fortune hunter.[6]

A key motive was indeed money. In 1708 Louis XIV's sister-in-law, Madame, reckoned that very few courtiers at Versailles were really rich.[7] French nobles under the social compulsion to spend lavishly on clothes, houses, carriages, and other luxuries looked to the crown for the help that they considered their just reward in return for military or domestic service. Soliciting Louis XV and his ministers for favors, members of the Flemish noble family of Croÿ pointed to "the services, losses and misfortunes of this House," which included "thirty or so Croÿ killed in war" as well as the ravaging of family properties by troops.[8]

A related factor was honor. Each generation in a noble family felt obliged to add luster to the family name by winning new distinctions. These were precious bargaining chips on the aristocratic marriage market. Emmanuel de Croÿ gives many details of how he hounded Louis

XV's ministers over the years in pursuit of honors and graces for himself and his family.

Croÿ was a decent sort, a family man in love with his wife, a soldier who fought with distinction in the Seven Years' War, and a man of his time and class in his obsession with genealogy, in his case a conviction that he descended from Attila the Hun.[9] In 1763, when he sought to marry his son into a branch of the sovereign Salm family, the prince de Salm insisted that Croÿ should first obtain the "honors of the Louvre," which would confer on the wife of the Croÿ heir the coveted right to be seated at the French court.

Croÿ appealed to his friend the prince de Soubise, a member of the royal council and a personal favorite of Louis XV, whose consent Soubise duly obtained. Later that year the whole Croÿ family went to Versailles to watch Croÿ's new daughter-in-law, fresh from her convent, "take her stool" for the first time under the royal gaze, which intimidated the shy bride.[10]

As this episode shows, for noblemen like Croÿ, attendance at Versailles was a family duty. Madame Campan, one of Marie-Antoinette's head tirewomen, observed in her memoirs that "people who devote themselves to service in courts often talk while there of their children and the sacrifices they are making for them."[11] For the aristocratic courtiers of Versailles, family feeling extended to all those of the same blood in the male line who formed the extended membership of their "house." When the baron and baronne de Montmorency died within weeks of each other in 1749, all the Montmorency males, some fifteen of them, turned up at Versailles in deepest mourning to thank Louis XV for his condolences.[12]

This clan sentiment was extremely strong. Provincial cousins looked to their more successful kinsfolk at Versailles for worldly help, although few could match the spectacular rise of the duc and duchesse de Civrac, a Versailles phenomenon in their day. The clever, pretty daughter of a Bordeaux notary married a country squire who, although poor, was a Durfort, distant relation of a powerful court family known for its extensive ramifications. Armed with the antique parchments proving her husband's lineage, she went to Paris, where she was welcomed with open arms by his kinsfolk, with whom she ingratiated herself so sucᶜully that in due course they found her a prestigious post in the ͟household of one of Louis XV's daughters, Madame Victoire.

At Versailles, she "navigated her ship so well" that she became a favorite of this princess, who obtained a dukedom and the Vienna embassy for her husband, despite his supposed lack of gray matter. To cap it all, the newly created duchess married her son to the heiress of the Durfort-Lorge branch, the family of Saint-Simon's wife. In 1774, by means of this marriage, the son succeeded to the prestigious title of duc de Lorge. Saint-Priest, a former minister of Louis XVI, held up Madame de Civrac as an example of how "talented women" got on at the court of France.[13]

As a system of government, Versailles stood for clientship and patronage. In the seventeenth and eighteenth century great nobles were patriarchal figures. Their influence was based on family, friendship, and property. These in turn surrounded them with networks of protégés of all ranks. Lords and ladies felt a Christian duty to protect even humble dependents; the duchesse d'Aubigny, for example, solicited Louis XIV for a reduction in the taxes paid by the peasants on her ducal estates.[14] Grandees protected men of letters and lesser nobles. The prince de Croÿ used his contacts at Versailles to advance various "private affairs" *(affaires de particulier),* as he called them: army commands and pensions for members of the Flemish noblesse, or an introduction to Madame de Pompadour, Louis XV's mistress, for the author of *How to Make Houses Fire-Proof,* which the scientifically minded Croÿ had helped to correct.[15]

The most powerful patrons were royal princes, especially ones whose hereditary networks of influence had survived the latest growth spurt of the modern state under Louis XIV. During his reign, successive heads of the house of Condé frequently interceded at court to secure pensions, obtain a favorable outcome in a lawsuit, or promote in other ways the interests of clients, especially ones in Burgundy, where the Condé were hereditary governors.

In the next reign the duc de Penthièvre, Louis XIV's grandson, enjoyed the second-largest private fortune in France. His inheritance included the governorship of Brittany. As governor, the duke was the king's representative at crucial meetings of the Breton assembly, or Estates, when the king's tax demands were presented to the province.

This preeminence in the affairs of the province, where he also owned large properties, made him the natural patron of the Bretons when they came to Versailles. It also conferred on him a leading role in the protocol that surrounded these visits. As early as the age of thirteen he was presenting the deputations from the Breton Estates to Queen Marie Leczinska in her audience chamber at Versailles.[16] In 1738 he gave a dinner for eighty-four members of the Breton deputation. His family papers record another dinner for upwards of 350 people in 1772: this too was for a Breton deputation.

The duke possessed an establishment at Versailles to match the demands of entertainment on this princely scale. As grand huntsman he had, in addition to a town house, an official mansion at the Kennel; in the palace, he inherited the ground-floor lodging once belonging to Madame de Montespan, his grandmother, with its imposing vestibule adorned with marble columns and statues of classical deities. That he offered large-scale hospitality in this grandiose setting is shown by the contents of the kitchens attached to the lodging, which included four fish kettles, thirteen spits, fifteen pie dishes, thirty-seven casseroles, and forty-one cooking pots.

This vertical world of patronage, with its relations of dominance and submission, is captured by the dining arrangements at these ducal feasts. On such occasions the pious Penthièvre, for all that he was remembered posthumously as "humble of heart," was a staunch—and probably unthinking—upholder of hierarchy. In 1772 the diners sat at five tables. But the duke's was decorated ten times more expensively than the rest and monopolized the fish—a delicacy—and the best wines (Bordeaux, Graves, Volney, Chambertin, and Tokay).[17]

In pursuing their selfish interests at Versailles, courtiers of the sword nobility naturally sized up their targets in military terms. Ministers had to be "attacked." But they exercised the art of war above all in the pursuit of royal favor. Anyone who was decently dressed, and a good many who were not, could gain entry to the public parts of Versailles. But to gain social access to the monarch was a different matter. For this, presentation was a necessary preliminary.

Grandees presented their children to Louis XIV with no ceremony. Late morning, after the council, when Louis stepped into the gallery on his way to mass, was a favored time. In 1691 the sixteen-year-old Saint-Simon was presented in this way by his father as an aspirant to service as a royal musketeer. Noting the youth's short stature, Louis rather crushingly replied that "he thought me puny and delicate in appearance."[18]

Louis XV turned presentation into a formal ceremony. An ordinance of 1759 decreed that no married woman could be presented unless her husband's family had been noble since before 1400. This regressive measure, which tended to entrench the social isolation of the monarchy, aimed at keeping away members of families ennobled more recently through office-holding. The king's genealogist had a reputation for incorruptibility in the verification of family titles, but the rules were not infrequently ignored by the king himself, who had the final word, in the interests of favoring such and such a person.[19]

Women were presented in the king's study, usually by their mother-in-law. Under Louis XVI this ceremony took place on Sundays after vespers. Presentees were traditionally required by court etiquette to wear black. The fashion-conscious Marie-Antoinette permitted color, which encouraged the ambitious presentee to pay exorbitant sums to be dressed by the queen's favorite dressmaker, Rose Bertin, so as to ensure an outfit to the queen's taste.[20]

Courtiers turned out for the spectacle. The journal of the duc de Luynes is scattered with blunt appraisals of presentees: "a lovely complexion and an agreeable face" (Mademoiselle de Tonnerre); "small and ripe-looking, although only thirteen" (Madame de Helmstadt, a child bride); "white but small, the nose too long; in all, not pretty" (the duchess of Berwick); "large, with a pleasant expression and no air of embarrassment" (the marquise de Broglie).[21]

After the one ordeal, the young women faced a second. By tradition they were expected to take the collection in the chapel on one of the high days when king and court used the two spiral staircases to descend for the service from the gallery to the nave. It was the prerogative of the first lady, the queen or dauphine, to make the nominations. Magnificently dressed and sporting the family jewels, they again had to endure the scrutiny of all as they passed with the collecting bag from one courtier to the next, curtseying each time, remembering to approach the princes in the right order, and all the time having to manage their huge panniers and long train. Hézecques, Louis XVI's ex-page, thought that coquetry and ambition helped these débutantes to weather their rite of passage.[22]

For men there was less formality. They too had to "make their proofs," and under Louis XV noblemen still brought their sons into the palace to be presented. The duc de Luynes judged males as well: "two brothers and very young; the elder has a large mark on his forehead which reaches the eye; the second is rather fine-looking" (the sons of the new baron de Montmorency).[23]

But mostly men were presented to the king when he was hunting. At Versailles this formality took place at the designated hunt rendezvous in the neighboring woods, after the presentee had first given his name to the guards' captain in waiting. He was then permitted to follow the hunt on horseback and, at the end, to ride back to the palace in one of the king's carriages.[24] From 1715 a register was kept of these so-called carriage entrées, recording 1,942 presentees up to March 31, 1789. The three "hunt débutants" who followed Louis XVI on that day turned out to be the last before the Revolution. Among them was the chevalier de Saint-Simon, a kinsman of the courtier-duke.[25]

A Saint-Simon might set little store on presentation as such. But lesser nobles based in the provinces placed a high value on the ceremony at Versailles. The ritual marked a family as "being known, and of passing for people of quality." These are the words of the abbé de Saint-Exupéry, author of a surviving letter that preserves his eyewitness description of the presentation of his kinswoman, Marie-Louise de Cugnac, in 1757.

The abbé breathlessly informed his brother that Louis XV had carried off some of Marie-Louise's rouge on the tip of his nose as he gave her the customary kiss, and that an attendant of the duchesse de Luynes had done her the honor of addressing her. For a brief moment his letter sprinkled some stardust from the court on the family seat in remote Périgord. As the timid wife of a minor officer in the royal hunt, however, Marie-Louise had neither the funds nor the wit to transform herself from a "presented lady" into a "courtier."[26]

Even for the presented noble, gaining closer access to the monarch was far from easy. Inside the palace, all members of the royal family were shielded from overexposure to their courtiers by a system of so-called entrées. These restricted the right to enter the royal rooms to an inner circle of family, household officers, ministers, and favorites, whose names were carefully recorded on registers kept by the first gentleman of the bedchamber or, in the queen's case, by the superintendent of her household. As usual, it was up to the ushers guarding the doors to police the system.

At Versailles the entrées determined who could (in court language) "follow" the king in his own palace, and above all how far they could penetrate into his "interior," as his more private quarters were known. There were essentially six sorts of entrée, graded on the principle that the greatest privilege was to be in the king's company for the longest time and with the smallest number of other courtiers. Three of the six admitted their holders to the royal bedchamber at the ceremonies of the *lever* and *coucher,* and to the next-door study for the *botté* and *débotté,* when the king's hunting boots were put on and removed. A fourth allowed its holders to follow the king into the official study after the *lever.*

The holders of the vastly more exclusive "grand" entrées had the right of admission, albeit only at certain times, to the king's "interior." This was a hidden world, unseen by the vast majority of courtiers, entered through doors off the official study. Under Louis XV precisely four courtiers possessed these entrées: the grand chamberlain, the first gentleman of the bedchamber, the grand master of the wardrobe, and the head valet.[27]

Most exclusive of all were the entrées that Saint-Simon called "by the back staircase" *(par les derrières).* This was the king's private staircase on the north side of the Marble Court, used by the monarch when he went out for a walk in the park or to go hunting; in its final form under Louis XVI, it can still be climbed. Flanked by a ground-floor guardroom, it led up to the king's private rooms on the first floor above. In Louis

XIV's time the first-floor landing was separated from the official study by a billiard room, where the king also kept his pet dogs.

These entrées allowed their holders to come and go with the utmost familiarity, morning and afternoon. Only the powerful head valets seem to have enjoyed them by right of office. For others it was a sign of the highest favor. Holders were entitled to a passkey, an object of enormous significance, as can be gauged by the fact that Louis XV himself made the wooden box holding the key that he gave to his young cousin, the duc de Penthièvre.[28]

Louis XIV did not invent the entrées, which already existed under his predecessors on the throne. Nor were they even peculiar to France. In ancient times, leading Romans were greeted at dawn by their dependents, who were likewise admitted in successive waves. The "first entrée" at Versailles recalls the "first admission" *(prima admissio)* at the *lever* of the Roman emperors. Louis XIV elaborated an older system and used it as a way of distinguishing the officers of his household and favored individuals.[29] Since Versailles aspired to be "Rome in one palace," Louis was conceivably alerted to the etiquette of the Caesars by his scholars, using it as a conscious model.

The cardinal importance that Louis XIV attached to the system is shown by his decision to enlarge his second, or inner, antechamber, which in 1701 became the Bull's Eye, which still exists today. After Louis XV's return to Versailles in 1722, the entrées remained so central to the mechanism of the court that the young king found himself trapped by them when he decided that he could no longer stand the extreme cold in his great-grandfather's bedchamber.

This was in 1738, when he was twenty-eight. A smaller, more modern bedchamber was created two rooms away, in Louis XIV's former billiard room. But the sequence of spaces needed for the entrées could not have been re-created in the new location without a drastic rearrangement of the first-floor rooms. Louis XV was obliged each morning to get out of his new bed, cross the study in his dressing gown, and climb into Louis XIV's four-poster to await the parting of the curtains by the head valet, which signaled the start of the ceremonial *lever,* doing the same in reverse for the *coucher*: there was no question of changing the court entrées. Louis XVI in turn maintained this curious charade of the two bedchambers.

The entrées gave their holders precious opportunities to approach the king in pursuit of their "affairs." For instance, in 1771 the political enemies of the disgraced duc de Choiseul, once Louis XV's prime minister in all but name, pressured the king into asking for the duke's resignation from his lucrative post as colonel-general of the Swiss Guards, but to do so without offering adequate compensation. The idea was to push the duke into a show of defiance that would prompt his fall into a deeper disgrace, maybe even a spell in the Bastille.

Instead, the exiled duke outwitted his enemies by nobly opting for resignation pure and simple. But his problem was how to deliver his letter of resignation. Louis XV had ordered him to deal solely with the duc d'Aiguillon, his successor in the war ministry, and Choiseul doubted whether this sworn enemy would pass on the letter. He entrusted a friend, the duc du Châtelet, with the task of delivering it in person, a mission not without risk for du Châtelet, should he anger the monarch in its execution.

Arriving at Versailles, the duc du Châtelet made use of his study entrées. Just before an early-evening council he took up his position in the open portal between the study and Louis XV's new bedchamber, knowing that the king would shortly come this way for the meeting. From his vantage point the duke watched as Louis XV entered his bedchamber by an opposite door and walked toward him. "He could not go past without squashing me." The duke then advanced to meet him, made a brief but dignified speech, and handed over the letter. Louis put it in his pocket and proceeded into the study.

Thanks to his friend's study entrées, Choiseul had outmaneuvered his tormentors at Versailles, prompting one of them, the comtesse de Marsan, to complain that it was "impossible to make this man unhappy!"[30]

Without the entrées, the would-be courtier had little choice but to resort to ambush. Saint-Simon never had any entrées. He stayed at Versailles because he believed that Louis XIV expected his courtiers to be in constant attendance and that absenteeism would threaten the duke's patrimony, or that part of it dependent on the king's goodwill, namely, his governorships of Senlis and Blaye, which Louis XIV had allowed him to inherit on his father's death in 1693.[31]

For several years Saint-Simon was out of favor with the aging Louis XIV, who saw him, not without reason, as a troublemaker over the niceties of ducal rank. Saint-Simon was determined to explain himself. But his difficulty was that the old king, happy enough to display himself in the carefully staged ceremonies of the court, was not in the habit of chatting with his courtiers.[32] He was also parsimonious with the private audiences that courtiers, as one gentleman to another, had a right to request of their king. It was precisely for this reason that the entrées were so valued. According to Saint-Simon, whenever a holder of the entrées approached Louis XIV to speak, the other courtiers would move aside.[33]

Like other noblemen in his position, Saint-Simon would wait in the gallery to intercept Louis on his way back from mass. In 1702 he handed the king his letter of resignation from the army in this way. The timing was unfortunate, just after the outbreak of the War of the Spanish Succession, and the duke later heard that an irate Louis had commented, "Here is another deserter!"[34]

The following year he got into more trouble by fanning a quarrel between the duchesses and the princesses of Lorraine over taking the collection in the chapel. In order to try to exculpate himself, the duke waited on the king as he ate the less formal dinner known as the small dinner setting (*diner au petit couvert*) in his bedchamber. As the king rose to go into the next-door study, Saint-Simon asked leave to follow him. "Without answering he made a sign for me to enter and walked over to one of the window-embrasures." These recesses in many of the more important rooms at Versailles were a routine setting for tête-à-tête conversations. There they talked for half an hour and the duke left looking extremely pleased with himself, convinced that his explanations had satisfied the king.

In 1708, with France doing badly in the War of the Spanish Succession, the foolhardy duke bet some friends that the besieged town of Lille would fall to the enemy. Through his spies Louis XIV was duly informed of this defeatist wager, and Saint-Simon fell into the deepest disgrace yet. He decided he had to confront the king, but once again faced the problem of how to approach him.

This time he felt the need of an intermediary. He lit on Georges Maréchal, the Saint-Simon family doctor who also happened to be Louis XIV's chief surgeon, liked by the king for his honesty and plain-spokenness. The doctor broached the matter with his august patient, who said that he would see Saint-Simon whenever the duke wished.

This still left Saint-Simon having to approach the king to arrange the time of his audience. Once again he seized his opportunity when the king dined alone in his bedchamber, an occasion to which the first gentleman in waiting would allow the usher to admit "known people" like the duke. Saint-Simon provides such detail that the scene can be exactly reconstructed. Louis dined as usual with his back to the fire. Saint-Simon took up a position on his right, "with my back to the balustrade." Toward the end of dessert, the duke advanced to the right side of the royal armchair and respectfully asked for a time. Louis, "not in the least annoyed," named the next morning.

The audience duly took place, lasted over half an hour, and once more Louis XIV's charm left the duke convinced that he had repaired the damage, even though his one specific request, for a lodging in the palace, was politely refused.[35]

At Versailles, the use of intermediaries to try to gain access to the monarch was universal. There were the obvious targets for this kind of attention, the troika of leading household officials, ministers, and favorites. But even the slightest preference accorded by the monarch to the lowliest servitor identified a potential target for favor seekers.

Louis XIV showed a great partiality for the bearer of the front poles of his sedan chair, a man called d'Aigremont, who used to open the chair's door for him. Once, as he did so, d'Aigremont presented a written request for a benefice from an abbé in the royal chapel. An inadvertently comical exchange followed, with the puzzled d'Aigremont misunderstanding the angry monarch's accusation of "simony" (trafficking in church offices) for one of "ceremony."[36]

This ceaseless quest for brokers gave Versailles much of its day-to-day animation. Of one marquis who spent his time "courting the notice of ministers and high-ranking persons," Saint-Simon acidulously noted,

"No man ever made so many daily journeys backwards and forwards through the château of Versailles and up and down its staircases."[37]

In doing so, the marquis, like countless others, was helped by the layout of the interior. This centered on what the architectural writer under Louis XV, Jacques-François Blondel, called the "gallery of communication, which conducts under cover from one end of the château to another all the persons attached to the service of the prince, as well as those from outside who come to visit this immense palace."[38]

Blondel must have meant the first-floor "thoroughfare" formed by the two open-sided galleries, or loggias, that ran the length of the north and south wings, respectively. They were built to withstand heavy use. In a memoir of 1682, Colbert worried about the thickness of the marble paving, "because all the lackeys will be continually using these galleries."[39]

On joining the central block, a part of the palace with no public corridors, these galleries communicated with each other—as they still do—by a serpentine sequence of public rooms made up of the king's antechambers, the Hall of Mirrors, and the state apartments.

This public walkway is rarely mentioned in the journals and memoirs of the time, probably because it was taken for granted. We catch a glimpse of its use by Saint-Simon in 1701 when he observed Louis XIV's doctor having an epileptic fit in the king's antechambers: "I saw Fagon lying all unbuttoned, with his mouth open, giving every appearance of a dying man." The duke happened to be returning via the royal antechambers from the apartment of his friend the duc de Beauvilliers in the south wing to the rooms of his father-in-law, the maréchal-duc de Lorge, in the north.[40]

In both wings this main thoroughfare gave access to the various public staircases that permitted circulation between the different floors, chiefly the Princes' Staircase in the south wing, which still exists, much remodeled, and its counterpart halfway along the north wing, a grand staircase destroyed in the 1830s.[41] These staircases in turn communicated with parallel galleries on the ground floor of the two wings, and with the attics, full of courtiers' lodgings.

When the monarch was in residence, by day this arterial system fairly bustled with courtiers, sedan chairs, servants, tradesfolk, soldiers, and visitors, all making their way around a palace comparable, as Hézecques, Louis XVI's ex-page, put it, "to a vast labyrinth, owing to the number of galleries, corridors, small staircases and apartments which it encloses."[42] Along these thoroughfares circulated a larger population than many a small town in eighteenth-century France.

Courtiers often heard the latest news or bumped into each other in the galleries of the two wings. People regularly relieved themselves behind their arcades, perhaps encouraged by the poor lighting. Just how stygian the corridors were is shown by Saint-Simon's story of the light from his torchbearers suddenly revealing his enemy, the duc de Vendôme, feeling his way down a staircase in the darkness. Under Louis XIV the main galleries were lit by candles, replaced in 1747 by oil lamps. Even so, they remained gloomy, and right up to the Revolution royalty and courtiers moved about at night lit, like Saint-Simon, by servants' torches.[43]

In other ways, too, the galleries and corridors resembled streets. They led to different quarters of the palace, with their own names. The accommodations at the extremity of the south wing on the town side were known as the Superintendency. The halfway block linking the two sides of the north wings, where Saint-Simon had his lodging when he finally obtained one from Louis XIV, was known as the Large Pavilion. Courtiers would trade lodgings so as to group themselves together. Under Louis XIV the Noailles family took over enough of the attic in the north wing for the corridor in this part of the palace to be nicknamed Noailles Street.

Unusual comings and goings in one of these "neighborhoods" aroused suspicion. On his way to a clandestine rendezvous with the duc de Beauvilliers in the south wing, Saint-Simon encountered two courtiers who "plagued me with questions because they met me in a corridor where they thought I had no business to be at that hour."[44]

Nosey parkers, not to mention the king's spies, had courtiers constantly looking over their shoulders. Saint-Simon reveals the dangers posed by servants, whose livery as they waited outside a door announced the presence of their masters and mistresses inside. In 1706 the duke received a visit in his borrowed rooms in the palace from the papal nuncio, come to divulge that Louis XIV planned to nominate the duke to the Rome embassy. As the news was still secret, the nuncio "begged me to bolt the door and that of my antechamber as well, lest anyone should see his footmen."[45]

The arteries of Versailles with their many staircases and lesser corridors were ideal for engineering "chance" encounters. In 1708 Saint-Simon's friend the duke of Burgundy, Louis XIV's grandson, returned from the war front under suspicion of cowardice. From a first-floor window, Saint-Simon saw Burgundy's carriage arriving in a courtyard below. Eager to demonstrate his loyalty to the compromised prince, the duke positioned himself ostentatiously at the top of the Princes' Staircase, and was ready with a low bow as the prince ascended.[46]

Mentioned here for its sheer oddity, finally, is the use of the palace galleries by Louis XVI's brother, the clever and exquisitely polite comte de Provence, to stalk his sister-in-law, Marie-Antoinette, for whom he burned with confused feelings. In the 1780s, when the prince was lodged in the Superintendency, he used to patrol the south wing's first-floor gallery in the hope of encountering "Rhodopovna," his code name for the queen, on her way to see her children, also lodged at the far end of the south wing. Halfway down the gallery with her footman, the queen would suddenly find her brother-in-law issuing from a side staircase, his prize for this subterfuge a few moments in her company and the chance to kiss her hand.[47]

After the monarch in person, the ministers were the principal target for people seeking to influence royal decision making. The four secretaries of state, respectively for foreign affairs, war, the navy, and the royal household, each occupied half of the two ministers' wings flanking the outer forecourt. Each ministerial unit included a ground-floor antechamber and study, where the minister received callers, first-floor reception rooms for entertaining, private rooms on the floor above, and offices for the clerks in the attics.[48]

These quarters were furnished by the royal Furniture Office. This allowed for a prompt evacuation when a minister was disgraced, as happened with increasing frequency during the mid-eighteenth century.

When Louis XVI sacked the comte de Saint-Priest, his own effects were taken from Versailles to Paris in a single cartload.[49]

In his private journal Croÿ gives numerous details of his relentless attendance on the ministers in pursuit of his various "affairs." These often hinged on the outcome of a minister's session with Louis XV, who liked to work in the evenings. Croÿ once kicked his heels for an hour, from ten to eleven at night, in the antechamber of the minister for war, Argenson, awaiting his return from the king. Another evening he had himself driven out from Paris and sat in his carriage, drawn up in the ministers' courtyard, waiting for Argenson to appear.[50]

Croÿ also found opportunities to buttonhole ministers during court ceremonies. Once he was able to approach Argenson in the chapel.[51] After obtaining the study entrées in 1762, he was delighted by their utility. He could sit down in the official study, whereas everyone else had to stand during the *lever* in the bedchamber. More to the point, when he first made use of his privileges at Louis XV's *lever,* Croÿ found hardly anyone else in the study apart from princes of the blood and ministers, a state of affairs "very agreeable and convenient for conducting business."[52]

The ministers were expected to entertain in their quarters, and their dinners and suppers provided another opportunity for courtiers to raise their personal affairs. In 1789 the then war minister, the marquis de La Tour du Pin, offered official dinners for twenty-four people twice weekly, men only.[53]

Croÿ regularly frequented the ministerial dinner tables. Sometimes he just took a café au lait at the coffee hour, a recognized moment for making courtesy calls. In spite of the obligation for men to be in full court dress, these could be relatively relaxed occasions. A minister might discuss government business. In 1757, at one of his dinners, the new war minister, the maréchal de Belle-Isle, aired his plans for military reform. These left Croÿ "grumbling in a corner," since they dashed his son's hopes for the command of a regiment at the age of seventeen.[54]

Up above, in the attics of the ministers' wings, were the bureaux of ministerial clerks, each ruled by a head clerk *(premier commis),* roughly equivalent to the English "first undersecretary." For people pursuing their business, the head clerks mattered, not least because they stayed on when their superiors were sacked.

Their influence was often belied by their working conditions. In 1748 Le Boulanger, a head clerk of the minister for the royal household, complained that his office in the attics of the south ministerial wing had never been repainted since the palace had been built, that it was black with chimney smoke seeping through cracks in the walls, and that there were not enough shelves for the minister's papers.

In 1785 things were no better in the attics of the next-door war ministry, where seven or eight clerks worked in one room for a head clerk whose adjacent office was so dark that he was obliged to use candlelight in daytime, so as "to arrange and keep in the order which is indispensably necessary all the documents which come and go daily."[55]

Under Louis XV some bureau chiefs were lucky enough to be transferred to the two next-door ministries built between 1759 and 1762 on what was then the rue de la Surintendance and now the rue de l'Indépendance américaine, where they still stand. A measure of the burgeoning bureaucracy in eighteenth-century France, they were built mainly to reunite under one roof the archives of the ministries of war, the navy, and foreign affairs. In 1762, when Louis XV paid a tour of inspection, the architect gave an adventurous demonstration of the efficacy of the fireproofing—the building materials were mainly brick and iron—by setting fire to a pile of wood and straw in one of the rooms.[56]

In July Croÿ rated the new buildings among the finest "in the world," especially the Foreign Affairs Library, shown to him by the minister in person. Arranged as a gallery of interconnecting rooms, it made "the richest enfilade which I have seen." With the exception of this superb library, the modern visitor to these buildings may find the prince's enthusiasm a touch hyperbolic. It can partly be explained by a military man's fascination with the maps and models up in the attics. Once, Croÿ happily spent two hours listening to an explication of the model of the naval base at Toulon by its maker, Monsieur Groignard.

Croÿ assessed the new accommodations for the bureaux from the courtier's viewpoint. "You were only let in between midday and two o'clock, so that the clerks were left free to work."[57] A contemporary engraving showing a cutaway view of the new ministry depicts some of these spacious new bureaux along with their antechambers, where visitors of both sexes sit and wait in postures meant to suggest boredom.[58]

In the mid-eighteenth century the French writer Charles Pinot-Duclos credited some of the head clerks of his day with more influence than the grandest noblemen.[59] The truth of this claim is shown by an episode at Versailles in 1737. The duc de Fitz-James arrived by sedan chair at the war ministry to complain to a head clerk about some leave given to a captain in the duke's regiment without his consent. In the ensuing altercation, the duke called the head clerk a "varlet." For insulting a royal servant, Louis XV sent this grandson of James II of England to cool his heels in the Bastille.[60]

Around 1900 a French historian came across three hundred or so letters in a secondhand shop comprising the personal correspondence of one Armand Nogaret, a head clerk under an eighteenth-century minister of the royal household, the duc de La Vrillière. The letters show that Nogaret lived well above the means of a head clerk, with numerous servants, horses and carriages, and a sumptuously furnished country house. All this was paid for by bribes, with the duke himself not above accepting a cut of the profits from the sale of offices such as the magistracies of Toulouse, known as *capitouls,* and sought after because they ennobled their incumbents.[61]

Nogaret was found out and sent to trial. But there are sufficient glimpses of activities of this kind to suggest that the machinery of power and influence at Versailles habitually worked in ways that today we would regard as corrupt. But modern attitudes are not necessarily a guide to the values and ideals of Versailles. Nogaret may simply have been excessive. As the ancient Roman emperors reminded their provincial governors: "Neither everything, nor every time, nor from everyone."[62]

Part of the temptation lay in the fact that petitioners outside the charmed circles of the court needed support if they were to approach the sources of power, the king and his ministers, without protection. Every day subjects of the king arrived at Versailles, many on foot, in the hope of a hearing. The usual route was a petition, which the illiterate could pay a public writer to compose on their behalf. A rare surviving example from 1695, probably read by Louis XIV himself, takes the form of a piece of paper folded in half so as to produce four sides for writing.[63]

How to put these petitions into the right hands was a problem. Only the bold, not to say brazen, could pull off the stunt of the self-styled "comtesse" de La Motte, the adventuress who went on to embroil Marie-Antoinette in the Diamond Necklace Affair. In the early 1780s she staged a fainting fit, clutching her petition, in the antechamber of Madame Élisabeth, the king's sister. The princess was duly handed the petition to read and sent its author on her way with a gift of two hundred francs.[64]

In 1699 a respectable academic from Douai, Louis Monnier de Richardin, followed a more conventional, but still fraught, route. He found out by chance from a military engineer, whom he met in a ministerial antechamber, that petitions were accepted in a ceremony that took place on Mondays in the king's outer antechamber, the one where he dined publicly at the grand dinner setting *(au grand couvert)*. The minister for the interior usually presided over the reception of petitions, but sometimes, Monnier learned, Louis XIV himself was present, seated in his armchair at the table on which the petitioners placed their requests. These were then put into a large velvet sack and distributed to the relevant ministers.[65]

Under Louis XVI, returning the deluge of petitions occupied a whole bureau with its head clerk.[66] Unsurprisingly, some petitioners tried to reach the king directly through the officials closest to him. A surviving petition reveals its route into Louis XIV's hands by its author's praise for his head valet, Bontemps, hailed as "illustrious Maecenas" and "Prodigy of the Court."[67]

Solicitors without connections were exposed to the full force of the ministerial temperament. At Versailles Monnier de Richardin found himself at the receiving end of an unexpected tirade against his university by the war minister, Barbézieux, before an antechamber filled with more than fifty people. The bishop of Arras told him afterward that Louvois, the minister's father, was the same: whenever he opened his door, everyone in the antechamber "trembled."

An anecdote in the memoirs of Alexandre de Tilly, one of Marie-Antoinette's well-born pages, shows what a difference a protector made. Tilly was approached in his lodgings in the Small Stables by a provincial lawyer, a connection of Tilly's father, come to Versailles to solicit for a lucrative vacancy in Alençon.

Tilly obtained Marie-Antoinette's written support, and together he and his protégé went to see Miromesnil, the Keeper of the Seals. Tilly having announced their business, the minister promptly berated the young lawyer for his temerity in demanding a post that he had done nothing to merit.

This point of view reflected the increasingly meritocratic ethos of the royal administration at Versailles, to which courtiers were unsurprisingly resistant: "The king is master of his graces," Louis XVI's brother the comte d'Artois once reminded a minister, who coolly retorted: "Positions are not graces, one merits them."[68]

But ministers held their posts only for as long they pleased their royal master: they knew better than to upset powerful figures at court, especially in an age when the comfortable pensions paid to ex-ministers meant that there was rarely a shortage of rivals and would-be successors. When Tilly handed over the queen's letter, Miromesnil's demeanor completely changed. "My happiness is to obey the orders of the queen." Tilly's man got his position.

For his services, Tilly had accepted in advance three hundred gold louis, which he treated as a loan and did indeed repay.[69] The agreement was formalized before a notary, a practice among the influence-trafficking courtiers of Versailles that went back to the time of Louis XIV. The very openness of this practice suggests the lack of a guilty conscience about such transactions, which covered not only intercession by courtiers, but also the sale of insider information, often about positions and offices about to become available. Saint-Simon, for instance, although he despised his influence-trafficking fellow courtiers, was not above paying 3,500 livres for a tip-off about a regiment for sale.

These "advice givers," as they were called, were considered a new type of courtier by the celebrated authoress Madame de La Fayette in *La princesse de Clèves*. Her novel appeared in 1678, just as Louis XIV was embarking on his huge expansion of Versailles. The existence of these "advice givers" shows how much more centralized France was becoming under Louis XIV: after 1682, Versailles was the greatest information exchange in the realm. In the mind's eye the ministerial bureaux in the palace forecourts must be peopled with her "marquises and countesses" laying siege to the ministerial bureaux, humbly supplicating the clerks for tip-offs.[70]

This lucrative business attracted fraudsters who preyed on the vulnerable. One such was the Swabian baroness who arrived at Versailles and rented rooms in the Hôtel de Fortisson, a reputable establishment two streets away from the palace, used among others by the prince de Croÿ. In 1782 this pretty thirty-six-year-old inveigled her way into one of the king's coaches in a royal procession escorting the sovereigns to Paris.

Meant to advertise her supposed entrée at the court to passersby, this bold ruse was her undoing: someone recognized an unauthorized person in a royal carriage and told the police. Their search of her rooms at Versailles unearthed a coffer full of polite but noncommittal replies from ministers and prominent courtiers to her letters of solicitation on behalf of her clients. After an enforced spell in the Bastille, she prudently left France for Brussels.[71]

It was a commonplace in the eighteenth century that the courtier at Versailles resembled, as Dufort de Cheverny put it, "a being in servitude."[72] Outsiders witnessed behavior that seemed to bear out this stereotype. Monnier de Richardin, a spectator at Louis XIV's *lever* in 1699, savored seeing the "very submissive and humble air under the gaze of the Prince" adopted by the governor and the lieutenant-general of Flanders, respectively the maréchal de Boufflers and the comte de Montbron, "who are so very much the masters in our region."

As the contrasting deportment of these two grandees suggests, French nobles were the match of their monarch when it came to putting on an act. Dissimulation was "the great art of courtiers," according to one of Marie-Antoinette's favorites, the baron de Besenval, not least because the disappointed faces of those whose requests had been refused embarrassed the monarch, who by definition could not make everyone happy in the distribution of graces.

The seasoned Besenval makes a number of other observations about the pitfalls awaiting the courtiers of kings. Asking for favors was always dangerous, because at best the monarch would reply "I shall see"—as both Louis XIV and Louis XV were wont to do—and at worst he would be annoyed. The same was true of ministers.

There were almost no safe subjects of conversation. Politics were out of the question, since the monarch could not discuss the business of his government in public and would fall silent. Religion had to be avoided too, since by his position the king was obliged to respect it; to forget oneself in this matter was to risk a royal reprimand.

Gossip was harmful, since one word was enough to prejudice the monarch against someone and obstruct his career. Of course, this did not stop the courtiers from doing each other down. A friend of Madame de Maintenon, the marquise d'Heudicourt, always interrupted with a "devastating *but*" whenever she heard someone being praised before Louis XIV and his second wife.[73] Ministers were always at risk from gossip put about behind their backs. In 1708 the younger Pontchartrain, minister for the navy, lost a much-loved wife. But his father exhorted him to take no more than two days off from Versailles because "the tongue and the envious and malign character of the courtier is only curbed by one's presence."[74]

Given these constraints, courtly conversation tended to have a superficial quality. Successful courtiers were masters of the anodyne. Marie-Antoinette's friend Marie-Thérèse de Lamballe was reputed to have no opinions of her own, and fell silent whenever the discussion became serious.[75]

A gift for harmless wordplay was an asset. In the days of Madame de Montespan, a more open-minded Louis XIV used to set rhymes for his courtiers to match, including salacious ones, rewarding one courtier who excelled with a coveted lodging at Versailles.[76]

Louis XV was something of a wit. To an Anglophile courtier who implicitly criticized absolutist France by announcing that he had been in politically liberal England to learn "to think" *(penser),* the irritated monarch, as he turned his back, replied "Horses?"—punning on the verb "to groom" *(panser).*

Courtiers needed a quick wit in response to a royal sally. Louis XV once asked the marquis de Bièvre, known for his bons mots, for a pun. "On what subject, Sire?" "I don't care; on me, if you like." "Your Majesty is not a subject" came the rapierlike reply.[77]

After the Revolution, a former courtier, the duc de Lévis, wrote, a touch defensively, that only people ignorant of courts would assume that all courtiers were servile. At Versailles, he claimed, there was "submission without baseness, deference without abjection."[78]

He may have had in mind the likes of the prince d'Hénin, guards-captain to the comte d'Artois and member of an illustrious family that the hyper-aristocratic Saint-Simon considered good enough for his daughter. Provoked by his royal master, Hénin once said: "Please remember, if I have the honor of serving you, you have that of being served by me."[79]

In fact, courtiers did resort to flattery. From their viewpoint it was as much a weapon of empowerment as a demonstration of baseness. But its deployment required artfulness, since the king was brought up to beware of flatterers, a subject on which ancient writers such as Tacitus or Plutarch were eloquent. When Louis XIV asked the duc d'Uzès when his pregnant duchess would give birth, the reply—"When you wish it, Sire"—was inept.[80]

Besenval claimed, somewhat unfairly: "Old wars, ancient history, events already in the past, science and literature, could furnish topics of conversation: but where are the courtiers with enough education to discuss them?"[81] Some courtiers had their own libraries at Versailles. The comte de Coigny, more polished than Uzès, used to find out the bookish Louis XVI's current reading, then steer the conversation at the *coucher* to related topics. The tactic paid off, because Louis often singled him out to hold the candle.[82]

Perhaps the knack when speaking frankly to royalty was to do so in such a way that the monarch could not be sure whether or not he should be offended. Once, at one of Louis XVI's suppers at Versailles, the young Marie-Antoinette was playfully pelting the monarch with bread. Turning to the comte de Saint-Germain, an old soldier, the king asked him how he would comport himself on campaign if under attack from projectiles. "Sire, I would spike the cannon" came the brusque reply.

Louis kept smiling. But others present were sure they had just heard a none-too-veiled reference to the childless state of the royal marriage.[83]

# 6.

# *"All the pleasures"*

EIGHTEENTH-CENTURY COURTIERS remem-
bered Louis XIV for providing "all the pleasures" for the nobles who
courted him at Versailles. Used to the diversions of Paris, France's great
lords had needed some persuasion to decamp from the capital.[1] With
the move of 1682, Louis responded by offering a weekly schedule of
diversions at Versailles. This was a novelty at the French court.

These entertainments centered on the new type of reception called
Apartment. Under Louis XIV, Apartment took place on Mondays,
Wednesdays, and Fridays. From six or seven in the evening until ten,
when the king left for his supper, the whole court gathered in the Hall of
Mirrors and the king's state apartments, all brightly lit for the occasion.
There was a concert and dancing in the Salon of Mars, fitted up with two
marble galleries for musicians, one on either side of the chimney piece.
Card tables and billiards were set up in other rooms, and copious
refreshments were available in the Salons of Venus and, appropriately,
Abundance. The atmosphere was notably relaxed. As one courtier noted
in his journal, "All who came were completely free to amuse themselves
exactly as they pleased." These entertainments played their part in habit-
uating the nobility to Versailles.

On Tuesdays and Thursdays Louis XIV sent his coaches to Paris to
bring professional actors with their costumes and props from the
Théâtre Français to entertain the court. In the absence of a proper theater, the troupes performed in the improvised Comedy Room. Between
1682 and 1715 some twelve hundred comedies and tragedies were
staged in this cramped theater, created in 1682 by enclosing an open

passageway on the ground floor of the building that links the south wing with the central block.

Under Napoleon, this theater was demolished and the original passageway has since been restored. The so-called Comedy Bookshop now marks the site of the stage. The passage proper used to house a horseshoe-shaped auditorium, two superposed boxes in each of the passage's arcades, and a royal box at mezzanine level, opposite the stage. In 1688 a countess, forgetting how low the ceiling was, fractured her skull as she got up to leave one of the upper boxes.

Earlier in his reign Louis XIV had been an avid patron of innovatory theatricals, prompting a flowering of French dramaturgy under the aegis of exceptional playwrights who have since become classic, notably Molière and Racine, who was also the king's official historiographer. The young king harnessed the talents of both for his outdoor fêtes at Versailles, which premiered their new works, including the comedy-ballets that Molière supplied in collaboration with the gifted Jean-Baptiste Lully, superintendent of the king's music until his death in 1687, fourteen years after Molière himself. These spectacles did much to foster the dreamlike atmosphere of these fêtes: works like the comedy-ballet *Georges Dandin,* staged at the fête of 1668 in a temporary theater devised by Vigarani, its rustic exterior blending into the surrounding trees and leading the astonished visitor into a lavish interior glittering with gold, crystal chandeliers, and magnificent tapestries.

Philippe Beaussant has pointed out that the repertory of plays in the later reign lacked the creative sparkle of Louis XIV's younger days. After 1682, the monarch commissioned no new plays among the hundreds of comedies and tragedies performed in the Comedy Room down to his death in 1715. In later life, more troubled and more pious, he seems to have lost his youthful appetite for this type of spectacle.

The schedule of entertainments was reinstated after Louis XV's return to Versailles in 1722. In 1752 Luynes records the custom *(usage)* as: plays on Tuesdays, Wednesdays, and Thursdays; concerts on Mondays and Saturdays; and gaming on Fridays and Sundays.[2] In the eighteenth century the full Apartment was confined to extraordinary celebrations such as royal marriages.

Alterations to the Comedy Room allowed the auditorium and stage to be converted into a ballroom, but had the effect of making the theater even smaller and more cramped, so much so that the guards posted when the monarch was present had to be relieved at the end of every act to avoid fainting fits.[3] On one occasion in 1763, as many as 350 people, ballet dancers and spectators alike, are known to have assembled here under the eye of the monarch. Each box held ten or twelve courtiers, the obligatory hoop skirts of the women no doubt lifted up under the arms while their wearers were squashed into their seats.[4] For courtiers, the heat and the crush were offset by the knowledge that the sovereign could see them all from the royal box. In spite of its obvious limitations, this theater remained the setting for ordinary court theatricals at Versailles as late as the reign of Louis XVI.

The registers of the plays performed under Louis XV survive.[5] They show that the troupes from Paris gave as many as seventy-six separate performances at Versailles each year, with little sign that wars prompted the monarch to make cuts in these "pleasures." The court liked to replay the classics, with Molière the most performed playwright, and Racine coming in third. Every courtier was a critic: of the play *Maximien* by La Chaussée, staged in March 1738, Luynes noted, "It was much admired, although the lines are not as noble as tragedy demands."[6]

After the king married, it was his queen who normally chose the repertory; it was then up to the first gentleman of the bedchamber, who oversaw the Entertainments Office, to implement them. He in turn delegated the practicalities to a lowlier official, the intendant, whose duties included everything from arranging the sets to dealing in person with recalcitrant stars like Mademoiselle Dangeville, who refused a summons to appear at Versailles in 1763, claiming that this would prevent her from being in a fit state to open in a new play the next day in Paris. Louis XV laughed at this refusal.[7] But it was symptomatic of the continuing subordination of "Court" to "Town" in matters theatrical: in the eighteenth century, new plays normally opened first in the capital.

The same could be said for opera. Louis XIV was a passionate music lover, and his palace at Versailles was full of music and song, from the fairy-tale operas staged in the grounds during the early fêtes to the chamber and sacred music of later years. But Louis XIV's enlarged Versailles could never hope to rival Paris as the capital of the French lyric stage until or unless the full-scale theater in the north wing, on which work had stopped in 1689, was completed. Simple operas could be staged in the Comedy Room.[8] But the dazzling stage effects adored by seventeenth- and eighteenth-century audiences required a wide stage with wings and vast spaces above and below to house the complex machinery of beams, ropes, wheels, and pulleys. All this was obviously out of the question in the provisional theater. As will be seen in a later chapter, this deficiency would be partly remedied in the following century.

Louis XIV has been called a born dancer. He repeatedly danced in public until the age of thirty-one. Thanks to his personal patronage, the French style of formal dancing became a prestigious element in the cultural package that France exported to an admiring Europe.[9]

Louis XIV was keen to promote dancing among his courtiers for ethical reasons. The charter of the Royal Academy of Dance, which he founded in 1672, proclaimed the virtues of the dance: it formed the body; it was a natural preparation for bearing arms; and it was especially "advantageous and useful" to the nobleman in royal service, who could apply its lessons both in war and the court entertainments of peacetime.[10]

Dancing was held to mitigate, even if it could not conceal, congenital defects. Saint-Simon said of the comte de Brionne, son of Louis XIV's grand equerry, that "he was considered the best dancer of his day, although not very tall, and on the stout side." Such was the enduring importance of dance at Versailles that under Louis XVI there were special balls for the royal children, like the one given in her rooms by the king's maiden aunt, Madame Victoire, in 1786, an opportunity for the rising generation of royals to practice their court minuets.[11]

Given the weight of expectations, dancing at Versailles under the appraising eye of the court was never just a pastime. The going was particularly tough for a newcomer. Not long after his own arrival at Versailles, Saint-Simon saw a young nobleman make a fool of himself at a ball by his ignorance of the right moves, provoking howls of laughter that drove him from the court for good. Nothing had changed under Louis XVI, when Monsieur de Chabannes, "handsome, young and rich," slipped while dancing at one of Marie-Antoinette's balls and compounded his gaucheness by swearing as he fell. Socially, he never recovered.

These balls were no less challenging for women. In 1786 the energetic moves of the new Swedish ambassadress dislodged her lofty headgear, the kind then known as a *pouffe*. People gathered round in anticipation, and only "the respect due to the locale" (the palace of Versailles) prevented booing. At Versailles the dance was a social performance that helped to define who belonged and who did not, beyond the formal requirements of presentation.[12]

The most daunting occasions were the dress balls. Most of the people present were spectators, who had to stand when royalty took to the floor. The dancers were named in advance, no one could dance before anyone else, and one type of dance would follow another in a strict order. This type of ball was a feature of royal marriage celebrations.

On these occasions Louis XIV asserted his authority over his court by naming the dancers, such as the pairs who danced the opening *branle,* an old-fashioned processional dance requiring participants to dance two by two before the king. In 1692 the seventeen-year-old Saint-Simon was named, thereby dancing at his first royal ball: "My partner was Mademoiselle de Sourches, daughter of the Grand Provost; she danced beautifully."[13]

Dancers had to be able not only to execute the intricate moves of the dances, but also to observe the rules occasioned by the presence of royalty. Under Louis XIV the male dancer began the minuet by bowing to the monarch, then to his partner, and then replaced his hat to dance. Under Louis XV, the quicksand of etiquette had inexplicably shifted: the man was now supposed to keep holding his hat until after he had come face to face with the seated monarch during the first turn.[14]

The seating plan survives for the ball that Louis XIV hosted in the Hall of Mirrors for the marriage of his grandson, the duke of Burgundy, to Adélaïde of Savoy in 1697. In the middle of the gallery a dancing area of some fifty-two by nineteen feet (sixteen by six meters) was defined by a rectangle of significantly different forms of seating: on one of the short sides were placed the royal armchair for the sovereign and stools for the royal princes and princesses; there were more stools down the long sides for the dancers; the rest of the courtiers were assigned banquettes and tiered seating in the window embrasures. The violins and oboes of the king's music were in an adjacent room, its doors wide open. Illumination was by lampstands dotted among the seats and concentrated on four big tables at the outer corners.[15]

The semblance of order and harmony on these occasions was not infrequently undermined by poor crowd control. At the Burgundy ball, the king himself was discommoded by the crush of courtiers looking for seats; his son Monseigneur was "knocked and trampled on."[16] The blame for this sort of chaos usually lay with the first gentleman of the bedchamber, who was responsible for arranging most court festivities. It happened again in January 1739, when Louis XV was prevailed upon to hold a splendid ball at Versailles. The timid young king—twenty-nine at the time—disliked appearing before strangers, but had been persuaded to show himself in this way to the Parisians, who were invited in large numbers.

The venue was the newly decorated Salon of Hercules. Its vast square made it much better for dancing than the Hall of Mirrors, which was too narrow. The workmen of the Entertainments Office installed wooden grandstands on the two short sides, and a longer one beneath the great painting by Veronese. In front, opposite the fireplace, were placed the royal armchairs.

The first gentleman on this occasion was the handsome duc de La Trémoille, whose competence some contemporaries doubted: "Of what use to him are his wit and his face? He does ill wherever he is."[17] Having opened the doors too early, the duke was disconcerted to find the grandstands filled not with courtiers, but with faces "hardly known" at Versailles—people from Paris, that is, who had left no room for the ladies of the court. The king himself had to come and tell the unwanted guests to give up their seats, which they only did—understandably—under visible sufferance, one woman daring to parley under Louis XV's nose. In "public relations" terms, the event was not a success.[18]

On the eve of the Revolution, Marie-Antoinette's balls at Versailles were often sparsely attended, partly because Parisian women were not always made to feel welcome. When the mother of the memoirist

Victorine de Chastenay found herself at one of these balls, she was one of only twelve ladies, the princesses of the royal family included.[19] Less blasé about her public image after the Diamond Necklace Affair, the beleaguered queen tried to make these events more agreeable. The old Comedy Room was extended on these occasions by the set builders of the Entertainments Office. Charming wooden rooms sprouted up on the south side of the Royal Court; the momentary effect on the architectural perspective must have been odd, to say the least.

Drawings and descriptions show that these wooden rooms were the last word in style and luxury. Artists painted the interiors with trompe-l'oeil cornices, columns, and wainscoting in colors of green, brown, terra-cotta, and pink. A huge pane of transparent glass—something of a novelty at the time—allowed people in one room to watch the dancers in another. A buffet was loaded with fresh fruit and pastries, separated by antique urns filled with liqueurs, not to mention a midnight supper. Dancing went on until dawn, with jets of water playing all night to freshen the air, and tirewomen on hand to repair ladies' dresses.

But etiquette remained adamantine. Only presented nobles could enter freely and dance. The effect of this restriction is shown by an episode related to her daughter by the marquise d'Osmond, a lady-in-waiting of Madame Adélaïde, Louis XVI's aunt.

The marquise had a sister, married to a leading magistrate of Bordeaux, a man proud of his nobility. Being of the legal kind, his nobility did not predate 1400, barring him and his wife from presentation at court. One winter the marquise arranged for her sister, visiting from the provinces, to be admitted to one of the queen's balls. Since she could not be presented, she attended only as what was called a "gawker" in the condescending argot of the court *(en bayeuse)*.

At the ball Marie-Antoinette asked the marquise who her companion was. The situation explained, the queen obligingly led the king away so that the marquise could show her sister the ballroom without the risk of a socially awkward encounter with royalty. The marquise's brother-in-law, told of the episode, was humiliated: the sovereigns had to leave a room so that his wife could enter it! Elected to the Estates-General a few years later, he became an enthusiastic supporter of the Revolution.[20]

This kind of social humiliation arose because the etiquette of eighteenth-century Versailles had frozen the rigid hierarchies of the age of Louis XIV. In 1784 Besenval could claim that "the barrier which separates the robe nobility from the court is so strong that everything which pertains to the former seems foreign to the latter."[21] The court of Louis XVI made no attempt to integrate the different elites of French society at the time. As opposed to the more mixed society of Paris, at Versailles the robe and the grand bourgeoisie—the world of finance and big business—remained socially beyond the pale.

One chink in the protective social armor of Versailles was the masked ball—the very opposite in spirit of the staid dress ball. To conceal their identity, dancers wore the domino, a half mask worn with a cloak. Not only the court but people ineligible for presentation, the Parisian upper bourgeoisie, were admitted. The only precaution taken by the palace was to require one member of each group of masks to unmask, give his name, and take responsibility for his fellows.

Masked balls brought something of the risqué thrill of Paris's opera balls to Versailles. In a rigid society of ranks, distinctions were leveled. The maréchal de Tessé, who commanded in the War of Spanish Succession, once fell into conversation with a man who turned out to be his cook. This anonymous atmosphere was sexually liberating, especially when combined with the surreal magnificence of the state apartment at Versailles and the excitement of the dance itself.

Unsurprisingly, masked balls were particularly popular with the younger royals. Louis XV liked them, turning up as a bat or a clipped yew tree, in tribute to the topiary of his gardens. Handsome and popularly rumored to have a wandering eye, he became a target for masked women who fancied their chances with the sovereign. It was at a masked ball at Versailles in 1744 that he was said to have met the lovely Madame d'Étioles, a rich Parisian bourgeoise ineligible for presentation.[22] She went on to become Madame de Pompadour.

With a whiff of chauvinism, Saint-Simon blamed the practice of gambling for high stakes on the bad influence of Mazarin, the Italian cardinal at the helm of state during Louis XIV's minority. According to the duke, Mazarin not only enriched himself in this way, but sought to ruin his enemies among the upper nobility, "a policy . . . continued long after his death."[23] Saint-Simon believed that Louis XIV was not averse to seeing his courtiers gamble away their money. He had set the example by playing for high stakes in the days of Madame de Montespan. Gambling was already entrenched at court when he formalized it in Apartment.

Whether his motives were as sinister as Saint-Simon implies is questionable. Moderate gambling was recommended to the future Louis XVI by his confessor, no less, as "one of the most honest and innocent amusements at court." In a world where a privileged few enjoyed a surfeit of leisure, gaming tables helped to dispel boredom and prop up conversation, although not always successfully, according to Voltaire, who wrote of "boredom increasing each time money was put down" at the formal gaming parties at Versailles.[24]

Voltaire knew the palace well. As Louis XV's royal historiographer, he received a lodging in the north wing, where he complained about the stink from the nearby latrines.[25] In referring to the boredom of gambling, he may have had in mind the card parties hosted by the virtuous but unexciting queen Marie Leczinska. As one courtier noted, "People were allowed in to watch this rather sad spectacle, but apart from a few old courtiers and some officers and captains of the bodyguard, no one was minded to go there."[26]

As ever, gamblers were tempted with the chimera of easy pickings. Saint-Simon's journal-keeping rival, the marquis de Dangeau, studiously applied himself to winning, with stupendous success. In 1676 Madame de Sévigné watched him playing at Versailles in a game of counters called reversis. "I wondered at how foolish we are compared to him. He thinks only of his game, and wins where others lose; he neglects no opportunity, profits from everything, and is never distracted: in a word, he defeats bad luck by playing well; thus two hundred thousand francs in ten days, a hundred thousand écus in a month, and all this written down in his receipt book."[27] Even Saint-Simon, generally not kind to Dangeau, conceded that his play was honest.[28]

The reign of Louis XVI illustrates the different styles of gambling at Versailles. For his ex-page Hézecques, Louis XVI was "a friend of morality." He shunned the fashionable games of chance, such as pharaon, and rarely exposed himself to a greater loss than two louis. His disapproval of high stakes was well known. He once sent four young gentlemen back to their regiments after they lost well over a thousand louis between them while gambling at one of the queen's balls.[29]

At his weekly suppers in his private apartments on the first floor, all was propriety. Guests retired from the dining room to play harmless "society games," as they were called. One room offered billiards, a fixture at Versailles since the time of Louis XIV, who was a devotee no less than Marie-Antoinette. Another room, spanning the public passage to the gardens, was devoted to gaming. Orders for forty-five gilt-wood chairs indicate the numbers expected at the tables. Here, surrounded by paintings of French victories in the present and previous reigns, the comte de Provence, the king's younger brother, would organize a whist party and the king sit down to his favorite trictrac, a game rather like backgammon.[30]

On Marie-Antoinette's side of the palace, the scene was different. The queen played publicly three evenings a week—on Wednesdays, Saturdays, and Sundays—when a large round table was set up in the middle of the Salon of Peace, a lofty room that had been annexed to the queen's apartment by closing the open entrance from the Hall of Mirrors with a double door inside a movable frame.[31] As in the time of Marie Leczinska, the queen's game *( jeu de la reine)* was an established time for the eligible to pay their court. Under Marie-Antoinette, presented women sat on the stools edging the room. Those who wished to play took a seat at the table when the queen sat down. Sometimes they placed money on behalf of others, including the men, who stood behind them.[32]

If contemporaries are to be believed, under Marie-Antoinette the risk was not so much of tedium as of financial ruin. The Austrian ambassador reported to her mother, the empress Maria Theresa, that by allowing high stakes the queen was keeping the presented nobility away, since respectable people feared being pressured into playing.[33]

These high stakes reflected less the queen's personal passion for gambling than a wish to keep up with the fast set. Her own losses were relatively modest, not least because she was careful with her money, a somewhat surprising fact given her reputation for extravagance. But the impression given to onlookers was different. Long after, Madame de Boigne, well informed thanks to her courtier-mother, paints a vivid picture of the queen of France at a table piled with money belonging to her subjects, wearing an eager expression that left no doubt that she liked to win.[34]

Court insiders had been reporting episodes of cheating since the time of Louis XIV. Saint-Simon claimed that the princesse d'Harcourt, a member of the inner circle of Louis XIV and Madame de Maintenon, cheated more or less openly at the royal tables.[35] Then there were the professional gamblers, Parisians ineligible for presentation at court under the normal rules. Madame, Louis XIV's sister-in-law, commented on the disrespectful atmosphere at Monseigneur's private gaming parties in his ground-floor rooms at Versailles. "People are wanted who can play for high stakes, but the best-born people are not the richest. So they play with every sort of riffraff."[36] Under Louis XVI, men with false titles of nobility were admitted to the queen's public table to hold the bank, for example, the Monsieur de Chalabre who had "no right to bear this fine name."[37]

The difference between the two reigns was that public opinion had since come into being in France. The appetite for court news and gossip was fed by samizdat publications like the *Secret Memoirs* circulating under Louis XVI: one inflammatory item reported on court duchesses cheating at the queen's game. When the comtesse de Provence, Marie-Antoinette's sister-in-law, alerted the bankers, they felt obliged to reply, out of respect for the queen, "Madame, we notice nothing."[38]

Hunting, according to Louis XVI's confessor, was a "true sport of kings."[39] In the Salon of Diana at Versailles, Louis XIV gave an elevated tone to this ancient royal pleasure. The ceiling décor surrounding the goddess of the chase juxtaposed scenes of ancient monarchs hunting threatening animals (the boar, the lion) beside one of Caesar sending Roman colonists to Carthage. Hunting and colonizing were twinned as aspects of the monarch's civilizing mission.

The ancient traditions of the royal hunt could be said to justify this view. Down to the Revolution the royal wolf hunt did in fact continue to perform a community service. The master of the wolf hunt sent his people and hounds to the rescue of provincials beleaguered by the creatures that, in 1709, "ate the royal courier from Alençon and his horse too." Successful hunting parties brought their trophies back to Versailles. In 1765 Horace Walpole saw the infamous "beast of Gévaudan" in Marie Leczinska's antechamber, where the public could contemplate its stuffed form while watching the sovereigns eat.[40]

At Versailles the hunt establishment that Louis XIV built up had no rival in Europe. To ensure a well-stocked hunting ground, from 1662 onward he embarked on a program of expropriation, justified by the need to provide for the monarch's "diversion." The land taken over in this way was planted with coverts for the game and cut through with rides. These were an expensive feature, which Saint-Simon contrasted unfavorably with Louis XIII's simpler taste for hunting in open countryside.[41]

The final result was the Grand Park, the closest thing in European history to the vast paradises or hunting grounds of ancient Persia. The Small Park alone encompassed an area much larger than today's gardens. The Grand Park, which framed it, covered eight thousand hectares and was surrounded by a wall nearly twenty-seven miles (forty-three kilometers) long, of which flinty stretches can still be seen on the modern road from Versailles to Marly.[42]

It was the job of the game wardens to keep the enclosure stocked. Acts of God were a setback, for instance, the torrential rain that turned out to have drowned nearly all the game birds when Louis XIV went shooting on July 17, 1692.[43] Game management also required a rigorous guard to deter illegal hunters. In an entry for January 1738, Luynes notes the seizure of two men caught in the bold act of using sulphurous smoke to stun pheasants in the park.[44] The reservation for the king's sole use of an area of countryside the size—in Saint-Simon's words—of a "small province" did not ease the lot of the local peasantry. After August 4, 1789, when all hunting preserves were abolished, poachers were prompt to sack the Grand Park for its game.[45]

Louis XIV remained an avid hunter even in older age. In 1708, when he turned seventy, he was out hunting on 118 days of the year: 63 shoots, 49 stag hunts, 5 outings with the falconry, and a boar hunt. Partly he loved simply being outdoors. "The king went shooting, despite the vile weather," as Dangeau typically records for January 29, 1692.[46]

As with all his actions, however, there was also a strong whiff of "reason of state." The hunt establishment was another chance to show off the king of France's resources. Hunting consumed these rather like the ritual destructions that anthropologists call potlatch. All France joined in sending an annual tribute of falcons to the king, of which perhaps just three or four were used in falconry, while the rest were killed.[47] On the hunt itself, thanks to vigorous beating, the scale of the slaughter could be spectacular: Louis XVI and his brothers used to kill up to fifteen hundred "pieces" on one day.[48]

Louis XIV used the hunt as one of his ways of maintaining a large following of courtiers by creating trifling distinctions that played on human vanity. He invented the "frock coat by royal warrant," a blue coat lined with red, with a red waistcoat and distinctive embroidery, announcing the wearer's right to follow the royal hunt whenever the wearer wished. Its origin lay in the early 1660s, when Louis XIV gave these coats to the ten or so courtiers allowed to follow him to Versailles from Saint-Germain. The young king displayed his innate flair for courtly "trifles" as soon as he began his personal rule.[49]

Since anyone could follow the royal hunt, these coats served to single out their wearers as part of the official suite, distancing them from the run of presented nobility, whose only privilege on these occasions was a seat in the royal coaches on the return. But no one could shoot without the monarch's express permission, a sufficiently momentous event for Luynes to record the fact in his journal.[50]

In the eighteenth century the royal hunt loomed larger than ever in the life of Versailles. Louis XV hunted on average three times a week, Louis XVI as much, if not more. The hunt even impinged on social life in the capital, where it gave rise to all-women suppers (*soupers de femmes*) on Saturday nights because husbands had gone to sleep at Versailles for Sunday's hunting.[51] An innovation of Louis XV in the

1730s, the hunt suppers (of which more in due course) had made the royal hunt even more of a target for the assiduous courtier.

The spiritual and musical performances in the chapel at Versailles were much commented on in their day and, for many, were a real source of pleasure. Louis XIV, a great lover of music, turned this chapel of the enlarged Versailles into a national center of excellence for French church music.

The year after the move to Versailles, he presided in person over a nationwide competition to find four new masters of music to serve by quarter in the royal chapel. Candidates from the dioceses of France had to submit sample compositions in sealed packets, and the monarch drew lots to decide the order in which they would perform in his presence.

Of the four winners chosen by Louis one, the twenty-five-year-old Michel-Richard Delalande, a Parisian organist, became the king's favorite composer of motets as well as other types of music. These choral compositions on scriptural texts accompanied the daily celebration of royal mass. Louis XIV considerably enriched their sound by obtaining permission from the archbishop of Paris—in whose diocese Versailles fell—for the chapel musicians to accompany them with violins, oboes, and other instruments.[52]

To a Protestant ear used to hearing less decorated music in church, the effect could sound secular—like "a concert of music," as one visitor from England said of Louis XVI's mass.[53] In 1699 Monnier de Richardin found the overall effect sublime, "serving to raise the heart towards God."

Monnier was surprised to see a girl among the chapel singers. These typically numbered around thirty at Louis XIV's daily mass, including six or eight boy-sopranos serving by semester and recruited from parishes all over France. At Versailles they received board, lodging, and an education, in effect forming a little choir school. After the last chapel was built, classrooms in the annex were set aside for their lessons in Latin, French, and music.[54]

Such was Louis XIV's interest in this choir that he personally auditioned each new recruit in the state apartments. His great-grandson

Louis XV did not listen to music for pleasure. But for reasons of royal prestige, the musical traditions of the chapel were upheld after Louis XIV's death by Delalande and his successors. In 1741 the choir was shown off to the Turkish ambassador, who as a Muslim listened unseen from a room in the chapel annex. In 1764 the choir won the approval of the Mozarts, generally rather critical of French music. During a visit to Versailles with his seven-year-old son, Mozart senior took his "little man" daily to hear the motets, rating the choir "good, excellent even."[55]

Today one of the most eye-catching items in the chapel is the organ. Miraculously, it survived the Revolution more or less intact, thanks to a former countertenor in the chapel choir who managed to persuade the authorities that the organ was a national treasure. The royal organist who inaugurated this instrument in Louis XIV's presence on Easter Day 1711 was François Couperin, one of the supreme exponents of the French school of organ playing.[56]

An item of liturgical furniture that failed to survive the Revolution was the gilt-wood pulpit. Carved with scenes of Christ preaching, this was originally attached to a pillar on the north side of the nave, where traces of the steps can still be made out.[57] Sermons were, in their way, one of the entertainments of Versailles. Performances were no less a subject for discussion than the previous night's play. Preachers were supposed to pay a compliment to the king or senior royals present in the chapel, before launching on their theme, which by convention was allowed to include mild criticism of the monarch, as at the ceremony of the *cène.*

Indeed, fiery sermons were especially licensed during Lent, in the period of penitence in the run-up to Easter. During Lent 1751 a Jesuit, Father Griffet, preached on the woman taken in adultery, and thundered against "present practices." The unmistakable reference was to Louis XV and his official mistress, the marquise de Pompadour, both of them married to other partners. Their relationship revived the double adultery of Louis XIV with Madame de Montespan.

*Passato il periculo, gabbato il santo* (When the danger is past, God is mocked): the baron de Besenval's cynical judgment on Louis XV's religion was by no means unfair. But religious feelings, once again, are complex. In 1751 the monarch rearranged his beloved hunting so as not to miss a single one of Father Griffet's twice-weekly sermons.[58]

As for the marquise, she was unflappable. Under the eyes of the court she continued to attend the royal chapel. But the following year she obtained Louis XV's permission to construct her own tribune. This small room—it still exists—was rather like a private box, in her day made snug with curtains, a bearskin rug, and a stove. It looked down into the nave through a false window, and through the glass the courtiers could just make her out, prayer book in hand. The whole scene was an example of the "mixture of piety, pomp and carnality" on display at Versailles; Horace Walpole "could not help smiling" at this curious ambience when he visited soon after.[59]

Versailles, and above all the king himself, were as likely to intimidate simple preachers from outside the world of the court as they were to prompt fire and brimstone. In 1738 Luynes witnessed a Franciscan monk so overcome with stage fright in the pulpit that he "took ill and twice vomited," hitting the dress of the marquise d'Armentières, seated below. Louis XV had inadvertently provoked this extraordinary scene by his presence a few feet away in his armchair, having come down to the nave, the custom when there was a preacher.[60]

Inside the vast palace the courtiers had their own social routines. They assembled to pay court at the *lever,* the king's mass and meals, the evening entertainments, and the *coucher.* In between they visited one another. The habit of paying calls began with the royal family. Memoirs show royalty inviting themselves for meals with their courtiers, dropping by unexpectedly, and even letting themselves in by the front door. Louis XIV's daughter the duchesse d'Orléans visited the Saint-Simon lodgings on her way to supper with her daughter, whose rooms were nearby, and ended up staying for two hours. When the duc de Berri, Louis XIV's grandson, called on the duc and duchesse de Saint-Simon, he felt free to enter every room. The memoirist complained that he was no longer master of his bedchamber or his study.[61]

Illness and accommodations ranked high among motives for royal visits. Marie Leczinska, Louis XV's queen, would call in person up to twice a day, as well as sending handwritten messages, if one of her ladies was unwell. In November 1786 Marie-Antoinette came in person to look over the new quarters of the princesse de Lamballe on the ground floor of the south wing and gave orders to hurry the installation of a dining room.[62]

At Versailles, where the courtiers were all related to one another, callers were often visiting family. Croÿ was frequently in the rooms of the marquise de Leyde, a Croÿ cousin in the service of Madame Infante, Louis XV's eldest daughter. His journal shows him attending her toilette in her lodging in the Small Stables. One time he was comforting her after her son ran off to Amsterdam with an actress. Another time he was summoned to consider a proposed match between his son and a Noailles, an idea scotched by Croÿ's mother, the dowager princess, who disliked the family.[63]

The convenience of Versailles and the concentration there of aristocratic women, accomplished brokers of matches, made the palace a marriage market. The Noailles project having come to nothing, Croÿ set his sights on a grander match with a daughter of the prince de Carignan, kinsman of the king of Sardinia. Accordingly, he went to call on the prince's mother one evening in her rooms in the Government Wing. But his efforts foundered in Turin, the other arm of this negotiation: the prince de Carignan's German wife, described by Croÿ as saintly and extremely haughty, would permit only a member of a sovereign house for her daughter. "A fine pipe-dream has vanished," he confided sadly to his journal.[64]

Great families would normally seek the monarch's permission for a marriage. This was not just a formality: in 1743 Louis XV refused a request from the duc de Bouillon to marry his son into the princely Arenberg family because the then head of the Arenbergs was fighting against the French in the War of the Austrian Succession.[65] At Versailles the king and royal family signed the marriage contracts of members of their households, both grandees and lowly servitors. Sometimes courtiers celebrated family marriages in their palace lodgings. "The marriage of Monsieur de Lillebonne with Mademoiselle de La Feuillade took place on Tuesday 13th [June 1752] in the rooms of Madame de La Feuillade, and the next day the wedding party was in the rooms of Monsieur le duc d'Harcourt, where there was music and a very large and very good supper."[66]

After kin came friends. Madame de Genlis recalled that, before the Revolution, "friendship was a far more exacting business": "The slightest incident obliged one to write, or to go and pay a visit. If a woman at supper complained of migraine, men and women were obliged to send for news of her the next day even if they hardly knew her; if she kept to her bedchamber, visiting her three or four times a week was obligatory, as was sending for news daily."[67]

At Versailles these elaborate rituals helped to keep useful friendships on their mettle. Saint-Simon, an only child, badly felt the need for trustworthy friends. He became extremely close to the upright duc de Beauvilliers, a minister of state high in favor with Louis XIV. Their relationship had been sealed at Versailles by mutual pledges during a furtive meeting "in a narrow dark corridor" behind the chapel of 1682, where the Salon of Hercules is now. This ended in "declarations of undying affection, with offers to assist me in matters great and small, and a mutual determination to regard ourselves thenceforward as father and son, bound in indissoluble union." In the 1770s, it was this sort of strong bond with his friend du Châtelet that Choiseul called on in the affair of his regiment.[68]

Under Louis XIV and Louis XV, some leading courtiers kept open house. For a quarter of a century the lodging of François VII de La Rochefoucauld, Louis XIV's grand master of the wardrobe, was one of the centers of the court, handily located right underneath what in 1701 became the Bull's Eye, with windows overlooking the Royal Court. He welcomed all comers from morning to night, keeping an excellent table in what must have been one of the first private dining rooms at Versailles, installed in 1684. Saint-Simon never went, because the duke's servants were too free in their ways for his taste. But it was a mecca for "the bored and the unoccupied of the Court," and its disappearance when the duke retired left a "great void" at Versailles.[69]

Under Louis XV, the lodgings of the duc de Gesvres, one of the king's first gentlemen, played much the same role. His third-floor rooms at the extremity of the Old Wing came with an outdoor terrace looking over the Ministers' Court, which the duke, who had a passion for flowers and birds, enlivened with aviaries and trellises.

Besenval, nothing if not a man of the world himself, classified Gesvres as "one of these rare beings which appear in the world from time to time." "In public he had all the mannerisms of a woman; he wore rouge; he could be found in his rooms either in bed playing with his fan, or working on his tapestry. He liked to get involved in everything; his character was precisely that of a frivolous chatterbox."

The pious, respectable duc de Luynes and the womanish Gesvres might seem unlikely friends, but Luynes held him in high regard. What brought the two men together was Gesvres' astounding memory and its application to, "not the sciences or literature," but the facts of Louis XIV's court, which Gesvres was old enough to remember, and to "the parentage and genealogy of all those who lived at the Court and in the Town." Here was the stuff of conversation at Versailles, at least in some quarters.

Gesvres ended up a kind of social arbiter to whom all the newlywed women were brought to be presented. His rooms at Versailles were full from the moment he woke up until bedtime, he wrote and dictated surrounded by a numerous company, and he gave a big dinner daily. To support this way of life, he had a large household of gentlemen and well-born page boys, and spent "prodigiously."[70]

In the eighteenth century, women ruled polite society in Paris. This was the age of the salon, in reality a private house whose hostess, usually well born and invariably well off, "received" on certain days, often over a dinner or supper. Certain salons became social centers, the place to see and be seen, to practice the social graces—above all, conversation—to meet the right people, and, for the well-born young, to be polished up by sitting at the feet of acknowledged models of grace and style among their elders and betters. Artists and writers in search of aristocratic patrons gravitated toward the salons, as did distinguished foreigners, including the ambassadors.

In the eighteenth century this elitist world of the Paris salons was of a piece with the court. Neither Louis XV nor Louis XVI had the political will or the personal authority to keep their courtiers on a short leash at Versailles, as Louis XIV had done. "Court and Town," meaning Versailles and Paris, now described a united society: the same people "were courtiers at Versailles and society folk in Paris." In one view, the only difference was that "people intrigued at Versailles, and amused themselves in Paris."[71]

Parisian hostesses included officeholders in the queen's household at Versailles. One of the most formidable hostesses of the 1770s was the twice-wed maréchale de Luxembourg, a granddaughter of the duc de Villeroy, Louis XV's governor. For fifteen years she was a palace lady of Marie Leczinska, commuting for her monthly week of service from Paris to a lodging in the north wing. After her second marriage in 1750 to a captain of Louis XV's bodyguard, she had the use of his rooms in the same part of the palace, and hung on tenaciously to a pied-à-terre when he died sixteen years later.

The maréchale was a larger-than-life figure. Born in 1707, she was a true child of the Regency, a period resembling the 1960s, at any rate in Paris, for its atmosphere of sexual liberation. Madame de Boufflers, as she then was, supposedly took full advantage. Following her debut at Versailles, the following ditty, somewhat lost in translation, made the rounds:

*When Boufflers appeared at the court*
*She was seen as the mother of love:*
*Everyone tried to please her,*
*And everyone in turn had her.*

In later years, thanks to her name, wealth, judgment, and quick wit, she became respectable, indeed a social power, metamorphosing into the "oracle of *bon ton*." She presided over one of the most fashionable Paris salons, with a character so mellowed that her granddaughter, whom she raised herself, was seen as a "masterpiece of education."[72]

The commuting palace lady was a stock figure of eighteenth-century Versailles. In keeping with Louis XIV's strict control of courtiers, in his day the ladies in the suites of the royal family lived permanently at

Versailles. When Louis XV married Marie Leczinska, the old rules were changed to suit the then chief minister, the duc de Bourbon. He wanted his mistress, one of the new queen's palace ladies, to be able to come and go at court without having to ask for leave. The palace ladies started to divide themselves into groups: each group served for one week only, after which its members were free until their next week of service. Under Louis XV, the same usage spread to the households of the royal princesses and remained in force down to the Revolution.

The abbé de Véri, a close observer of the court of Louis XVI, claimed that these ladies-in-waiting, numbering over sixty-six in 1774, only "camped" at Versailles. Their real life was in Paris. Since, in his view, aristocratic women could flower as hostesses only in their own homes, Versailles was socially the poorer as a consequence. The starting point for this analysis was Véri's assumption that "(with the partial exception of England), women form the heart of society." His point was amply borne out by the flourishing salon scene in eighteenth-century Paris.[73]

There were exceptions. The prime court positions for women required a more constant presence at Versailles. This was true above all of the governess of the royal children. The comtesse de Marsan raised the future Louis XVI and his siblings, retaining the girls after the boys were handed over to governors at the age of six, as was the custom. She occupied the official apartment of the governess at the extremity of the south wing, one of the nicest in the palace, the air scented in summertime by the nearby Orangery.

The countess was gatekeeper for all visitors to the royal children. They lived next door in an enfilade of interconnected rooms, their walls padded to prevent injury when the young ones played. Such was the public interest in these children that, in 1770, the countess had a wrought-iron barrier installed in front of the French windows onto the garden terrace to prevent the curious from peering or, indeed, just wandering, into her rooms.[74]

Surrounded by adulation, the royal children had a deserved reputation for precocity. In 1755, when the ambassadors came on New Year's Day to pay their customary court to the duke of Burgundy, elder grandson of Louis XV, they expressed the wish to be standing before him on the same day in eighty years' time. Aged all of four, the little prince replied, "with a proud and imposing expression which astonished": "Why not in a hundred years' time?"[75]

The countess's rooms were one of the centers of the court. Courtiers came to watch the royal children eating at table or dancing at children's balls. Not a beauty ("as for the face, there is nothing to say," Luynes wrote after her presentation), the countess was good company in her younger days. As governess, she maintained a table at royal expense on a scale that can be judged by the silverware stolen from her rooms in 1755: fifty-four plates and two or three dozen place settings.

As piety and, some said, prudery took hold in later years, she turned into the "plotting, vindictive and dangerous" woman whom the Austrian ambassador warned the newly married Marie-Antoinette not to cross. Her rooms became a bulwark of the *dévots,* the courtiers who worked in vain first to avoid, then to reverse, the expulsion of France's Jesuit priests in 1762. After Marie-Antoinette became queen, the countess retired to Paris. When the loyal Croÿ visited her there in 1782, he found a suffering old woman, "tired of life."[76]

The pious comtesse de Marsan was a pure product of the world of hierarchy. She was called *hautaine* (haughty), an adjective that aristocrats of the time did not see as derogatory. Courtiers joked that the devout, Catholic, countess even thought her family good enough to marry into the Holy Family. Supposedly she was planning a match between Jesus and a princess of her house, to save the bachelor Son of God from any risk of a misalliance![77]

From her windows higher up the side of the hill she looked down on a Versailles salon quite different from hers in atmosphere. It came closest to the traditional picture of the salons of eighteenth-century Paris: assemblies of talented people of mixed backgrounds amusing themselves in sparkling conversation under the aegis of a clever, charming woman.

Élisabeth de Laborde was a cousin of Madame de Pompadour. She was married first to one of Louis XV's head valets, then to Louis XVI's director of royal buildings, the comte d'Angivilliers. Her appearance was striking: she was tiny, her lined face framed by floor-length hair adorned with flowers and feathers. She was excellent company, amiable and well informed without letting it show too much. In conversation, she spoke "with elegance, justness and clarity; people always wanted to hear what she had to say."

She lived in an annex of the palace on the rue de la Surintendance. In those days the building—it still stands—was linked by a covered corridor to the extremity of the south wing, allowing visitors from the palace to enter without braving the elements. In rooms plagued by rats that gnawed at her furnishings, she received "artists, scholars and writers," as well as ambassadors and "the best company of the court." Among her regulars were Choderlos de Laclos, author of the sensational novel *Dangerous Liaisons,* and a certain Monsieur Saint-Germain, an eccentric who claimed to be three thousand years old and to have watched Alexander the Great's entry into Babylon.

Despite the charms of her salon, hierarchical Versailles kept her at arm's length because she was not from the social cream, as she revealed by her overobliging manner toward court grandees. Handing down not so much the truth as the prejudices, probably from her mother, Madame de Boigne classed Madame d'Angivilliers with the "secondary inhabitants of the château," the people who found all the doors of the court grandees closed to them.[78]

The garden front around 1695. Architecturally this is the most successful part of the palace. But the style and materials clash awkwardly with the Paris front *(below)*. RMN/© FRANCK RAUX

The Paris front in 1722. At its core is the red-brick château of Louis XIII, which Louis XIV would have liked to demolish. His successors both planned a major rebuilding of these façades, but only had enough funds to make a beginning. RMN/© DANIEL ARNAUDET

Hall of Mirrors, ceiling: Louis XIV crosses the River Rhine as a triumphant Roman imperator, his chariot pushed by Hercules. RMN/© GÉRARD BLOT/HERVÉ LEWANDOWSKI

Shock and awe. Enthroned on a temporary dais in the Hall of Mirrors, Louis XIV receives envoys from Persia in a carefully staged ceremony in 1715, a few months before his death.
RMN /© GÉRARD BLOT

The Menagerie of Louis XIV today. The surviving pavilions formed part of the royal dairy favored by the duchess of Burgundy, Louis XV's mother. TONY SPAWFORTH

An original shutter is all that remains visible today on the site of the vanished bath apartment of Louis XIV. TONY SPAWFORTH

The bedchamber of Louis XIV, ceremonial heart of the palace down to the Revolution.
RMN/© DANIEL ARNAUDET/JEAN SCHORMANS

The next-door Bull's Eye antechamber, a palace crossroads thronged with watchful "idlers."
RMN/© GÉRARD BLOT

Under the monarchy, galleries like this one in the south wing were the thoroughfares of the palace, full of people and bustle, and none too clean. TONY SPAWFORTH

In the eighteenth century, hygiene at Versailles made gradual advances. Alongside the traditional close stool *(right)* appeared the bidet *(left,* made for Madame de Pompadour). The setting of this modern display is a former privy of Louis XV. RMN / © HARRY BRÉJAT

The "ceremony of the Order": In the chapel a teenage Louis XV confers the Holy Ghost on novices wearing their traditional Louis XIII-style costumes. RMN / © DANIEL ARNAUDET

A masked ball in the Hall of Mirrors, Carnival 1745. Anonymity and the admission of commoners gave this kind of court entertainment a decidedly erotic frisson. Note the figures in "Turkish" dress.
RMN/© MICHÈLE BELLOT

LEFT: The false window in an aisle of the royal chapel behind which Madame de Pompadour sat in her "niche" during services. Courtiers could just make out her hands piously thumbing her prayer book. TONY SPAWFORTH

RIGHT: Chest of drawers from Madame du Barry's opulent lodging at Versailles. Those seeking the king's favor were obliged to climb the stairs to this new center of power. RMN/© DANIEL ARNAUDET

Marie-Antoinette's artificial grotto in the Trianon grounds. With two separate entrances, its layout prompted speculation about the queen's morals. TONY SPAWFORTH

Marie-Antoinette's state bedchamber, where she gave birth to her four children. On October 6, 1789, she escaped her assailants through a concealed door to the right of her bed. RMN/© J. DERENNE

# 7 ·

# *Comforts, or Lack of Them*

THERE WAS no parallel in Europe for the living arrangements of Versailles. They brought together a ruling dynasty, a swollen household of domestic employees, and a system of government in a single, vast complex. Beyond the palace, the major annexes formed small worlds of their own, each a community centered on a chapel. The chapel in the Grand Commons survives; once there were others in the Grand Stables, the Small Stables, and the Kennel.

The palace proper resembled a vast apartment block. Apart from the royal family, most of the residents were senior members of the household. On each floor, living units of varying size, some 350 in all, were arranged along tiled corridors and given a number.[1] Each door had a key, to be handed in when the lodging was vacated.

In the eighteenth century the lodgers found the aging palace increasingly uncomfortable in spite of the limited spread of more modern comforts such as bathrooms and water closets. But the practical advantages and social prestige of a base in the palace ensured that, down to the Revolution, every vacancy gave rise to "a series of intrigues and solicitations over who should have it."[2]

Rank and status dictated the location and quality of lodgings at Versailles. In the royal family itself, everyone except the king and queen was liable to be moved around the palace as they gained or lost seniority. Louis XVI's brother the comte de Provence shared an apartment with his governess on the ground floor of the south wing until the age of six, another next door as he grew up; when he married, he and his wife qualified for the traditional apartment of the dauphin, where they remained for twelve years, until a dauphin (the elder son of Louis XVI) dislodged them in 1786 to rooms back in the south wing.

Louis XIV envisaged Versailles as a residence for all the Bourbons, including his adult bastards—six of them—by Louise de La Vallière and Madame de Montespan. Seventeenth-century France was unusual in the number of branches of the royal family. Saint-Simon points out that no younger son in the Spanish branch of the Habsburgs ever produced descendants.[3] By contrast, in 1710 the Bourbon-Condé and Bourbon-Conti families alone numbered thirteen; the family of Louis XIV's brother, the Orléans, added another seven.

The Condé and Conti branches had both supplied rebels in the civil war of Louis XIV's childhood. For reasons of state, Louis XIV encouraged the numerous princes and princesses of the blood to live at Versailles and to treat it as a kind of family headquarters. He wove them into his immediate family by arranging intermarriages with his legitimized offspring, celebrated in the royal chapel. They were expected to turn out for ceremonies and state occasions, as well as family events: the princesses of the blood, for instance, were alerted when the queen went into labor and would set out for Versailles to witness the birth.

In return, they all received royal subsidies and honorific distinctions. At Versailles the guards always presented arms when a prince or princess of the blood passed through the guardrooms. They profited from their rank in all sorts of practical ways, too. Despite their past (or because of it), the Condé princes had a reputation for fawning and for making constant demands, over and above the substantial profits from their post of grand master of the household.

So that they could play their part in court life, Louis XIV assigned members of these families some of the best lodgings at Versailles, in prime locations overlooking the gardens. In 1700 the prince de Condé, son of the rebel prince, was able to give a party for the whole court in his rooms on the ground floor of the south wing, offering dancing, supper, and booths of exotic merchandise. Saint-Simon says that "there was no crowding" although his rooms were "few and small": perhaps, but only relatively, compared with other princes.

A rare engraving of a princely interior at Versailles depicts a fancy-dress ball in 1695 in the lodging of Condé's son, off the same gallery.

The room could almost be one of the salons of the state apartments: high, decorated ceiling; sculptured cornice, and eight or more chandeliers. Sixty-five or so onlookers line the dance floor, mostly on grandstands.[4]

Until Louis XV's wife produced a dauphin, the heir to the throne was the king's second cousin once removed, the son of the Regent. Although Louis XV made a point of numbering the cadet branches among "our family," in fact their relations with the monarch deteriorated from the mid-century on. The prince de Conti became the talk of Versailles in December 1756 when he abruptly removed his possessions, gave back his lodging, and announced that he was never coming back to the palace after falling out with Louis XV over foreign policy.[5]

Later in the reign there was a more serious rift when the princes reverted to their old ways by siding with the Parlement of Paris in its dispute with the crown. Coincidentally, by the 1760s the numbers of the royal family had shot up dramatically. As the grown-up children of Louis XV, followed by those of his son, the father of Louis XVI, took up more and more space in the palace, the princes found themselves increasingly sidelined in the allocation of lodgings at Versailles. This was one reason why, under Louis XVI, they hardly used their apartments except on days of ceremony.[6]

The case of the Orléans family is instructive. The branch's founder, Louis XIV's younger brother, Monsieur, occupied the whole first floor of the south wing with his wife and family. But by the time the fourth duc d'Orléans died in 1785, the family had been dislodged entirely from the garden façade and had to make do with rooms above the king's kitchen, overlooking a street and a busy courtyard.[7]

Obviously, this far less prestigious address hardly explains on its own why the future Philippe Égalité, the fifth duke, joined the Revolution in 1789. But perhaps it can be accounted among the least of the perceived slights that fueled his long-standing animosity toward Louis XVI and Marie-Antoinette.

Saint-Simon's living arrangements at Versailles reveal the extreme importance attached by a courtier to gaining, and keeping, a foothold in the palace. He states plainly what was at issue: "Not only to live at court, as I have always done, but even just to frequent it, is unbearable and impossible without a lodging."[8] The reasons are instructive: a lodging gave his wife somewhere to change her clothes, and allowed "us both to see our friends there."

Living in the town of Versailles was out of the question by reason of the daily inconvenience, "the thousand complications," and the interruptions to a palace-based social life "from which one imperceptibly draws so many advantages." As a result, Saint-Simon never made a permanent residence of his father's small town house nearly half a mile from the forecourt of the palace.

Like many of the noble dwellings at Versailles, this was more pavilion than mansion. A deed of sale from 1758 gives this cursory description: "carriage door, courtyard, mews, stables, buildings, garden and rear courtyard planted with fig trees."[9] This preference for the palace lodging over the town house reemerges from the valuation of the property of the duc de Chevreuse at his death in 1712. The contents of his Versailles house were worth 2,274 livres, those of his lodging, 5,324 livres, over twice as much.[10]

Saint-Simon never held a *charge* (an employment at court), the prime qualification for board and lodging under the royal roof. As not infrequently happened at Versailles, at first he lodged with a relation, his father-in-law, the maréchal-duc de Lorge, a captain of the royal bodyguard, who had rooms in the north wing, which Louis XIV reassigned after the marshal's death to the new duc de Lorge. He, in turn, let Saint-Simon stay on because *his* father-in-law, Michel Chamillart, as war secretary had a larger apartment at the other end of the palace, which he offered the new duke and his duchess.

The duc de Saint-Simon stayed on in the late marshal's rooms until 1709, when Chamillart was disgraced. Louis XIV then reclaimed the ministerial apartment lent to Lorge, who in turn needed back Saint-Simon's lodging. At this point Saint-Simon, who had his own difficulties with Louis XIV, contemplated retirement from the court.

A powerful friend, the chancellor Pontchartrain, came to his rescue with the offer of "a large and fine chamber" along with a secondary room, or *garde-robe.* He suggested that the ducal couple could use these by day, even if they did not want to sleep there. The two rooms were in the north ministers' wing, up in the attics, lit by one of the dormer windows, still extant.

The following year the fortunes of the ducal couple rose abruptly when Louis XIV, who had a high opinion of Saint-Simon's virtuous duchess, offered her the post of lady of honor in the household of the duchesse de Berri, wayward wife of his third grandson.

Service in lesser royal households was less honorific than in the sovereign's. Saint-Simon fulminated privately against a "position so far beneath persons of our birth and rank." He managed only a middling bow of gratitude to Louis XIV when, under strong pressure, he and his wife accepted. In fact, the duke was not entirely blind to his interest: there was also no long-term advantage for his family in entering the service of a younger son's wife. At the duchesse de Berri's death, her royal household would be dissolved and her officials would lose their places.[11]

Louis went out of his way to sugar the pill by giving the duc and duchesse de Saint-Simon one of the nicest lodgings in the palace, conveniently sited across the corridor from the princely couple, whose vast apartment accounted for twelve windows on the first floor of the north wing overlooking the garden. For Saint-Simon, existing occupants were dislodged and rooms knocked together to form what courtiers called a "semi-double": each large room was paralleled by two floors of smaller ones, created by the insertion of a mezzanine, or entresol.

The duc and duchesse de Saint-Simon had a row of five large rooms along one side of a public corridor. The middle one was a shared antechamber, flanked on each side by a study and bedchamber for the two occupants respectively: at this date aristocratic couples did not normally share beds in France. These rooms were doubled by entresols, gloomy and secretive, reached by doors concealed in the paneling.

Here Saint-Simon had a back study that his friends called his "workshop," where he kept his writing desk, some chairs, and some books. It was ideal for secret meetings. Saint-Simon tells us about one, during which he and the king's confessor had locked themselves in and were talking "nose-to-nose" across the table by the light of two candles when suddenly the duke heard royalty—the Berri couple—enter the next-door study.

The duke and his visitor froze, until Saint-Simon's duchess rescued them by leading the royal couple into her own rooms at the other end of the lodging. The two then went back to arguing church politics, until eventually Saint-Simon let the priest out by a small door from the back study onto the corridor.[12]

Outside the royal family, few noble courtiers were as comfortable as the duc and duchesse de Saint-Simon were from 1710 on. Lowlier servitors were mostly housed in very different conditions in the outbuildings. In the Grand Commons, the worst lodgings were crammed beneath an original roof—since destroyed—of the mansard type, with two slopes. Behind the lower and steeper slope were two floors of lodgings sharing dormer windows that let light into the upper rooms at floor level only. These rooms were about five or six feet high.

Above them, under the gentler incline of the upper slope, was a final floor of wedge-shaped rooms whose occupants could just about stand upright by the door. The records name some of the occupants of these dark, airless, and for the most part unheated spaces: François Courtois, pastry maker; La Branche, floor polisher; Léon Hébert, linen draper; François La Guaisse, wine waiter; Bonaventure Testu, kitchen boy; the widow Poupion. In such conditions, people lived outside as much as possible, in the wine shops and, in fair weather, on the streets of the town.[13]

Sanitation, or lack of it, did something to level these differences in living conditions. Although French people of the time saw Louis XIV's Versailles as a gold standard of refinement, older habits died hard. Versailles "cheerfully accepted" the princesse d'Harcourt, whose obnoxious behavior—she sometimes relieved herself in her skirts, nonchalantly leaving a foul trail behind her for the servants to clean up—was like a throwback to a less polite age, when aristocrats had bothered themselves less with self-restraint.[14]

Even members of the royal family—women as well as men, the king included—thought nothing of giving audiences or chatting to intimates while installed on the closestool. In 1723 the high-living Regent received Saint-Simon in this way at Versailles the morning after one of his late-night suppers, horrifying his friend by his befuddled manner and thick voice. Within a month the Regent was dead.[15]

The privies of Louis XIV's Versailles have so far escaped close study. In the eighteenth century there were public latrines placed in the corridors and stairwells of the palace, the Grand Commons, and the other annexes: these latrines consisted of a room with a wooden seat, or *lunette,* closed by a cover in a vain attempt to shut in the odors, and connected by a waste pipe to a cesspit. Some were kept locked and the key distributed to nearby residents.[16]

Versailles was no different from Paris in the squalor of this type of latrine. For instance, in 1785 we find seven lodgers in the attics of the Grand Commons, among them one of the king's dressers and one of the queen's chaplains, petitioning for the closing down of a fourth-floor privy because "the smell penetrates the lodgings . . . and infects furnishing, clothes and linen," as well as "serving certain riff-raff who use it as a meeting place."[17]

Noble courtiers fared no better. In 1766 the king's daughter, Madame Adélaïde, demanded new rooms for a lady-in-waiting lodged above the queen's apartment, "far too near the privy." Two years earlier the comtesse du Châtelet, who lived in the attics of the south wing, complained of the smell from the nearby privy and also—a glimpse of the cheek-by-jowl living at Versailles—of the fact that she could be seen in her cabinet from its window.

To the smell was added the risk of leaks, whether through the floor of latrines to lodgings beneath them, from which not even the rooms of the royal children were safe, or from iron or lead pipes prone to blockage and corrosion, like the ones that let their contents "leak and poison everything" in Marie-Antoinette's kitchen.[18]

If people found the latrines closed, they would relieve themselves in the public corridor, as happened in 1741 after a privy in the attics of the north wing was converted into a lodging. People did the same in the first-floor gallery of the south wing. When the newly married dauphin and dauphine were lodged here in 1745, iron barriers were placed in front of the arcades opposite their rooms "to prevent indecency and dirtiness." In 1762 the comte de Compans complained about the passersby and kitchen boys who "attended to their needs" in an inner courtyard in the same wing, "often breaking his windows," presumably because he remonstrated with them. Bombelles, an admirer of Versailles under Louis XVI, wrote in his journal that more effort could be made to address the "dirtiness" of the public galleries.[19]

In 1742 the master of the wolf hunt, the marquis d'Heudicourt, who occupied attic rooms in the south wing, took a fatal fall down the stairs on the way to the public latrine, "apparently having no other privy." This was unusual: noble lodgers generally possessed at least their own closestool, a chair with an upholstered seat and a receptacle that could be emptied and cleaned. They were still in use at Versailles in the 1780s, no doubt widely, since they crop up in the possessions of people as different in standing as a lady-in-waiting of the comtesse d'Artois and a captain in the French Guards.[20]

At Versailles chamber pots were common as well, if not universal, and in the eighteenth century, despite attempts to stop the practice, servants on the upper stories frequently emptied them into the interior courts below. The dauphine Marie-Antoinette was once hit as she crossed the king's inner courtyards beneath the numerous windows of the king's mistress, Madame du Barry. Since she and the mistress were scarcely on speaking terms, an indignant Marie-Antoinette suspected foul play and complained to Louis XV—pointlessly, for obvious reasons.[21]

Under Louis XV Madame du Barry seems to have been one of the few inhabitants of the palace, apart from royalty, to benefit from a civilizing invention imported to eighteenth-century France from England, the water closet. The bowl was flushed by tap water supplied from an overhead tank, and the waste was piped to a cesspit. In 1738 Louis XV had one of these "English places" *(lieux à l'anglaise),* as they became known, fitted up in a small room *(garde-robe)* off his new bedchamber.

The great advantage of this new device was the absence of smell. A luxurious installation of marble, porcelain, and mahogany, the king's was kept so clean that Louis XVI once sat down without noticing an enormous angora cat curled up contentedly in the perfumed bowl. When events galvanized the cat into attacking the sovereign from below, a dazed Louis XVI fled, stockings in hand, "ringing all the bell-pulls." Hézecques heard this story from the footman who ran to the king's rescue.[22]

At Versailles the new device quickly spread from the royal family to the princesses of the blood: Mademoiselle de La Roche-sur-Yon, sister of the prince de Conti, must have had hers well before 1747, when she asked for it to be relocated. By 1788 Louis XVI was providing his footmen with one, its marble basin recycled from the queen's rooms.[23]

~~

In Louis XIV's day most French people conceived water as positively bad for health. At Versailles the court was fixated on appearances, maintained by washing eyes, teeth, and hands, by products such as the white wax that Mademoiselle d'Elboeuf applied to her teeth, and above all by the whiteness of the linen or lace at one's neck and cuffs.[2]

The remedy for Louis XIV's tendency to perspire was, not a wash, but a change of shirt. A clean shirt was a symbol of royal propriety, and this helps to explain the solemnity attached to the royal shirt at the ceremonial *lever*. First the head valet presented it to the grand chamberlain, who in turn handed it to the most senior prince of the blood present, who finally offered it to the monarch.

Another aid to propriety was scent. Louis XIV's apothecary and his assistant had the job of making up the sachets to perfume the king's clothes, linen, and wigs, a task done at Versailles in their large laboratory overlooking a courtyard in the south wing.

The linen, if not its wearer, was frequently washed. Louis XIV employed two laundresses, literally "whiteners," for this purpose. In the next reign Queen Marie Leczinska's laundress washed her mistress's linen in the Lake of the Swiss Guards. In the reign after that, the washed linen of various royal princesses was discreetly hung out to dry in the surrounding avenues of trees.[25]

Baths did exist at Versailles under Louis XIV, who installed three of them in his magnificent ground-floor bath apartment of the 1670s, including a huge octagon of Rance marble in which several people could sit at the same time on a marble ledge. These "pleasures of the bath," as they were euphemistically known, were sensual. The whole apartment, Pierre Verlet suggested, should be considered "an annex of the kingdom of Madame de Montespan," the king's mistress. In the chamber next door to the baths was a full-size bed.[26]

After the end of their relationship, Louis completely gave up this apartment, not before removing many of its ornaments. In 1684 the octagonal tub was buried, and in due course forgotten, beneath a raised floor in what became a bedchamber. Louis XIV continued to bathe occasionally. An official list of 1699 records that he and Monseigneur took a hot bath "when necessary" in their bedchambers—so in a portable tub, and not regularly. Perfume, considered therapeutic then, was also burned during the bath, suggesting that the aim of such immersions was chiefly medicinal.[27]

The young Louis XV was in the vanguard of a patchy revival of bathing in eighteenth-century France among the sophisticated elites of court and capital. One of his first orders at Versailles, when he was thirteen, was for a bathroom. Although this was later destroyed, the technology remained essentially the same for all bathrooms at Versailles: water carriers emptied their casks into a cold-water tank, which supplied a boiler heated by charcoal.

This first bathtub of Louis XV, made from heat-retaining copper, was on rollers, and the young monarch modestly bathed in a bath shirt; later, Marie-Antoinette wore a similarly buttoned-up garment on bathing days in her Versailles bedchamber, when this same type of bath was rolled out. In Louis XV's later bathrooms, the baths were plumbed in, the supply of hot and cold water controlled by taps, and the wastewater evacuated to a discharge pipe on an outside wall and thence to a drain.[28]

The destruction of nearly all of the bathrooms of Versailles in the 1830s has fostered the myth of an unsanitary palace. In the second half of the eighteenth century, residents whose lodgings possessed them included the comtesse de Noailles, wife of the governor of Versailles; the princesse de Lamballe; and Louis XVI's foreign minister, Vergennes, and his countess. These last two had lived in Constantinople and, like other Europeans of the time, may have become habituated to the watery therapy of the Turkish hamam.

At Versailles bathrooms were probably never widespread outside the royal family and certain favored courtiers. They were expensive and sometimes difficult to install, the water heaters were a fire hazard, and their flues threatened the appearance of the palace. In 1765, forty years after Louis XV's first bathroom, his Buildings Office was still refusing them to princesses of the blood on grounds of cost.[29]

Louis XV's Versailles also promoted a new French fashion for intimate washing in the form of the bidet. By 1789, its use had percolated down to junior officers of the French guards stationed at Versailles.[30] In some models, the bowl could be removed and a vertical syringe inserted for self-medication with the enemas beloved of doctors of the times.[31] This operation could now be performed privately: a far cry from the days of the duchess of Burgundy, who had herself syringed by a servant in Madame de Maintenon's room under the nose of Louis XIV. The king—himself a martyr to the constant purging prescribed by royal doctors wedded to the ruling medical theory of bodily "humors"—could not help laughing when he found out what she was doing.[22]

Louis XIV's engineers performed wonders to bring water to Versailles. Two huge water tanks at the extremity of the north wing have given their name to the adjacent street, the rue des Réservoirs. Most tourists have little idea as they stroll the parterre and forecourts that beneath their feet are yet more reservoirs; even less that, for miles around, the countryside was once laced with a system of ponds, ditches, and aqueducts, all aimed at supplying the gardens, the palace, and the town. But neither Louis XIV nor his successors solved the fundamental problem: a lack of a natural supply of drinking water at Versailles.

By the mid-1750s a network of lead pipes delivered mains water to over sixty outlets in the courtyards, ground-floor kitchens, and offices of the palace.[33] But demand exceeded supply. In 1762 Marigny, the director of the royal buildings, was unable to send more water to the king's kitchens because there were "already too many outlets in the château for the little water available to distribute."[34] Under Louis XVI the periodic removals of the court to Fontainebleau and Compiègne were partly the result of water shortages at Versailles.

In the early 1770s, when the dauphin, the future Louis XVI, lived on the second floor above the queen's apartment, he relied for the delivery of water on one "Bury, water-carrier."[35] Water carriers were employed at Versailles because the upper stories of the palace lacked a mains supply. A pump-fed reservoir existed at roof-level above Louis XV's apartments, supplying his private kitchens. But this facility was never extended throughout the palace, whether from fear of frozen pipes and damage to the décor, or simply because existing arrangements were adequate by the standards of the day.[36] Eighteenth-century Paris, after all, relied on an army of twenty thousand water carriers.

All over the palace, lodgings were provisioned in this laborious way. Each had one or more copper "fountains," storage vessels with feet, a lid, and a tap. Madame de Châteauroux, Louis XV's mistress briefly in the 1740s, kept two in her antechamber, one with a capacity of around eight bucketfuls of water. They were refilled by a carrier who had to negotiate his load up the back stairs to the duchess's second-floor rooms, above the king's.[37]

The proud duchess, who belonged to a well-entrenched court family, the Mailly-Nesle, had agreed to become the king's lover on the condition "that the king should openly hold his Court in her apartment, and sup there with the same publicity." Louis gave her an apartment, but at first withheld a kitchen. Holding out for all her demands, "Princess," as her lover nicknamed her, refused to join him for supper in the royal rooms or even to let him bring his supper up to her rooms.

Instead, she sent out to the then equivalent of take-out, the *traiteur,* who sold cooked food from premises in the town. Without her own kitchen, her only other culinary resort was the soup that her women rustled up in the tiny rooms where they also slept.[38] Other courtiers improvised in the same way. In 1768 an undergovernor of the royal princes, the comte de Fougières, complained to Marigny, "[I am obliged] to make my bouillon in my bedchamber."[39]

A private kitchen was an extreme rarity under Louis XIV. The monarch expected courtiers to take advantage of the hospitality that he offered at the "tables of honor." These were provisioned by the royal kitchens and hosted in his name by leading officers of the household. In addition, certain key officials were paid extra "to do honor to the Court" by hosting tables in their apartments.

This tradition was maintained in the following reigns: Marie Leczinska's lady of honor, the comtesse de Noailles, often had twenty-five guests for supper. She was also obliged "by etiquette" to receive visits from new ambassadors when they made their entry at Versailles. For this, she complained, her drawing room was too small, obliging half of the English ambassador's suite "to wait in the little antechamber with the lackeys."[40]

A few noblemen kept open house at Versailles from their own funds. In the eighteenth century this tradition of noblesse oblige flourished among the successive princes of Lorraine, who held the post of grand equerry. Luynes comments on the "extremely grand" dinners, with costly and recherché dishes, hosted by "Prince Charles" of Lorraine (who died in 1751) in his vast apartment in the Grand Stables. Under Louis XVI the marquis de Bombelles ate "one of the best dinners to which I have been invited for many years" at the table of Louis XVI's grand equerry, the prince de Lambesc. As often at Versailles, conversation did not sparkle: Bombelles rated its level "probably beneath the cook."[41]

Then there were the "secondary" tables at the Grand Commons. Because these were frequented by the lesser officers of the royal household, they were considered socially beyond the pale by the court nobles, who would "rather eat a chicken bought from the rôtisserie" than be seen there.[42]

Saint-Simon and his wife were among the lucky few to whom Louis XIV granted a kitchen of their own, three floors below them in the courtyard. A surviving plan shows a spacious room with a bread oven and a massive chimney-breast along one wall, used for roasting meat directly over the fire with spits and chains. Along another wall stood a masonry stove, its burners (ten of them) fueled by charcoal and suitable for slow cooking by the barbecue method. In a next-door room steps led down to a cellar.[43]

In the eighteenth century more courtiers demanded cooking facilities, if only a *réchauffoir,* or warming kitchen, for reheating meals prepared elsewhere, like the one on which the comte d'Agoult, a guards officer with rooms in the Old Wing, warmed up the food delivered from his unit's headquarters in the town. In 1746, when the duchess of Berwick's kitchen was given to another courtier against her wishes, she felt so aggrieved that she gave up her lodging and retired from Versailles.[44]

The eighteenth-century trend toward cooking meals in the palace lodgings gave rise to new inconveniences inside the cramped building, such as warming kitchens and sculleries improvised in blocked-up arcades in the public galleries; kitchen refuse thrown from windows; and tubs of dirty kitchen water left in the corridors.

In Louis XIV's Versailles, residents relied for warmth on smoking fireplaces that roasted those who went too close and left the rest of the room unheated. In 1709, one of the worst winters in living memory, icicles fell into Saint-Simon's wineglass as he ate before the fire in the duc de Villars' bedchamber. On the other hand, that same winter, at table with the royal family before the chimneypiece in the king's outer antechamber, Madame developed "a migraine, a cough and a cold" from sitting too close to the "terrible fire."[45]

The spread of stoves was one of the ways in which eighteenth-century Versailles became more comfortable. But the request in 1773 from the comte de La Marche, a prince of the blood, was one of a number refused, always for the same reason: "The king completely disapproves . . . of the establishment in any part of the château of Versailles of stove-pipes leaving by a window and climbing the whole height of the building. . . . Their aspect could only be shocking in buildings such as those of Versailles."[46]

Another improvement was the double window, a second frame fitted from the inside, an ancestor of today's double glazing. Courtiers pleaded for them on the grounds that otherwise their lodging would be "uninhabitable in winter." Under Louis XV a bill for two double windows cost 770 livres—a sizable sum that explains why, as with other improvements, not everyone had a right to them. The queen's ladies-in-waiting counted among those who did, Madame Victoire's among those who did not. Along with winged armchairs, their disappearance after the Revolution was lamented by Gaston de Lévis, a former courtier, in his old age.[47]

In the summer, sunshine made some rooms at Versailles unbearably hot. In the eighteenth century courtiers pestered the director of royal buildings for *persiennes*, a type of detachable shutter first introduced at

Versailles in the rooms of the dauphin, father of Louis XVI. Loosely inspired by Islamic woodwork, these grilles of beveled, vertical rods admitted enough daylight for reading and could be kept inside when not in use.[48]

In the eighteenth century this advance in comfort must have modified the external appearance of Versailles. So did progress in glassmaking, which also helped to make the interior less somber. The original windows of the palace had been fitted with small panes of glass. After the mid-eighteenth century these were gradually replaced by large squares of Bohemian glass, which made an apartment "less sad and lighter," as one courtier put it.[49]

~

Distinctions of dress played a key role in setting the French elites apart from the lower orders. Over and above this traditional role of rich apparel, Louis XIV successfully promoted costume as a means of advertising the French luxury industries: in this sense, too, Versailles was meant to be a showcase. He and his entourage set French styles on the road to European supremacy, a status they continued to enjoy well into the twentieth century. In 1711 *The Spectator* of London mocked the type of the modish Englishman, who "can inform you from which of the French King's Wenches our Wives and Daughters had this Manner of curling their Hair, that Way of Placing their Hoods."[50]

As the official residence of the monarch, Versailles had the strictest dress code of all the royal palaces: "Everyone who appears before the king or before us is in *grand habit,*" wrote Madame in 1702.[51] This ruling applied to the upper servants known as *femmes de chambre,* except that they were not entitled to a train. The standing of these sometimes influential women, who could be recruited from the lesser nobility, is not exactly captured by the literal translation "chambermaid." They were far too grand to do the cleaning that this English word implies: the archaic "tirewoman," a type of lady's maid, better captures their role of personal servant and (often) confidante rolled into one.

For court ladies, this costume remained essentially the same down to the Revolution: a short-sleeved bodice baring the shoulders over a laced corset stiffened with stays, a skirt with three petticoats but no underpants. For those entitled to a train, its length depended on rank, from around thirty-six feet for the queen to ten for a duchess. The grand habit was accessorized with gloves, jewels, and the bands of black lace in the hair known as "hanging whiskers."[52] Pins, not buttons or zippers, held this constricting costume together.

Under Louis XV the *grand habit* was toppled as the ordinary costume of court women under the influence of Madame de Pompadour, a more stylish clotheshorse than even Marie-Antoinette. It remained de rigueur for presentations and ceremonies. But court women now routinely wore a more comfortable sleeved robe, put on like a jacket, with large pleats in the shoulder and panniers. Worn with a corset, embroidered and garnished, this so-called *robe à la française* was a dazzling sight in its own right. In eighteenth-century Parisian society, it constituted formal attire for balls, the theater, and elegant suppers.

Male costume at Versailles was every bit as superb as its female counterpart. At the end of the 1660s Louis XIV led male courtiers in abandoning the old doublet and *rhingrave* (a kind of skirt) for the ancestor of the three-piece suit, a combination of frock coat, matching breeches, and waistcoat known as the *habit complet à la française*. Surviving examples are a revelation for their color, richness, and the quality of the craftsmanship.[53]

Noblemen rounded off the look with red heels, a cane to steady themselves, and the all-important sword. Now usually a "town sword," a decorative marker of noble rank, it was worn by all gentlemen in the royal household, down to the bearer of the monarch's chamber pot.

The total effect of this costume was not only visually stunning but socially intimidating. In 1783 the vicomte de Narbonne, son of a lady-in-waiting at Versailles, donned "a green habit with gold embroidery, a black waistcoat and breeches since the Court is in mourning, with a large hat and a very long sword," to call on a Parisian financier who had insulted him. In a period when Louis XIV's ban on dueling was ignored even by members of the royal family, the financier had grounds for alarm at this vision of the armed courtier. He regained his composure only when Narbonne, savoring the moment, nonchalantly requested a favor instead of a rendezvous.[54]

It follows that storage of clothes was an important consideration for the residents of Versailles. In 1755 the wife of the palace governor kept her *grands habits* in two large armoires in her husband's rooms. Vermin could be a problem, even for royalty. In 1758 the dauphine, mother of the future Louis XVI, demanded "urgent and indispensable" measures against the rats and mice threatening to "gnaw and ruin" her linen, stored in the attic of the south wing.

Marie-Antoinette was the first and only truly fashion-conscious queen of France in the sense that her innate love of appearances was fed by a contemporary revolution in the textile industry, marked by the appearance in the 1760s of the Parisian *marchandes de modes*, ancestors of the Parisian couturiers. Rose Bertin, the queen's "minister of fashion," was the most famous of these shrewd businesswomen, succeeding in orchestrating a "total change" in the dress of Frenchwomen, from which she profited handsomely.[55]

At Versailles the queen had her clothes housed in three large rooms beneath her first-floor apartment, each furnished with wardrobes, sliding shelves, and a large table on which assistants adjusted costumes before they were taken up to the royal rooms. After use, the garments had to be stored flat on individual shelves, since they were "garnished with flowers and pompons which prevent them from being placed one on the other without completely ruining them."[56]

Clothes were the major expense of court life. In 1788 they accounted for almost a third of the annual expenditure of the rich duc de Saulx-Tavannes, Marie-Antoinette's gentleman of honor: twenty thousand out of sixty-two thousand livres.[57] Strict sartorial conventions for different activities and times of day help to explain why. Under Louis XV, a lady-in-waiting of Madame Adélaïde complained that she had to change dress four times daily.[58] In addition, Louis XIV and Louis XV both expected courtiers to wear gorgeous new clothes for royal marriages. Saint-Simon writes of the need for "many different costumes" for the various festivities marking the wedding of the duke of Burgundy.[59] Clothes for all the different degrees of court mourning were a further charge for habitués of Versailles: at her death Madame de Pompadour's mourning outfits filled a trunk.[60]

The financial strain sometimes showed. At a ball in the Hall of Mirrors in 1751 the marquis d'Argenson saw "handsome clothes, but most of them old and well known," which he put down to courtiers' shortage of funds.[61] Poorer courtiers risked debt to keep up appearances. When Louis XVI complimented a courtier on his costume he wittily replied, "Sire, I owe it."[62]

Clothes apart, the sojourns of Saulx-Tavannes at Versailles in 1788 cost him three thousand livres, or just under 5 percent of his expenses for the year. Before the Revolution, an annual income of this order was enough for over 40 percent of French nobles to live on modestly but decently.[63] With annual revenues of ninety thousand livres, the duke was vastly richer. By his own plutocratic standards, however, he was not spending lavishly when he visited Versailles. At court he lived under the royal roof and largely at royal expense, down to a monthly entitlement to two dozen candles for lighting.

Nor did he keep a "table" at his own expense, perhaps the most extravagant form of noble display at Versailles. In 1688 François VII, duc de La Rochefoucauld, was obliged to stop offering meals on an open-house basis in his lodging at Versailles, an economy that allowed him to dismiss forty-two servants. He told Louis XIV that the cost of these meals had "ruined" him. He felt the dishonor so keenly that he had his old dining room completely altered so that nothing reminded visitors of his old generosity.[64]

In the eighteenth century courtiers became less willing to subsidize the magnificence of the court in this way. When planning for the future Louis XVI's wedding festivities began in 1768, one suggestion put forward was for a chivalric tournament along the lines of the brilliant fêtes of Louis XIV's youth. But the idea got nowhere, since there was no longer any prospect of the leading courtiers "sacrificing" twenty thousand livres on the costumes and accessories that such a pageant entailed.[65]

Generalizing about the fortunes of the courtiers is not easy. But some clearly had nowhere near the means of a Saulx-Tavannes. The marquis de Bombelles was a career diplomat, his wife a lady-in-waiting of Madame Élisabeth, Louis XVI's sister. The marquis came from an impecunious military family, and he and his wife had little income apart from their earnings in royal service. In 1783 he needed a royal intervention to stave off his creditors.

In 1782 the Bombelles were living in furnished rooms overlooking the place d'Armes with one live-in servant and no carriage, paying a large annual rent of eighteen hundred livres. This figure reflected the exorbitant cost of lodgings close to the palace in a town notorious for its prices, where even the daily hire of a sedan chair to be carried to the palace could tot up ruinously.

More than once the princess made gifts of clothes to the marquise, "knowing her shortage of funds," including, for the balls of the carnival season, a *grand habit* in silver and gold costing five thousand livres. After befriending the grand equerry, Bombelles was able to borrow the king's horses to pay visits in the neighborhood of Versailles (one of the many small abuses in the grand equerry's department). He complained of the difficulty of making economies in his establishment at Versailles, even though living "as simply as possible."[66]

From the sovereigns downward, the lifestyle of the elite residents of Versailles was entirely dependent on an army of domestic servants. It was only at the last minute that noble servitors were interposed to perform honorific tasks such as handing the king his shirt or the queen her drink.

Since everyone in the royal household "served" the monarch, this distinction between honorific and subaltern positions is rather confusing, as indeed it was at the time. The shortsighted Louis XVI once made a low bow to one of his wife's tirewomen, confused by her court costume. The tirewomen and the valets, who also wore court dress, were the upper servants of royalty. The royal footmen, their lower status revealed by their livery, were the equivalent of a nobleman's lackeys.

These lackeys were a familiar sight by the fire in the guardrooms of Versailles, spending so much time there that quarrels broke out over who was hogging the warmth. This enforced idleness while they awaited the return of masters and mistresses from attendance on royalty helped to give the impression of a palace filled with loungers.

In this period an entourage of liveried manservants was a tool of aristocratic display. The uniforms were often based on the armorial bearings of employers, and individual liveries were well known to habitués of Versailles. Saint-Simon tells how the duchess of Burgundy, a friend of his wife, once recognized a footman in the Saint-Simon livery as she passed through her guardroom. She stopped to ask him where his mistress was, assuming that the duchess must be somewhere nearby.[67]

The king's livery was worn by the footmen in his service known as *garçons* (here meaning domestics): a navy blue frock coat, the cuffs and pockets in red velvet, with braiding of white and red chevrons on the sleeves and double braiding of red velvet and white cables around the edges. A surviving example from the end of Louis XIV's reign shows that these liveries were made from cheaper woolen serge, easily distinguishable from the fine fabrics of the courtiers.

Royal footmen tended to be of a certain age; the leading nobles in the royal household would obtain these posts for them as a kind of pension. Marie-Antoinette caused adverse comment by breaking with this tradition and appointing her footmen for their looks, which she enhanced by incorporating an abundance of silver thread in their clothing. The liverymen of elite households had a justified reputation for their insolence—enough to prompt the occasional blow at Versailles from a guard officer's baton. With their airs the queen's haiducks, as they were sometimes known ("haiducks," like the queen, being Germanic), were no exception, something that "displeased the people."[68]

At Versailles domestics inhabited a kind of parallel universe of service corridors, back stairs, and lackeys' antechambers, to be summoned either by voice or by the bellpull. Physically, they were always close at hand. Confident of their places at the social pinnacle, the sovereigns could behave familiarly with servants. Only an unlocked door separated the private quarters of Queen Marie Leczinska from the room of the king's head valet, Bontemps, who would pass the time here with his wife and friends. Despite their presence, the queen refused a proposal to put a bolt on the door from her side.[69]

Louis XVI, brusque and tongue-tied with the court, liked to play rough games with the servants. An eyewitness remembered how he used to return from soirées in the queen's rooms by the back stairs, passing en route a service chamber where valets, cleaners, and lamplighters took naps. Here, the king loved to join the pages in attacks on the sleepers, roaring with laughter after targeting the loudest snorers with water.[70]

Inside the palace the networks of gossiping servants provided an important channel for information. As Saint-Simon says, "One sometimes learns from servants things which are believed to be closely concealed." A duke at his toilette is told the news by nervous servants that his daughter—an abbess in holy orders—has just given birth. A close follower of Louis XIV's wars, Saint-Simon hears that secret preparations are under way for the duke of Burgundy to serve at the front, his servants having learnt it in turn from the coach maker fabricating the vehicles for the prince's use in the war.[71]

Sexual predators were among the greatest dangers faced by female servants. At age eighteen, Marie-Madeleine de Mamiel, a tirewoman in the household of the comtesse d'Artois, one of Louis XVI's sisters-in-law, arrived from the provinces under orders from her naïve mother to "have no truck with men" apart from a mutual friend. This friend was a dashing bodyguard of the comte d'Artois over twice her age, by whom she became pregnant less than a year after her arrival in Versailles. In this case her lover, fortunately unmarried, did the decent thing and led the young tirewoman, seven months pregnant, down the aisle.[72]

Working from necessity in a despised calling, some servants fell prey to the opulence that surrounded them. At Versailles they were the usual suspects in cases of theft or burglary, a sufficient worry in the eighteenth century—despite the fact that the palace bristled with guards—for the Royal Buildings Office to fit security locks to the doors of the sovereigns and royal family.

Luynes describes a theft in 1754 from the lodging of the marquise de Durfort in the north wing, on the street side. A *secrétaire,* or lockable desk, had been forced and cash and diamonds stolen during the night, apparently while the marquise and her husband were asleep.

An insider job was suspected because the marquis kept a fierce guard dog on the premises, and it had made no noise, as if it knew the thief. The Durforts, we learn, kept five or six servants at Versailles, including two lackeys who had accompanied them that evening to a supper at the other end of the palace and returned with them to spend the night in the antechamber.

Initially, suspicion had fallen on an old retainer, who vigorously denied the charge, then on one of the lackeys, hired only three weeks earlier. In prison he made a written confession that led to the recovery of most of the loot, which he had either buried beneath a statue in the garden or thrown down a palace privy.[73]

Living conditions for servants at Versailles varied. Madame du Hausset, Madame de Pompadour's tirewoman, had her own apartment in Madame de Pompadour's town house, where she took her meals. Inside the palace, a manservant or tirewoman would normally sleep overnight in the entresols of the master and mistress. A restored tirewoman's entresol once forming part of Madame de Pompadour's attic apartment can still be visited at Versailles: a tiny, low room lacking any direct source of natural light, with an alcove for a bed and room for a few sticks of furniture but not much more.

The word *soupente,* meaning the space beneath a staircase, is often used to describe servants' quarters in the palace: in 1746, for instance, the marquis de Matignon requested alterations in his lodging to provide "a *soupente* for his cook to sleep in." If they slept in the palace, lower servants, such as the Durforts' two lackeys, rolled out mattresses in the antechamber, commonly called for this reason "the lackeys' antechamber."[74]

Treatment of servants varied. The figure of the overweening manservant was not unknown at Versailles, to judge from Saint-Simon's disapproving comments about the ménage of, once more, Louis XIV's grand master of the wardrobe, François VII, duc de La Rochefoucauld: "Having to mingle with the valets of an indulgent master, the consideration which they demanded and the airs which the chief among them assumed, kept good society away" from his apartment.[75]

Others were less indulgent. Louis XIV prided himself on never striking a gentleman in anger, but he was not above hitting a servant with his cane. Madame used to hear the disagreeable princesse d'Harcourt beating her women in the next-door lodging, and once one of them grabbed the stick and beat the princess in turn.[76]

In 1749 there was a shocking incident: while being shaved, a noble officer of the Stables killed a manservant with two blows of his sword. For a moment we glimpse the antipathy felt by many ordinary townsfolk to the occupants of the palace who, in more than one sense, constantly looked down on them. A threatening crowd of a thousand gathered, and a lynching was avoided only by the arrest of the officer and his dispatch to the Bastille. In 1789 the townsfolk would turn out to be enthusiastic supporters of the Revolution.[77]

# 8.

## *Behind Closed Doors*

IN THE seventeenth century, when Versailles was built, privacy mattered much less to the French upper classes than it did a hundred years later. On the first floor of the Envelope, the architect Le Vau did not trouble with corridors. The sole means of circulation were the state rooms themselves—"sumptuous public passages," as Hézecques called them.[1] The queen's bedchamber on the south side, in which all the queens who lived at Versailles actually slept, traditionally served as a shortcut from the Hall of Mirrors to the queen's antechambers.[2] In the wings, the galleries were little more than covered streets. Royalty, courtiers, and servants all lived on top of one another.

Everyone minded everyone else's business, helped by thin partition walls and windows overlooking courtyards. At the center of the palace, the Bull's Eye was a haven of watchful "idlers." In an age when foreign envoys were little more than spies, royalty was kept under a constant and continuous scrutiny. A pawn in the dynastic politics of France and Austria, the newlywed Marie-Antoinette hid letters from her mother the empress in her bed. One day a senior courtier of anti-Austrian persuasion, the duc de La Vauguyon, was surprised outside her door, his ear to the keyhole.[3] Her predecessor, Marie Leczinska, found "several holes" in a door in her private quarters. Louis XV's mistress, Madame de Châteauroux, was suspected: she apparently thought that the queen gossiped on the other side of this door about her and the king.[4]

In this atmosphere of constant surveillance, royalty and courtiers placed much stock on secure hiding places. The aptly named *secrétaire* was a popular piece of furniture at Versailles, combining a desk with lockable drawers for papers and other valuables and, in the fall-front variety popular with Louis XVI and Marie-Antoinette, a concealed safe. In 1769 Louis XV had a mechanical desk delivered that allowed him by one turn of the key to lock the rolltop and all the drawers inside simultaneously. When he pressed another lever, the inkwells slid over to side openings for the servants to refill while the desk remained firmly locked.[5]

"A king wherever he was and at all times"—for much of his adult reign Louis XIV made little distinction between public and private life. When he was ill, he made a point of appearing daily before the courtiers. Far from being an intimate retreat, his bedchamber was the center of court ceremonial. As the room in which he not only slept and ate but also gave audience, it was a shrunken version of the all-purpose hall of a medieval prince.

The courtiers came to Versailles to interact socially, not to be alone. At the turn of the seventeenth century the companionable habits of an earlier age lived on at Versailles. Two great ladies, the duchesse de Foix and the princess of Fürstenberg, shared not only their lodging but also its one large bed. Saint-Simon reports this in the most matter-of-fact way, adding that the princess was immensely rich.

"Family life" is a cultural construct. As we know it today, it hardly existed in the seventeenth century, at least not in the households of royalty. At Versailles, the first event in a newborn royal baby's life was to be swept off by the royal governess to the royal nursery in the extremity of the south wing. At Versailles the sovereigns had, not just separate bedrooms, but separate living quarters.

Marie Leczinska, Louis XV's virtuous queen, passed a great deal of her time on her own—up to five hours a day at Versailles. Once she and Louis XV stopped sleeping together, she still saw him every morning, but only at the *lever* with the other courtiers, when she could never speak to him privately. Much of their communication took the form of notes.

They ate together in public on certain days, usually in the queen's first antechamber. In this large room their armchairs would be set up side by side, with the backs to the fireplace, while they were served by a procession of officers of the Mouth in the ceremony of the grand table setting *(au grand couvert),* before rows of gawking spectators placed on wooden grandstands set against the walls.

For the rest, the neglected queen ate on her own in her bedchamber or invited herself with no warning to sup with the duchesse de Luynes, her lady of honor, in the nearby lodging in the south wing, which the duchess shared with her diary-writing husband. Here, in her "delicious armchair," the queen would play cards and say that she was no longer the queen.

To return to Louis XIV, Saint-Simon describes the family gatherings of the king's old age. Because he never acknowledged Madame de Maintenon as his wife, they never ate together in public. After his regular supper, taken at ten in his bedchamber before an audience of courtiers, he gave the following day's orders in the official study next door. Next, he went into the adjacent wig room, where he was joined by thirteen or so princes and princesses. He sat down in his armchair. The women sat on stools and the other men stood. A crowd of royal valets and footmen were on hand in the billiard room off the wig room. Because the enfiladed doors were left open, the courtiers in the bedchamber could not only see this gathering, but also overhear the king as he chided his daughters for smoking or settled quarrels of precedence within the royal clan.[6]

But the image of Louis XIV as a monarch enslaved by his public role should not be overdone. After his secret marriage to Madame de Maintenon in 1683, he spent an increasing amount of time in her rooms. In 1697 his eldest grandson, the duke of Burgundy, married a lively child bride from the house of Savoy who enchanted the aging king. Madame de Maintenon took her over and started to arrange entertainments in her own rooms for a select circle. It was here, if anywhere, that Louis XIV belatedly discovered the joys of family life.

He also had a more private domain on the north side of the Marble Court, entered from the wig room. Little known today since it vanished in the alterations of his successors, this was what courtiers called his "interior," "small apartment," or "cabinets." In the evenings Louis would often withdraw to these rooms with a smaller group, abandoning the rest of the court in the state rooms on the north side of the central block. Dangeau records midnight suppers here, as well as lotteries and balls.

This was also where Louis spent free time during the day, usually in the afternoon, in the company of the valets and footmen whose duties gave them a permanent entrée to this domain. Ill informed about a part of the palace into which he was never invited, the aristocratic Saint-Simon was outraged by the intimacy between the king and his servants. Louis, he claimed, loved them more than his own children.[7]

The layout of Louis XIV's small apartment is now known only from descriptions, plans, and inventories. From the wig room a door led into ten or so first-floor rooms overlooking the Marble Court on one side and the king's inner courtyards on the other. Above these there was a yet more secluded retreat in the attics. The first-floor suite began with the billiard room, where Louis also kept his pet dogs. Then came the private staircase from the Marble Court with its antechamber, followed by a group of rooms forming a semiprivate museum.

An avid collector, Louis XIV used these rooms to display his spectacular paintings, medals, and objets d'art, many of them transferred to Versailles from the Louvre in 1684. The rooms were almost as impressive as the collections they housed: floors of precious woods, mirrors, incrustations of ivory and lapis lazuli, and an abundance of gilt. One of the most sumptuous was a small gallery with a ceiling painted by Pierre Mignard, a rival of Le Brun. Precious objets d'art were displayed here on wall consoles alongside old masters including, as a description of 1701 records, "the portrait of Lisa, wife of a Florentine called Giocondo; by Leonardo da Vinci."

Louis XIV also transferred from Paris to Versailles the royal collection of coins and medals. These were kept in an opulent cabinet of curiosities entered from the first room of the state apartments, the Salon of Abundance, through an elaborate portal that still exists. The room overlooked the Royal Court, and Louis had a spiked gate built so as to prevent an intruder from scaling its balcony. He was in the habit of dropping by on his return from morning mass. Pincers, magnifying glasses, and a desk allowed him to take items from their trays in the twelve specially made cabinets and pore over them at his leisure, with a tame scholar in attendance.[8]

These rooms were not public, but they were not entirely off-limits, either. Louis would show off his collection in person to exalted visitors such as the exiled James II of England. For the ordinary sightseer without connections, access was harder. According to a German guidebook from early in the next reign, "It is normally very difficult to obtain permission to see this cabinet, unless by luck you can enter when a distinguished person is being shown round, or are known to the guardian."[9]

Louis XIV's courtiers stood a better chance of gaining entry, although not all were cultured enough to appreciate what they saw. Saint-Simon reports with relish the marquis de Gesvres, who told people that the various paintings of the Crucifixion, in fact by different hands, were the work of a single artist who signed himself "Inri."[10]

Louis XIV's cabinet of curiosities was a particularly luxurious version of the private retreats that became popular in fashionable French homes during the seventeenth century. It too had its daybed, along with mirrors and beautiful objects to stimulate daydreaming. But Louis did not possess the taste for solitude that was making inroads into other parts of his palace. His sister-in-law Madame, another neglected royal wife, relished being alone in her first-floor rooms overlooking the gardens. "I read, I write, I amuse myself with my engraved stones."[11]

When the Regent reinstated the court at Versailles in 1722, Louis XV was still only twelve. Orphaned from infancy and brought up by a governess and a governor old enough to be his grandparents, the new king grew into a handsome but diffident introvert, shy and tongue-tied to the point of rudeness. From an early age he was determined to ration his exposure to his court and to live as privately as possible.

Unlike Louis XIV he never showed a strong desire to rule in person, and until he was thirty-three he relied on a succession of chief ministers, culminating with the elderly cardinal de Fleury. While they got on with the job of ruling, the young monarch insisted on being "absolute master of all that concerns his personal life," brooking no interference even from the cardinal.[12]

The lengths taken by Louis XV to achieve privacy are shown by the little den that he created when he was twenty-two in the roof space above the Salon of War. Those visitors who looked up to admire its painted ceiling would have had no idea that the present king might, at that very moment, be occupying a series of tiny attic rooms over their heads. This retreat—now destroyed—was so private that we cannot say for certain that the king was ever there. Its added attraction for a monarch who loved hunting and the outdoors was the view from the windows, the only ones in Louis XV's private domain that overlooked the garden.

Louis XV's personal inclinations coincided with the temper of an age. Among the rich, public ostentation aimed at impressing inferiors was slowly giving way to a preference for a luxurious intimacy among one's own kind. In the late king's final years, this tendency can already be found among the younger generation at Versailles. His daughter the duchesse d'Orléans spent most of her day in a former privy entered from her bed alcove; she had converted this space into a tiny boudoir big enough for five people at most.[13]

At eighteenth-century Versailles this changing mood can be detected throughout the building. Over in the stables the pages moved out of their dormitories and into individual chambers. Courtiers wanted separate rooms for their servants. They subdivided lodgings to create small dining and reception rooms. They asked for a new palette of stylish colors such as gray, lemon, green, and mahogany. In interior décor, at Versailles as in Paris, grandeur was giving way to elegance.[14]

These new comforts allowed the courtiers to lead their own social lives inside the royal palace. In the next reign a conversation between Marie-Antoinette and Tilly, her page, which he later set down verbatim, captures this side to eighteenth-century Versailles:

> *"Good day. . . . Where have you dined?"*
> *"At Madame de Beauvilliers', Madame."*
> *"My Madame de Beauvilliers?"*
> *"No, Madame, Madame Adélaïde's."*
> *"She gives dinners, does she?"*
> *"Yes, Madame, at least to me. She knew me as a child and I don't put her out."*
> *"If Monsieur de Champcenetz were at Versailles, you could have dined with him. . . . Now there's good company!"*[15]

Courtiers now spent more time cultivating an inner life, to judge from a rising demand for bookcases. In 1744, the year of her sudden death, the indolent Madame de Châteauroux, Louis XV's mistress, somewhat surprisingly had eight hundred volumes on "different subjects of devotion" in her apartment at Versailles, where, according to Luynes, she passed her days in either her armchair, bath, or bed.[16]

In between helping the king in and out of the right sleeve of the royal jacket, the comte de Cucé-Boisgelin, first master of Louis XVI's wardrobe, could retire to his attic rooms in the north wing. Here, his library included antireligious works and a large array of the freethinking writers of the time, not only French but also English, which he read fluently.[17]

Bombelles scatters his journal with comments on the bestsellers that he was reading. They included works hostile to the world of the court, such as Mercier's *Tableau of Paris* ("his book contains some great and useful truths") and the anonymous *Private Life of Louis XV*. Putting this down in 1781, Bombelles reflected that Marie-Antoinette did not cost the French a sixth of the resources consumed by Madame du Barry, Louis XV's last mistress. An influential queen was unprecedented at Versailles. The reflex of even a well-disposed courtier like Bombelles was to compare Marie-Antoinette with the notorious royal mistresses of the previous reign.[18]

The interests and character of Louis XV are revealed by the alterations that he began to make to Louis XIV's private rooms. Over the course of the reign this domain saw a total transformation that continued under Louis XVI, as avid for privacy as his grandfather. What both kings sought here was an escape from the hidebound court officials, who ruled over the king's official apartment, and from the entrées. Louis XV also wanted somewhere at Versailles where he could receive the company of his choice in relative informality.

The end result of these yearnings was the creation of a private house within a palace, a house with its own budget and staff, headed by the king's first valet. Under Louis XV, this domain assumed the dual character that it would retain throughout the eighteenth century: first-floor "small apartments," and the far more private "small cabinets" on the floors above. Lack of space between the north façade of the Marble Court and the king's state apartments forced both Louis XV and his grandson to build upward. Both added extra floors round the inner courtyards. Some façades here eventually reached six stories.

By 1789, all this unplanned building had a bizarre impact on the appearance of the north side of the Marble Court, as if a small village had been set down on the roofs. After the Revolution, Napoleon's architect described what he saw: courtyards "burdened with structures with no order or symmetry, their roofs or terraces piled on top of each other," making a "real labyrinth from which the rainwater runs off with difficulty." This higgledy-piggledy silhouette was visible from the palace forecourts until well into the nineteenth century, when the graceless accretions were demolished in order to restore the original roofline of Louis XIV's palace. They had been tolerated under Louis XVI, not so much from indifference to the majesty of Louis XIV's creation, but because they were seen as more or less temporary, until the time when the Grand Project for modernizing the Paris side of the palace could be implemented.[19]

The removal of the top floors is an irreparable loss for royal history. It was up there that both Louis XV and Louis XVI found privacy, fresh air, and panoramic views. Both liked to walk on the roofs, where they could be alone, without even the guards captain-in-waiting. Louis XVI used to sit up there in an open-air armchair with a telescope, watching the comings and goings in the forecourts below.

What has survived of this domain is still atmospheric and evocative. On the first floor the rooms are more formal, with high ceilings, cornices, and gilding combining to create a stately effect. The cabinets, by contrast, are a warren of narrow corridors and stairs, with low-ceilinged rooms only five or six feet high and windows overlooking roofs, courtyards, and chimney stacks. Here and there in these small rooms the original décor survives or has been painstakingly revealed under later coats of paint: wooden panels painted in pastel shades of pink or blue and carved in the delicate, sinuous style named after the king who was its leading patron.

All the rooms were once furnished in the same light style, which could hardly have contrasted more with the ponderous furniture of Louis XIV's Versailles, exemplified in the two cabinets now at Alnwick Castle in northern England, their ebony a deep black, towering over eight feet in height, lavishly gilded and laden with swags, pilasters, and carved figures. These behemoths left Versailles because Louis XV disliked the old-fashioned furniture of his ancestor, sending much of it to the salesroom in 1741 and again in 1751.[20]

Louis XV started to personalize his great-grandfather's domain within a year of his return to Versailles. At the age of thirteen his passion for the hunt prompted him to have the walls of his inner courtyard decorated with plaster stags' antlers. In addition to this Stag Court (*Cour des Cerfs*), as it became known, in later years he arranged a trophy room, where real antlers from slaughtered quarry were put on display.

The child of an age of scientific and mechanical experimentation, he ordered a succession of workshops for his private use on the upper floors of the Stag Court. He began a tradition in the royal family of learning how to fashion wood or metal on a rotating wheel, or lathe. The king who once had a mild electrical current passed through a human chain of French Guards lined up in the Hall of Mirrors had his own chemistry laboratory.[21]

Louis XV's fascination with astronomy and chronometry prompted him to mount two solar clocks on the outside walls of the Stag Court, which the sun hit around midday. They thereby set the time for a wonder of Louis XV's Versailles: a seven-foot-high astronomical timepiece by the engineer and clockmaker Claude Passement. It marked not only the time of day but also the years and months, the phases of the moon, and the revolutions of the planets. Louis XV started the New Year's Eve custom at Versailles, maintained by Louis XVI, who also loved mechanical objects, of coming to watch the total change of the mechanism as the clock struck midnight in a room two doors away from his official study.[22]

Louis XV was intelligent and he liked to read, mainly books on history, geography, science, and religion. He would have enjoyed perusing Madame de Châteauroux's collection (an inheritance?), which may explain why she installed it at Versailles. Around the age of sixteen he had the first of a series of libraries installed in second-floor rooms overlooking the Stag Court. Others followed, including the only one that survives today, a large room in the attic above his official study. By his early thirties Louis had amassed over three thousand books. This was in addition to a hereditary palace library that included such heirlooms as the prayer book of his ancestress Anne of Brittany.

Louis XV also liked to write, a habit sufficiently novel in a French monarch for the marquis d'Argenson to comment on it more than once in his journal. "The King always works on his own for two hours at his desk on days when he doesn't hunt; he is always writing." Apart from official papers, he corresponded with a large circle of officials, friends, and family. The official study next to Louis XIV's bedchamber—the "grand bedchamber" as it had become known—was totally unsuited to this kind of private activity, because it was a court meeting place. Under Louis XV, Dufort de Cheverny used his study entrées to spend all his time there when not on duty. He lists nineteen or so other habitués who, along with himself, composed the "the study regulars."[23]

To get away from this ever-present crowd of courtiers, in 1735 Louis XV converted a corner of Louis XIV's museum into a study with windows over the forecourts; there, he worked with his ministers or on his own. Even there he was disturbed. He went on to destroy more of the museum so as to convert a more secluded space next door into a "back study," also with modern décor. This second retreat was also closer to two staircases crucial to Louis XV's privacy. One went up to his quarters on the floors above. The other, used by his private visitors, went down to the Marble Court.[24]

Most of Louis XV's correspondence is lost, apart from a batch of letters to his grandson, the infante Ferdinand of Parma. In these mainly brief missives the secretive Louis XV gave little away. But occasionally there are glimpses of life at Versailles. In early October 1766 he wrote from Versailles with news of the royal family and the weather: "We are mourning madam the comtesse de Toulouse [a favorite great-aunt] who died on the evening of 30th September. Her funeral procession passed by yesterday evening, and from a distance I saw it start on my way to the queen. The last few days have been hotter than summer; today an autumnal wind blew up, but the sun is shining."[25]

In writing to his grandson, Louis XV had politics as well as sentiment in mind. France was keen to maintain its influence over tiny Parma in northern Italy, now ruled by the king's Spanish cousins. In the manner of his times, Louis was able to express his family feelings more naturally than the stiffer age of Louis XIV. The prince de Croÿ was charmed by the sight of the king in his official study talking and playing with his children like "the best papa in the world." But Louis was not a family man in anything like the modern sense. Madame Campan, who used to read to the king's daughters, remembered him "seeing very little of his family."[26]

The real habitués of Louis XV's private domain were not his family but his small circle of cronies, including in time his mistresses. In the early days, while cardinal de Fleury governed, the young Louis XV was free to mooch around Versailles in the company of the "marmosets," as Argenson unkindly nicknamed his entourage of noblemen, "small in stature, well-powdered, and of very little merit."[27]

The eerily well informed Luynes, who was certainly not one of the king's circle, describes an evening in March 1737 that began with a private supper in Louis XV's cabinets. Then the king felt like some dancing and decided there and then to leave for the free and easy atmosphere of the Opéra ball in Paris. He went in person to wake up his guards captain, asleep in his lodging, and stood over him while he dressed.

Then he changed his mind after a courtier said that Madame de Chalais was having a ball for her daughter in the palace. Off the royal party went, Luynes fascinated by the details of the king's route: under the arched passage from the Royal Court to the gardens, past the Comedy Room, through a door into the ground floor of the south wing, and along the gallery before climbing the stairs to the Chalais lodging. The king danced quadrilles until around four in the morning, returning by the same route, escorted by the long-suffering guards captain.[28]

This could almost be a bored teenager. In fact, Louis had just turned twenty-seven, he had been married nearly thirteen years, and Marie Leczinska was pregnant at the time with their tenth child. But he seemed immature for his age, unlike the boy Louis XIV, bounced by civil war into precocious adulthood. Two years later, on a public outing to the military camp at Compiègne, "everyone noticed that he was a child from head to foot, amusing himself readily with childish things."[29]

Louis XV loved fine food and wines, as would his grandson. He lived in an age of culinary revolution and the first celebrity chefs, some of whom he employed. The upper classes now relished food for its taste as well as its appearance. When he was sixteen, Louis revealed the budding gourmet in him by taking lessons from an expert chef in a kitchen over the Stag Court, specially installed for this purpose. An order survives for the king's aprons, twelve of them, embroidered with the double V of Versailles. He wore them when he made omelettes.[30]

Louis was prompt to break with the established dining customs of Versailles. He did his duty and still ate in public, if less frequently than Louis XIV. In private, he adopted the newer fashion for a special room solely for dining. He was in his early twenties when he arranged a dining room for summer on a terrace over the Stag Court, and one for winter in the attics overlooking the Marble Court. These seasonal locales suggest a sophisticated comfort new to royal dining at Versailles.

These dining rooms were the first of a whole series as Louis XV chopped and changed his small apartments and cabinets over a period of more than fifty years. Three can still be visited, two on the first floor and another on the second, overlooking the Stag Court. The dining rooms were served by a succession of roof-level kitchens, offices, and sculleries, all now vanished. This was the domain of a line of head chefs, who were so important to Louis XV's personal comfort that they slept in their own quarters over the Stag Court.

Surviving menus from the royal hunting lodge at Choisy, by the Seine, give some idea of the fare at Louis XV's private dinners and suppers at Versailles. At Choisy, meals of some forty-four dishes were served in the extravagant French style *(service à la française)*: for each course an array of dishes was placed on the table, from which the diner selected according to taste.

Royal chefs had to be inventive, not least because the God-fearing Louis XV was a strict observer of the dietary rules of the church. Just how far royal cuisine had come from the gold-sprinkled medieval banquet is shown by the fare for meatless days. Louis XV might be served grilled salmon, sole with fines herbes, or skate in a black butter, dishes perfectly at home in a modern restaurant.[31]

Up in the dining rooms of the little cabinets, guests sat in no particular order, the chef brought in the dishes himself, two or three "blue waiters" served the guests, and the servants then retired. Bottles of wine were placed on the tables, and people helped themselves. Like any group of young people over food and drink, these occasions could be lively: "Much champagne wine was drunk, by the king too," notes Luynes. But he adds that by 1743, when Louis XV was thirty-three, he had stopped drinking. These occasions still lasted "long enough, but without excess."[32]

Louis XV understood why Louis XIV had built Versailles. In the best traditions of his predecessor, he used the privilege of admission to his private domain as a way of distinguishing people. He made clear that anyone could hope to be asked to the suppers that followed the royal hunt. In his memoirs the duc de Richelieu, one of the king's first gentlemen and a royal crony, described the new court ritual that developed:

> *In the evening the hunters who wished to sup with the king entered his (official) study if they had the entrée; if not, they waited in [Louis XIV's] bedchamber at the study door, where the king would come out to honor them with a glance and decide whom to invite. The usher read out the names in front of the hunters, who stood waiting in silence. Some were admitted, but most were sent away. All needed to have made prior supper arrangements, because none of them was a particular royal favorite.*[33]

Emmanuel de Croÿ was one of those who hoped that he might advance his various "affairs" by following Louis XV's hunt and becoming personally known to the king over supper afterward. To this end, he paid to maintain five hunting horses in stables at the hôtel de Fortisson.

But Louis XV kept the courtiers in a constant state of anticipation. Croÿ was by no means always named, as on Sunday, March 4, 1747. With a likable honesty he confessed to his journal: "I avow that at first I was foolish enough to be angry, above all from vanity, because the chevalier d'Ailly [a fellow Fleming] and Havré [his cousin] were with me, and I should have been greatly flattered to be nominated . . . in front of people who knew me." Here in a nutshell is the human craving to stand out from the crowd, a desire on which Louis XIV—and, it seems, Louis XV—played so shrewdly.[34]

One of the few to have left eyewitness accounts of these occasions, Croÿ comments on their relaxed atmosphere, which fostered the illusion of intimacy. But Croÿ also observed how the mature Louis XV maintained his dignity: guests never forgot that they were in the company of "the master." There was no dropping the royal guard, no lapse into discussing the affairs of the realm.[35]

The larger and very complicated question of courtiers and politics must be touched on here. Great noblemen looked back to times gone by when their class was actively involved in running the state. But Louis XIV made clear that, as far as he was concerned, politics were the business of the king and his ministers, not his household officials.

There certainly were courtiers intelligent and engaged enough to have opinions about how the kingdom was governed. But it is hard to judge how many, like Saint-Simon, were prepared to run the risk of airing their views. Saint-Simon did not dare to take his up with Louis XIV himself. But he cultivated a close relationship with the duke of Burgundy, who became dauphin in 1711 when his father, Louis XIV's only son, unexpectedly died.

Saint-Simon describes private audiences in the dauphin's ground-floor study at Versailles to which the duke was admitted by the prince's head valet. They discussed important matters: religious tolerance, the overweening power of Louis XIV's ministers, his elevation of his bastards, and a matter that obsessed Saint-Simon: the crown's political abasement of the dukes.

On these occasions the dauphin kept notes, and the duke flooded him with memoranda. The prince ignored Saint-Simon's advice to bolt the door, and once they were surprised by the dauphine, Louis XV's mother, luckily on her own. It was a frightening moment, given the nature of their conversations.

When the dauphin died unexpectedly the following year, Saint-Simon foresaw with horror the discovery of his writings in the prince's desk and his own ruin: Louis XIV would not tolerate courtiers meddling in politics. A friend in high places, the duc de Beauvilliers, now a minister, had the task of sorting the dauphin's papers in Louis XIV's presence. He saved Saint-Simon by reading out the financial documents in their entirety. Eventually, the bored monarch ordered him to tip the rest into the fire just as Saint-Simon's handwriting came to the top of the pile.[36]

The rising generation, eyeing their future prospects, naturally tended to group themselves around the dauphin of an aging monarch. According to Saint-Simon, in Louis XIV's old age both his son, Monseigneur, and grandson and next-in-line, the duke of Burgundy, were surrounded by "cabals" of courtiers anticipating their own moment in the sun. But courtiers did not form durable groupings supporting a particular policy or stance. Some contemporaries saw a "party of the devout" attached to Louis XV's pious queen and children. But a loose network of people who were like-minded only on a particular issue is not really the same as a party in the modern sense.

At Versailles courtiers certainly had views about ministers, because ministers were the conduits of graces, favors, and appointments. In the eighteenth century, contemporaries portray individual courtiers or whole court families as opposing or supporting different ministers. Leading nobles were particularly active during Louis XV's minority: "the Luynes, the Chaulnes, the Mortemart, the Charost, the duc d'Humières, the Saint-Simon, the Luxembourg, and all those who hold to these families directly or indirectly are for Monsieur Le Blanc and Desforts [two newly appointed ministers]," as a Paris informant wrote to the French ambassador in Vienna in 1726.[37]

All these families belonged to the noble elite of "dukes and peers" who were entitled by hereditary right to sit in the plenary sessions of the king's court of justice, the Parlement of Paris. From the mid-eighteenth century the attempts of the cash-starved monarchy to raise taxes brought it into increasingly bitter conflict with this body. In the crisis of 1771, when an authoritarian Louis XV took the unprecedented step of suppressing the Parlement altogether, a minority of ducal peers of

liberal persuasion joined princes of the blood in supporting the magistrates against the crown. Leading courtiers such as the duc de Duras,
one of Louis XV's first gentlemen, and the prince de Tingry, one of the
four captains of his bodyguard, briefly found themselves opposing the
government of their "master."

For the monarch to be influenced, it had to be possible to talk politics
with him. But the rules of court society made this a taboo area of conversation. Just how cautious courtly conversation was at Versailles is suggested by an episode in 1744, when Louis XV scandalized the kingdom
by recalling his recently exiled mistress, Madame de Châteauroux; he
had been prevailed upon to send her away during his life-threatening illness at Metz earlier that year. But Luynes notes a complete silence on this
shocking affair at Versailles: in the palace "ordinarily one talks little." By
this Luynes meant that the courtiers were not in the habit of openly discussing the king's affairs.[38]

What was said in private to the king is impossible to know. Historians have spilled much ink trying to gauge the influence on the king at
Versailles of favorite courtiers, mistresses, and family members. These
questions cannot be dealt with here. But French kings were taught to be
distrustful and wary, and neither Louis XV nor Louis XVI, for all their
portrayal in their own time and since as weak monarchs, can be assumed
to have been easily led. The year after Marie-Antoinette gave birth to a
son and heir, Louis XVI was overheard at Versailles loudly admonishing
her that "when a Dauphin had been born, it was no longer fitting to desire advantages to his detriment for the house of Austria."[39]

According to Madame de Boigne, on the eve of the Revolution, at
Versailles "no one thought about the general political situation." She re-
counts a conversation between her father and her mother's mistress,
Louis XVI's aunt Madame Adélaïde:

> *"Monsieur d'Osmond, is it true that you take the Leyden* Gazette *[a Dutch
> newsprint reporting French affairs]?"*
> *"Yes Madam."*
> *"And you read it?"*
> *"Yes Madam."*
> *"That's unbelievable."*[40]

This caricature may faithfully reflect the tone in the apartments of the king's reactionary aunts. But the courtiers were not an isolated caste. Not only were many well read, but as a group they belonged to "the Court and the Town," a social milieu in the Paris arm of which liberal ideas were freely discussed in aristocratic salons like that of the duchesse d'Anville. On the eve of the Revolution the political outlook of the residents of the palace defies simple generalization.

Under Louis XVI the monarch's retreat into privacy continued. Louis XVI's timidity is shown by his preference for even the builders at Versailles to be known to him: "The King always likes to see the same faces."[41] In May 1774 he took over his grandfather's small apartments and cabinets and enthusiastically set about making himself at home. Thereafter, hardly a year passed in which he did not make alterations and additions. Like Louis XV, he found it difficult to be truly alone even in his private domain. Not finding his predecessor's back study remote enough, in 1777 he created a new "private study" two rooms away in what had been Louis XV's last bathroom. Here, Louis XVI worked amid an incongruous décor of swimmers and water nymphs.[42]

Inside this domain Louis XVI the man expressed himself. He had the sort of mind that loved minutiae. Another enthusiastic hunter, he hung a staircase in the cabinets with framed statements of all his hunts since he was dauphin, detailing "the number, kind and quality of the game he had killed at each hunting party during every month, every season, and every year of his reign."[43]

He shared other interests with his grandfather. An avid reader in English as well as French, he enlarged the libraries, ending up with four. He too found relaxation in working with his hands, installing new workshops for turnery, woodworking, and physics, where he experimented with electricity, and lock making. A provincial aristocrat, the baronne d'Oberkirch, was given a tour of the king's cabinets by a friend, an undergoverness of the royal children. She was struck by "so great a king occupying himself with such little things!" Louis XVI lived in an age generally more critical of royalty, even among conventional thinkers like the baroness.[44]

Marie-Antoinette, a queen at nineteen, full of grace and charm, was locked into an arranged marriage that, year upon year, failed to produce offspring. Whether cause, effect, or a bit of both, Marie-Antoinette kept quite different hours from her husband, as a result of a frantic social life that she pursued at the expense of her duties as queen. She too shared her husband's preference for life outside the public eye. Far from disapproving, Louis XVI encouraged her within weeks of his succession by the gift of the Petit Trianon, a secluded house in the gardens that Louis XV had built for Madame de Pompadour.

At the time, rustic retreats were all the rage in fashionable society. The Trianon is only the most famous of a group of rural idylls that members of Louis XVI's close family built in the vicinity of the palace. In 1785 his brother, the comte de Provence, bought some land from the king near the royal kitchen garden. There, he built a pavilion and created his own garden of rare trees and plants, landscaped in the English style around a lake, a templelike folly, and a grotto in the English style. Now wild and overgrown, this little-visited spot is one of the most evocative and least-known remnants of royal Versailles.

Louis XVI allowed Marie-Antoinette to enlarge the private quarters of the queen in the palace itself. Under Marie-Antoinette the main entrance to this domain was by a door in the first of her official antechambers, guarded on the inside by her tirewomen. She herself used a door arranged in the alcove of her official bedchamber. There was also a kind of back door in a corner of the Bull's Eye, leading to the alcove door from the "private" side. Marie Leczinska used this route on her morning visits to Louis XV.

On the first floor the queen's private rooms were arranged around an inner courtyard known as the Dauphin's Court. This court was lighter then than it is now: the façades were raised when Versailles was converted into a museum in the 1830s. In Marie-Antoinette's day it was less dismal, too: the walls were decorated with ornamental trelliswork, and a first-floor terrace ran around two sides, filled with flowers and plants.

Just inside the door from her bed alcove, two staircases led up to the second floor and down to the ground floor respectively. Over the years, Marie-Antoinette extended her private domain by adding rooms on both these floors until she ended up with a rambling triplex extending on the floor above as far as the attic of the Salon of Peace and on the floor below to the Stag Court, where she had her own entrance. Most of this domain was destroyed by nineteenth-century alterations. Claustrophobic passages and staircases survive, as do remnants of a nest of small, superbly decorated rooms.

After the court removed to Paris on October 6, 1789, Hézecques, Louis XVI's page, was emboldened to explore behind the alcove door, "left open in the disorder" of the court's hurried departure. To his surprise, he discovered "an infinity of little rooms of which I did not even suspect the existence."[45] Besenval, a friend of Marie-Antoinette, had a similar reaction in 1778. Summoned by the queen to a private audience, he was led by her secretary "by several doors and staircases entirely unknown to me," to "an unsightly little door." There, the audience had to be aborted when the secretary, producing a key, found the door not only locked but bolted from the inside.[46]

This determination of Marie-Antoinette to guard her privacy at Versailles is shown in the eventual fate of the back door from the Bull's Eye. Marie Leczinska had tolerated the presence of a little retreat for the king's head valet in the first room behind this door. In 1779, five months after the birth of her long-awaited first child, Marie-Antoinette prevailed upon Louis XVI to cede it to her tirewomen. At the same time, she had the door "condemned from the outside," presumably by means of a lock or a bolt on the Bull's Eye side. Ten years later, this closed-up door for a brief moment would endanger her life.[47]

The life that the secretive Marie-Antoinette led in her private rooms is elusive. No eyewitnesses set down in any detail what they knew. She aspired to live in these rooms "like a private person," just as she tried to do on her visits to the Petit Trianon. She had a billiard table, a favored time killer among the French royal family. She had libraries, although Besenval, for a time one of her intimates, says that she "never read." She kept her collection of oriental lacquerwork here.[48]

In 1781, when she was nearly twenty-six, she finally gave France a dauphin after eleven years of marriage. As the mother of an heir to the throne, her position at Versailles was transformed. The next year she started to annex the ground floor to her domain. Here, most of the spacious ground-floor vestibule from the time of Louis XIV had already been partitioned into additional rooms for members of the royal family. Eventually Marie-Antoinette took over all the windows on the west, or principal, side of the Marble Court. In the south-facing rooms behind them she arranged another library, a new bathroom, and a second bedroom. Outside, railings were installed to protect, once more, her privacy.

Her desire to be undisturbed found its most extreme expression in her use of mechanical devices to isolate whole rooms from the outside world. In her boudoir at Trianon she installed a system of mirrors that rose from beneath the floor to cover the windows. Pierre Verlet, one of the great scholars of Versailles, could only speculate on what lay behind this compulsion of the queen to "stop up the chinks with mirrors."[49]

In 1780 Marie-Antoinette commissioned an artificial grotto for her English garden at the Petit Trianon. Her final choice from no fewer than seven models was a two-story confection of cyclopean rocks and flowing water, with an interior staircase linking its two entrances, both masked by rocks and vegetation. In the main cavern a crevasse at the head of a moss-clad "bed" was so placed as to allow the bed's occupant to keep a lookout for anyone approaching the hideaway. Hézecques records how, in 1789, these arrangements were enough to give even an ardent royalist food for thought.[50]

Most thought-provoking of all are the complex and—at the time— highly unusual locking devices that Marie-Antoinette put on the doors of her two bedrooms at Versailles. A letter of 1784 from her personal architect, Richard Mique, to the director of the King's Buildings refers to bills submitted by a locksmith, the Sieur Jubeau, for "locks and system of movement made in the château in the bedrooms of the Queen so that she can open and close the doors from her bed at will."[51]

All this leads into more speculative territory. Anecdote tells of a debate in a Parisian salon in the years around 1900. Guests discussed whether a historian should always tell all, or sometimes leave certain matters well alone: the delicate question of Marie-Antoinette's faithfulness to Louis XVI was offered as an example.[52] Whether from this sort of historical discretion or simply by oversight, Marie-Antoinette's curious bedroom locks have received little attention since Marguerite Jallut, a curator at Versailles and an expert on Marie-Antoinette, cited Mique's letter in a learned article published over forty years ago. Jallut made her own views plain six years later. She supposed that the queen's wish to secure her bedroom against unwanted intruders had to do with Axel de Fersen, her reputed lover.[53]

Privacy was in some ways the undoing of Versailles. The open style of holding court for which Louis XIV built Versailles vanished with his death in 1715, and with it, some of the raison d'être of the great palace. Louis XV hid from his courtiers and was less predictable. When he was young, courtiers could not always be sure of the times of the daily ceremonies: in 1736, for instance, Luynes notes that the almoners often waited two or three hours for the *coucher*.

When he was older, Louis XV would abandon Versailles for days or weeks on end, either for his other official residences or for one of his smaller country houses: in 1750, according to police records, he slept at the palace for only fifty-two nights. These departures, as always when the king was elsewhere, plunged Versailles into solitude.[54]

Even so, people could still pay their court "more or less daily" to Louis XV. Bombelles makes an unfavorable contrast with Louis XVI and Marie-Antoinette, who really held court only on Sundays, on the great festivals, and "sometimes" Tuesdays, when the ambassadors came to Versailles. On these occasions the palace would fill up as in the old days. On New Year's Eve 1784, the courtiers—"reliable in these matters"—counted record numbers of presented nobility at Versailles.

Weekdays were different. Early in the reign Marie-Antoinette was particularly elusive, with no fixed days or times when presented ladies from Paris could be certain of seeing her. As a result, and this was something quite new, Versailles was often deserted in midweek, even when the sovereign was in residence. In July 1783, Bombelles found himself the only person in the Hall of Mirrors when the queen passed by on her way to morning mass.

The summer was also a time when Marie-Antoinette's friends liked to go to their country estates. This was a new trend in the high society of court and capital. It reflected the new taste for nature and simplicity among a generation brought up on the writings of Jean-Jacques

Rousseau. At Versailles it contributed to the emptiness of the palace in the summer months.[55]

~

Nowadays it is recognized that the Revolution was triggered not just by social and economic injustices but also by stories and gossip.[56] The French equated a royal life lived in public with a morally reputable life. Since the sixteenth century they had tended to "put the worst construction on any desire for privacy evinced by their royal family."[57] As Marie-Antoinette's popularity plummeted in the aftermath of the Diamond Necklace Affair in 1785, her love of privacy played into the hands of her detractors.

After the liberation of the French press in August 1789, she became the object of a virulent outpouring of pornographic abuse. In one publication her rooms at Versailles were depicted as a bordello in which stark-naked courtiers and prelates took turns servicing the lustful queen.[58] This obscene material was mainly composed by male revolutionaries. For them, Marie-Antoinette was an unnatural creature by virtue of being a powerful woman and a foreigner. From their writings we learn about male sexual fears and fantasies, but not necessarily the historical Marie-Antoinette.

Just how ill informed these revolutionary hacks were about the queen's life at Versailles is shown by their omission of the one name that has always cropped up in discussions of the queen's private life and that was well known in court circles under Louis XVI. It is time to return to the subject of her bachelor friend Fersen, a handsome Swedish aristocrat.

The extent of the independence of Marie-Antoinette's life at Versailles on the eve of the Revolution—to put it no more finely for now—is shown by her plan in 1787 to have Fersen stay in her private quarters in the palace on his visits to Versailles. History would never have found out about this startling arrangement without the paper trail left by the Royal Buildings Office at Versailles: its officials were so bureaucratic that we can even follow the rounds of the palace window cleaners.[59]

An unpublished letter of October 14, 1787, written by one Loiseleur, a departmental underling to the director, transmits the queen's order for a stove to be installed "in one of her inner cabinets with heating pipes to warm a small room next door." This room was on the floor above her official bedchamber, the two linked by the poky staircase behind the queen's alcove door.

In 1970 two French scholars—Philippe Huisman and, once more, Marguerite Jallut—drew attention to the correspondence between this letter and a series of entries by Fersen in his letter-book, recording his missives to a certain "Joséphine," his code name for the queen. Two, dating from April 1786, discussed respectively a "project to lodge upstairs" and "what she needs to arrange for me if I am to live upstairs." On October 8, six days before Loiseleur's letter, Fersen wrote by an intermediary, asking for "Joséphine" to "arrange a niche for a stove."[60]

To understand the implications, it is necessary to take account of the rampart around French royal princesses formed by an ancient "etiquette of decency" aimed at protecting their virtue and reputations. Under Louis XVI this etiquette was still in existence. It was much stricter than the mores of fashionable society. Bombelles records how he used to have to retire whenever Madame Élisabeth, Louis XVI's unmarried sister, called on his wife in their lodgings at Versailles. Until she turned twenty-five, a royal princess could not be in the company of unrelated men.[61]

For the queen, whose chief function in the French monarchy was to bear the king's seed, this etiquette was strictest of all. But Marie-Antoinette's love of informality, combined with her influence over Louis XVI, enabled her to do away with the half of it. She dispensed with the old etiquette of always being followed around the palace by two ladies-in-waiting in *grand habit*: "One would repeatedly encounter the Queen in the galleries of Versailles going to Madame de Lamballe's or the duchesse de Polignac's followed only by a page, something never seen before."[62]

Malicious tongues could easily distort these informal ways as evidence of lax morals. In 1778 Marie-Antoinette provoked a scandal by her fondness for summer walks late at night, serenaded by the musicians of the chapel. Accompanied by her two sisters-in-law, she mingled on the palace terrace with the ordinary townsfolk admitted to hear the concert, but "without the entourage appropriate to a queen."[63] When the queen sat on a park bench, veiled and dressed simply, she was unrecognizable. Strangers sometimes sat down beside her and struck up a conversation.[64] A ministerial clerk, realizing who she was, later boasted about it in his bureau. The story rapidly spread from Versailles to Paris, and the queen found her virtue impugned in the public eye.

This particular episode boomeranged back on Marie-Antoinette in a very specific way in the Diamond Necklace Affair seven years later. Fraudsters led by a self-styled countess, one Jeanne de La Motte, had apparently duped the grand almoner of France, the credulous cardinal de Rohan, into paying out large sums of money to make a secret purchase of jewelry on behalf of none other than Marie-Antoinette—or so he was led to believe. The affair came to light when the jewelers complained to the king that they had handed over the necklace but not yet been paid. Marie-Antoinette's reputation suffered a crippling blow: the public was left with the false impression that her love of diamonds had led her into conduct unbecoming to a wife or a queen.

Allegedly to persuade the cardinal that she was indeed acting for the queen, La Motte hired an amiable Paris prostitute, dressed her up in a simple gown of the kind favored by Marie-Antoinette, and staged a solitary nocturnal meeting between her and Rohan in a remote corner of the gardens of Versailles: not on the terrace, which was too conspicuous, being illuminated by the lights of the palace, but in the unlit bosquets below. According to her trial affidavit, the prostitute, "hidden deep in shadows," her face masked by a black domino, handed over a rose to the cardinal, which he was meant to take as a token of affection from the queen.

Thanks in part to the damage done to Marie-Antoinette's reputation by her nocturnal strolls six years earlier, not only could a senior official in the royal household be conned into believing that the queen of France would consent to meet in the park in this indecent way, but so could the general public, as was clear from its support for the cardinal's innocence at his ensuing trial.

Louis XVI finally caught wind of this murky business in August 1785. Toward midday on Assumption Sunday, with the palace packed with sightseers, the unsuspecting cardinal, dressed in his full regalia and about to celebrate high mass in the chapel, was awaiting the king in his official study along with a crowd of other courtiers when he was summoned to the king's private quarters next door. Led into Louis XV's corner study, he was surprised to see a hatchet-faced queen there as well as the king.

Louis XVI confronted the stunned cardinal, who was then sent alone into Louis XV's next-door "back study": "You will find paper, pen and ink there; write down your statement, then give it to me; take all the time you need."[65] When the cardinal reemerged fifteen minutes later, Louis warned him that he was about to be arrested, then dismissed him. Coming out into the crowded Hall of Mirrors, the cardinal heard the humiliating cry "Arrest Cardinal de Rohan!"

Unfortunately for the king and queen, the arrest was bungled in at least two respects. The arresting officer under orders to escort the cardinal back to his palace lodging at one point was asked by his captive to lend him a pencil. Dazzled, presumably, by the cardinal's name and rank, in a moment of almost comic incompetence this junior officer obliged. The cardinal was then able to scribble a message ordering his servants to burn his Parisian papers, which they duly did, destroying any evidence that might have compromised their master's self-proclaimed innocence. As Besenval points out, the king and his ministers should have anticipated such a ruse by placing seals on all the cardinal's residences before the arrest took place.[66] At the ensuing trial, the lack of incriminating documents ensured the acquittal of the cardinal. As for the queen, the public drew its own conclusions.

In fact, Marie-Antoinette was more prudent in her behavior than gossip allowed, at least in public. This is shown by her attitude to dining etiquette at Versailles. Louis XVI had inherited from Louis XV the ritual of the royal suppers. His grandfather had transferred them in 1769 to a new suite of first-floor reception rooms, which he created by annexing to his "small apartment" a further seven windows along the north side of the Royal Court. In these so-called new rooms (salles neuves) Louis XV included two dining rooms, which permitted him to segregate royal princesses from nonroyal men at mealtimes.

A description by Croÿ of a supper that he attended in 1775 shows that Louis XVI maintained these arrangements:

*Not only the Queen, Madame de Lamballe and their ladies, but Monsieur
and Madame, Monsieur le comte d'Artois and Madame la comtesse
d'Artois, Monsieur le duc and Madame la duchesse de Chartres and their
ladies were there, with the result that there were sixteen ladies alone at the
large table with the king and his brothers. M. le duc de Chartres joined ours
in the other room, where we were seventeen men.*

As a prince of the blood, Chartres was not "family" in the narrow
sense.[67]

Even inside her private domain, Marie-Antoinette never ate with
men in the king's absence. According to Madame de Genlis, at her
fashionable Versailles brunches *(déjeuners-dîners),* her male guests ate
together in a neighboring room, and both sexes regrouped only after
the queen and her ladies had left their table.[68]

Marie-Antoinette's circle at Versailles formed an extension of French
smart society, in which adultery was not a taboo at this date. What
were styled "known liaisons," like that of Marie-Antoinette's best
friend, Gabrielle de Polignac, with the marquis de Vaudreuil, were not
uncommon. But there was an iron rule about discretion. In a society
that considered it "grossly insolent" for a gentleman to put his hand on
the back of an armchair occupied by a woman, a lover would never allow himself in public "even the most innocent familiarity" with his
mistress.[69]

Against this background the historian must weigh the fact that, in
1787, Marie-Antoinette offered rooms in her private domain to Fersen.
Her alleged partiality for him had given rise to court gossip in April
1779 (weeks, as it happened, before she tightened access to her private
rooms at Versailles); a journal entry of Bombelles shows that tongues
were still wagging at Versailles four years later.[70] There is no decisive
proof that the two were ever lovers, and there probably never will be.
In 2003 the originals of the correspondence between Fersen and the
queen failed, under expert examination, to yield the secrets of the era-
sures made at an unknown time and by an unknown hand, apparently
to protect the dead queen's reputation.[71]

Fersen was well known for his discretion. According to Madame de
Boigne, this explained why the "liaison, although known, never gave

rise to scandal."[72] By "known," she meant that it was known to, or sus-pected by, court insiders such as Tilly, her onetime page, or Saint-Priest, one of Louis XVI's ministers.[73] All things considered, Fersen's compli-ance with the "project to live upstairs," given its complete breach of the "etiquette of decency," is hard to square with the view that his relation-ship with the queen was strictly platonic. His and Marie-Antoinette's behavior in 1787 really only makes sense if both were playing for the highest stakes.

# 9 ·

# A Garden with Flowers

IN THE sixteenth century a French writer likened a court without women to a garden without flowers.[1] Louis XIV, a connoisseur of female charms, was well aware that women, his mistresses included, were among the attractions of his court. At a Versailles reception in 1676, Madame de Sévigné admired the magnificently adorned Madame de Montespan: "a triumphant beauty for all the ambassadors to admire."[2]

From the noblewoman's point of view, attendance at Versailles was a family duty. If she had a post in the household of the queen or a royal princess, a common ploy was to try to pass it on to the next generation, especially a son's wife. Women courtiers were skilled at networking, using informal conversations to plant ideas or take soundings while they sat with their needlework at court functions like the queen's game in the Salon of Peace.[3] Saint-Simon acknowledged the enormous help that his duchess provided to him at Versailles, "where she was universally loved, respected and admired, not least by the King himself."[4]

A formidable female operator often lay behind the entrenchment of a court family at Versailles. Marie-Françoise, maréchale de Noailles, was "the cleverest woman of our century" in the view of Luynes. She was a matriarch who thought only of "the establishment of her family and the enlargement of its fortune." Her weapons were reproductive stamina on a heroic scale—she bore her husband, the maréchal-duc, no fewer than twenty-one babies between 1673 and 1695[5]—and relentless matchmaking for the resultant brood of children. She had nine daughters who reached adulthood. With her eleven sons-in-law, courtiers took to referring to the Noailles as the "tribe."

Her biggest coup was to marry her son to Madame de Maintenon's niece, whom the childless marquise had brought up as her daughter and heiress—the bride came with a huge dowry of 800,000 livres, with a further 70,000 livres in jewelry.[6] The young couple joined the family circle of the old Louis XIV, with all the benefits that flowed from such intimacy with the sovereign. When she died in 1748, the nonagenarian maréchale had done her work well. A generation later, in the view of the Austrian ambassador, the Noailles were still "the most numerous and powerful of all the families at the court."[7]

The comtesse de Brionne, a widowed mother of four, used bold tactics. In 1761 she brought Louis XV round to appointing her as grand equerry, one of the prime *charges* of the royal household, always held by a male. This allowed her to keep the post in the family of her late husband, a prince of Lorraine, whose son at nine was too young to take over from his father. Her worry was that a temporary substitute would intrigue successfully to divert the post into the hands of another family. After overcoming the reflexive chauvinism of the court accountants, who protested that it was unheard of for the accounts of a court department to be signed off by a woman, the young countess went on to run the Grand Stables for nearly ten years.

She is said to have discharged with aplomb the ceremonial duties of the grand equerry. In 1763 Louis XV drove in state to the capital to celebrate the peace that ended the Seven Years' War. This peace was a humiliation for France, which lost its overseas empire to England, and many Parisians blamed the malign influence of Madame de Pompadour. It is unrecorded how they reacted to another sign of the power of women at Versailles— the king of France with a woman as grand equerry at his side.[8]

Traditionally the foreign princesses who married into the French royal family were pawns transferred to France at a tender age in a man's game of dynastic politics. Divided loyalties were hard to avoid. When France and the Palatinate were at war in the 1690s, Madame had to endure the sight of the paintings from her father's Heidelberg palace hanging as booty in her husband's apartment at Versailles. Long before Marie-Antoinette was accused of putting Austrian interests before French, the duchess of Burgundy used to rummage through the papers of Louis XIV on behalf of her father, the duke of Savoy.[9]

Never anointed or crowned, the queens who resided at Versailles played no formal part in the two ceremonies that did most to symbolize the power and mystique of royalty, the *lit de justice* and the royal touch. Even so, they were central figures in the official life of the palace. Admission to their rooms was governed by a system of entrées, just as on the king's side. The bedchamber was the setting for daily ceremonies: the queen's *lever* and *coucher,* and royal meals when the queen dined alone. In the next-door Salon of Peace Marie Leczinska and later Marie-Antoinette routinely presided over the "queen's game."

In the Room of the Nobles, the large salon between the queen's bedchamber and her first antechamber, the visitor can still make out a pair of hooks in the cornice midway along the north wall. These are the sole relics of a colored canopy, the equivalent of the English cloth of estate, under which Marie Leczinska and later Marie-Antoinette used to sit in an armchair for formal audiences. When the queen was in mourning, a black canopy was substituted, which she stood beneath while she received the condolences of the court.[10]

The duc de Luynes describes numerous audiences that took place in this room under Louis XV. His interest in them had a lot to do with the prominence that they gave to his wife, Marie Leczinska's lady of honor. She was entitled on these occasions to place her stool in the most honorific position, immediately to the queen's right, as in 1738, when the queen gave audience to the deputies of the Estates of Brittany, nobles, clergy, and commoners. Marie Leczinska heard their loyal speech sitting in her armchair in the middle of an arc of seated ladies on their stools, the nontitled ladies standing behind them.

Marie Leczinska and Marie-Antoinette were both patrons of the arts, even if eighteenth-century France no longer deferred to Versailles in matters of taste in the way that it had under Louis XIV. His successors did not seek to direct the French arts to anything like the same degree. In the 1780s the Parisian Jean-Sébastien Mercier, an anti-aristocratic writer with a sharp quill, claimed that "people no longer say, with an absurd emphasis, 'The Court has pronounced thus.'"

But Versailles did not forget its role as a showcase. Under Louis XV paintings by contemporary artists, such as an "Esther" by Dutroy or new tapestries from the Gobelins factory, were put on public display from time to time in the state apartments. Whenever the soft furnishings of the royal bedrooms were renewed, they advertised afresh the skill of the silk weavers of Lyon.[11]

In a Colbertian move, Louis XV had set up a French porcelain factory at Sèvres with the express intent of rivaling the much-admired Meissen ware of Saxony. At Versailles he instituted an annual display of its latest products, which the courtiers were put under pressure to purchase. Louis XVI maintained this custom. As Christmas and present-buying loomed, the porcelain went on display for fifteen days in Louis XV's three "new rooms." Here, Louis XVI would "enjoy watching the porcelain being unpacked and scrutinizing the crowd of purchasers."[12]

Visitors like Horace Walpole in 1765 could ask to see the king's pictures. These were kept in the vast headquarters of the director general of the Royal Buildings, on what is now the rue de l'Indépendance américaine. Nine rooms housed a considerable collection of the Italian and French masters. Choice items from time to time were taken off for display on easels in the apartments of the palace.[13]

But the retreat of royalty behind closed doors at Versailles meant that its private patronage of contemporary artists and craftsmen was now invisible to most visitors. Mercier again, on the Parisian sightseer gone up for the Whitsunday procession of the Holy Ghost: "The state apartments are opened for him, but the small apartments are closed, although these are the richest and most interesting."[14]

It was behind these doors that members of the royal family enjoyed the exquisite furniture, paintings, and bibelots produced by the French luxury trades, or experimented with new home technology such as the "Franklin chimney," fitted to a fireplace in the rooms of the comte d'Artois in 1781. This antismoking device was named after its inventor, Benjamin, the American scientist and diplomat lionized in Paris during the 1780s.[15] Much of the vaunted patronage of Madame de Pompadour and Marie-Antoinette boiled down to a keen interest in fashionable furnishings and objets d'art to decorate their apartments, houses, and gardens.

Music remained something of an exception in this tale of cultural concealment at Versailles. Marie Leczinska gave court concerts once or twice a week, either in the Salon of Peace or, for larger groups of musicians, in her large antechamber. In 1764 the seven-year-old Mozart, already a prodigy, played the harpsichord in the queen's antechamber, for which he received fifty gold louis.[16]

Marie-Antoinette picked up this musical baton. She was a keen musician, taking lessons in both singing and playing. A gouache by the painter Gautier-Dagoty from early in the reign shows the young queen at her harp in her bedchamber, a guitar on a stool nearby, two ladies-in-waiting on stools in full court dress, and a male singer thumbing his music.

In December 1774 Louis XVI asked his spouse to decide the traditional program of winter entertainments that played out at Versailles over the two or three months between the return of the court from Fontainebleau, usually in November, and the end of carnival sometime in February.

This gave the nineteen-year-old queen an opportunity to impose her musical taste on Versailles, and she seized the chance with gusto. She gradually phased out the Italian harlequins and columbines in favor of a young French composer of the moment, Modeste Grétry. His gamboling melodies perfectly complemented the comic-opera plots of peasants and cows popular at the time.

For serious opera, Marie-Antoinette had to bide her time. The problem was that the new opera house at the extremity of the north wing was ruinously expensive to use. It was only after she gave birth in 1785 to a second son—a further enhancement of her status at court—that Louis XVI, by way of a solution, approved plans for yet another new theater.

Marie-Antoinette was the driving force behind this venture. It was not as extravagant as it sounds, since the theater was a provisional structure of wood inserted into the empty shell of Gabriel's new wing on the Royal Court. The exterior of this wing had been finished in 1780. It was destined to house a grand new staircase to replace the Ambassadors' Staircase, but the funds, for the time being, were lacking.

This new theater was of the eighteenth-century court type, a horseshoe with five tiers of boxes capable of seating five hundred people. Unlike the old Comedy Room on the other side of the palace, it had all the necessary machinery below and above the stage—pulleys, cords, and frames for painted scenery—for mounting complicated operas.

This new theater encouraged an operatic renaissance at Versailles on the eve of the Revolution. Records show that as many as 311 performances were staged here in just over three years. But Versailles had lost its cultural authority. Madame Campan recalled in her memoirs that the "spirit of opposition which reigned in [Paris] loved to overthrow the judgments of the court." In the mid-1780s, it was almost enough for a work to have been written for the court to guarantee failure when it opened in Paris. Some of the opening salvos of the political revolution to come were fired across the lyric stage.[17]

At the heart of a royal marriage was the urgent need to produce offspring, preferably male. To this end, Louis XV's father-in-law had advised his daughter on her marriage: "You must no longer think of anyone other than him. . . . Your whole soul must lose itself in his." Marie Leczinska obediently produced ten children in ten years, all of them born at Versailles.[18]

In 1682 Louis XIV insisted that his first grandchild be born at Versailles. Since then, a royal tradition had grown up that all births in the direct line of succession take place in the principal residence. The setting for almost all these births was either the queen's state bedchamber on the first floor or the dauphine's on the ground floor below. These births were national events, especially when a son and heir was ardently awaited, as in 1778, when Marie-Antoinette became pregnant. On that occasion, society ladies from Paris established themselves at Versailles "for this great event."[19]

Luynes, who was there, describes the birth in 1750 of the first child of Marie-Josèphe of Saxony, Louis XV's daughter-in-law. It took place in the dauphine's bedroom, which survives with its dimensions intact but not much else. The birth was public, an old royal tradition to ensure that the child really was the mother's. The occasion was chaotic, and the normally rigid etiquette was momentarily thrust aside:

> *Everyone who was at Versailles gathered [in the early hours, when the pains began] in the large bedroom of the dauphine's apartment, as well as in her large cabinet and even the second antechamber; many ladies went into the*

*dauphine's bedroom wearing undress gowns, even though the King and*
*Queen were present.*

*At four in the afternoon the labor proper began, the king had both*
*leaves of the doorway opened, and a prodigious number of people*
*entered the bedroom, men and women, whether they had the entrée or*
*not; none of the Court people was refused. In spite of the presence of the*
*King and Queen, the men sat down, not only the medical faculty and*
*the guards, but also the princes and the officers of the service, the guards*
*captain, grand chamberlain, and the master of the wardrobe. They*
*even sat on the sofa opposite the dauphine, whose [bed] curtains were*
*open. . . .*

*The King kept getting up to report progress to the large cabinet. The*
*labor was strenuous and painful, but the dauphine made no complaint. At*
*six she gave birth to a daughter.*

Louis XV had commissioned a painter to celebrate the birth of a
hoped-for son to secure the succession. Natoire depicted Hymen, the
god of marriage, presenting to France an infant wearing the blue sash
of the Holy Ghost, which royal princes received at birth. This sash
could be painted out if the worst came to the worst and the baby was
female, as was the case this time. Five years later, in 1755, the little girl,
Marie-Zéphyrine, died without even being officially mourned since, to
achieve this distinction, French princesses needed to remain alive for at
least seven years.[20]

Until the late eighteenth century the birth of a prince provoked
popular enthusiasm. For spontaneity nothing could equal the scenes on
August 6, 1682, when the Bavarian dauphine gave birth at Versailles to
Louis XIV's first grandson, the duke of Burgundy:

*The rabble, not wishing to be outdone by the gentlefolk, in a kind of fury*
*broke all the windows in the Superintendency, [the part of the palace]*
*where Madame la dauphine had given birth; some clapped when the king*
*passed by, others lit fires, throwing on whatever they could find; they burnt*
*the cranes and the scaffolding used by the builders; some threw their own*
*clothes into the fire; in short, if they had not been prevented, they would*
*have burnt all the wood in the timber yards of Versailles.[21]*

In 1751, on the birth of another duke of Burgundy, Luynes records the perpetual "drums, violins and whoops of joy in the courtyards, galleries and garden terrace" from the guildsmen of Versailles. The year before, for Marie-Zéphyrine, the fishwives from Les Halles had given their traditional harangue before the newly born dauphin before ending up on the terrace for "a lot of singing and dancing."[22]

The royal household was no less enthusiastic. In 1751 the bodyguards gave a ball in the Grand Guardroom to which they invited the queen. It began at six and was still going on at four in the morning, when the dauphin, father of the baby, finally left—a mark of his bounty, adds Luynes, as this dour prince liked neither dancing nor late nights. There was more merriment on the parterre outside the windows of the baby's mother, where mounted huntsmen gave mock chase to a Swiss Guard wearing a stag's head.[23]

The duke of Burgundy died young and was succeeded as heir to Louis XV by his younger brother, the future Louis XVI, who married the Austrian archduchess Marie-Antoinette in 1770. For eight years the union failed to bear fruit. Part of the problem was Louis, who at first did not know—allegedly—how to bring himself to orgasm. Marie-Antoinette also had a mind of her own, despite her mother's conventional advice: "In everything the wife submits to the husband and must have no other occupation than to please him and carry out his wishes."[24] There are grounds for believing that she was not always the compliant figure constructed by Mercy, the Austrian ambassador, in his reports to the empress.

In 1775 Mercy blamed the lack of a pregnancy on the distance between the royal apartments. Louis had to suffer the "inconveniences" of reaching his wife's quarters via the back door in a corner of the Bull's Eye, a public antechamber full of prying eyes.[25] In June Louis took action. He ordered the construction of a serpentine corridor at entresol level beneath the floor of his official bedchamber and the Hall of Mirrors. This "king's passage," as it became known, began in a private corridor off his official study and emerged just behind the alcove door in Marie-Antoinette's bedchamber.

The real reason for this innovation seems to have been Marie-Antoinette's habit of sometimes bolting her bedroom door against her own husband. Circumstantial evidence comes from the dispatches of the Sardinian ambassador, who knew "for certain" that Louis XVI, one night at Fontainebleau in 1777, had "found the door closed." He meekly returned to his chamber. The point of the king's new passage would then be to prevent the idlers in the Bull's Eye gossiping about the monarch, not on his way to his wife's bedchamber, but on his way *back* with a speed that could only denote a refusal on her part. This was material for a major scandal.[26]

The travails of the royal marriage coincided with what some observers saw as a shift in public attitudes to royalty. In 1776 the abbé de Véri was struck by the public indifference to the birth of a son to the comte d'Artois, even though the event assured the future of the dynasty in the continuing absence of a dauphin. Seven years later Bombelles had a similar thought when Artois became the father of—admittedly—a baby girl: "Today the multiplication of the children of our princes seems more a charge than a pleasure for the nation." Confided to diaries, these contemporary impressions by supporters of the monarchy must be allowed their weight. Véri's was accompanied by a prescient prediction that France would one day be a republic.[27]

Growing disillusionment with the monarchy was a legacy of the reign of Louis XV. The king who once enjoyed the title of "Beloved" lost his early popularity among his subjects for a variety of reasons, mostly to do with his government's perceived misconduct of the country's affairs, but also to do with public criticism of the monarch himself and his entourage—especially the continuing scandal of his mistresses.

Royal mistresses were nothing new at Versailles. Louis XIV's womanizing was so notorious throughout Europe that it became a point of weakness on which foreign enemies could attack him in print. A Dutch medal of 1693 shows Louis fleeing back to Versailles from the front during the Ten Years' War in a chariot pulled by four women.[28]

Once Louis XIV had settled down with his second wife, the marquise de Maintenon, the moral tone of Versailles sobered up. In 1687 Madame complained that the king's piety had made the court boring and was driving people away. In the eighteenth century the formidable old king was remembered for his power to check loose-living tendencies among his courtiers "with a single look."[29]

This repressive atmosphere at Versailles prompted a backlash on the old king's death. When the boy-king Louis XV returned to Versailles in 1722, the reformed court brought with it the relaxed morals of the Regency. Matthieu Marais, a Parisian lawyer, heard rumors of "open debauch" at Versailles in the following months. The duchesse de Retz was said to have a lover on every floor of the palace.[30] We have already encountered Madame de Boufflers.

The sexual freedom of the time encouraged an upsurge among high-ranking males in what was then known as "the philosophical vice." Within weeks of the return of the court, a group of young lords, including three dukes, were caught engaging in "infamous acts" inside one of the fenced bosquets of the palace garden. Evidently they had transferred Parisian habits to Versailles. Reports of police spies show that, at this time, "sodomites"—to employ police language—frequented the gardens of the Tuileries, where aristocrats could enjoy casual encounters with males of varied social backgrounds. At Versailles the gardens were at best laxly policed, to judge from the eighteenth-century reports of thefts, muggings, and prostitution. And even a duke was hard put to find total privacy for acts that still carried the death penalty in France.[31]

This freer atmosphere was felt to threaten the moral health of the king himself. Charles, duc de La Trémoille, one of the first gentlemen and, at sixteen, two years older than his master, was abruptly exiled from Versailles in 1724 and quickly married off to a cousin.[32] The case for a royal wedding sooner rather than later was now pressing.

At the age of fifteen Louis XV was married to Marie Leczinska, an attractive Polish princess. For the first ten years or so the young couple were both in love, and the queen never ceased to be. But by 1738, when the king decided to move his bedroom at Versailles, the royal eye had already started to rove.

The official explanation for this move was the cold. There may have been other reasons. From his new bedchamber in Louis XIV's former billiard room, Louis XV could easily reach his private staircase three doors away, and thence his small cabinets over the Stag Court. Here, on the second floor, he had arranged yet another bedroom two years previ-

ously, decorated in pale yellow with damask hangings and taffeta curtains.[33] The palace paperwork improbably assigns this pretty chamber
to the king's chef, Lazur. In fact, Louis had fixed it up for secret trysts
with one of his wife's married ladies-in-waiting, Louise de Mailly.[34]

In the course of 1738 he and the queen stopped sleeping together
for good after Marie Leczinska was compelled to abstain temporarily,
following a miscarriage. She was too timid or modest to give her husband an explanation; he took offense at this refusal. The years of subterfuge with Louise de Mailly now stopped. In 1739 Louis installed her
in a second-floor apartment overlooking the Marble Court. The angle
room directly above his new study was the countess's salon, where she
received the king and his intimates.

In the next few years the king transferred his attentions to one of
Louise's sisters, who died giving birth to an illegitimate child, then back
to Louise, and then from Louise to a third sister, a lovely widow, "tall
and majestic," called the marquise de La Tournelle, sometimes "tender
like her heart," at others "proud like her name."[35] Evicting Louise from
her apartment, the thirty-something king for the first time became the
subject of scandal. "To choose a whole family," ran one rhyme, "is this
being unfaithful or constant?"

History's verdict on Louis XV's character has not been kind. He was
intelligent, but said to lack application. He was easily bored. He had
what is least unkindly described as an insensitive streak. Once he deliberately stepped on the toes of a courtier who suffered from gout, asking if
that was where the pain was.[36] He loved women and in adulthood grew
into a roué. But he had no interest in amorous pursuit—"gallantry," as
the French would say. He preferred to be served sex, as it were, on a plate.

Intrigue as well as lust fueled his affairs with the Mailly sisters.
Madame de Mailly was a protégée of Louis XV's chief minister, the cardinal Fleury. The cardinal's enemies at court sought to attack him by
undermining the position of his protégée in the king's affections.
There were those like the duchesse de Brancas who believed that Louis
XV's personality was such that he needed a more dominating and more
politically aware mistress to prod him into asserting himself so as to become truly the master of France. Then there was the fact that the sisters belonged to an illustrious court family, related to almost everyone

who mattered at Versailles, including the royal governess, the grand equerry, and two of Louis XV's first gentlemen. Their liaisons with the king were potentially advantageous to all these influential kin, who offered the sisters their tacit support.[37]

At first the king and Marie-Anne de La Tournelle—soon to become duchesse de Châteauroux—met surreptitiously in the lodging of an absentee bishop in the north ministers' wing. The duc de Richelieu, the type of the eighteenth-century rake and a royal favorite, played Cupid in scenes straight out of an eighteenth-century opera. "Shortly after midnight, the King went to Monsieur de Richelieu's rooms [in the south wing] where he found large wigs of the type which doctors were still wearing at the time, as well as black clothes and cloaks. Thus disguised they went to call on Madame de La Tournelle."[38] Without his guards captain in waiting to escort him, the king was unrecognizable, and Marie-Anne worried that his disguise would cause him to be accidentally run over by the carriages habitually driven "at full speed" in the Ministers' Court.[39]

The lazy Marie-Anne, pet dog habitually tucked under her arm, may not have been as in love with the king as her sister. What she sought was the power and plunder of a mistress's place. She asked for an official role at the court along with "a fine apartment worthy of her place." Bit by bit the king gave in to her demands, creating a nest of rooms for her in the attics above the state apartments. Her position being a family matter, a fourth sister was installed next door for support.

In 1743 Marie-Anne won a lift—an exceedingly rare luxury at Versailles—to save her the climb to her attic. A tower was built against a wall in one of the king's inner courtyards, with a small cubicle in the shaft which the marquise sat in while servants hauled her up by weight-and-pulley.[40] The following year she extracted a duchy and became duchesse de Châteauroux. In 1744 Louis fell dangerously ill and sent Marie-Anne into exile as a prelude to confession and the last rites. Unexpectedly recovering, he shocked France by recalling her to Versailles. But she unexpectedly died before she could resume occupation of her luxurious apartment.

Even before her death, Marie-Anne had sensed a rival in a certain Madame Le Normant d'Étioles. The rich and well-connected Jeanne-

Antoinette was a Parisian commoner. She too had family and kin, including two head valets at Versailles, to support her burning ambition to become the king's mistress.

The charms of Madame de Pompadour, as Jeanne-Antoinette became in 1745, were summed up by Dufort de Cheverny: "Every man would have wanted her as his mistress." Her longevity in the king's affections lay not in the sex, which fizzled out around 1750, but in her knack for making herself his indispensable friend. This she owed to her intelligence, careful education, and her indefatigability. A bourgeoise, she had to work to maintain her position, unlike her languid predecessor, to the manner born.

Her talent to amuse emerged in the success of her amateur theatricals at Versailles. She enhanced the house-party atmosphere of Louis XV's private domain by putting together an orchestra and a troupe of actor-singers. Professionals performed alongside a select group of courtiers, including two princes of the blood and the marquise herself, who usually took the leading roles.

The first venue was a wooden stage in the painted gallery of what used to be Louis XIV's museum. The old cabinet of curiosities, now emptied, acting as a dressing room. In 1748, needing more space, the king transferred the theatricals to the well of the Ambassadors' Staircase. Since this was still used every New Year's Day for the procession of the Holy Ghost, the stage, again of painted wood, had to be one that could be disassembled. Seats and stage were supported by the upper landing level, with the musicians placed on the lower one.[41]

Lasting just over three years, these private theatricals were an extravagance at a time when France was at war in Europe over the Austrian succession and the court as a whole (despite the war) was already enjoying the regular program of plays put on by the troupes from Paris. They helped to turn public opinion against the marquise.

At first the king installed the marquise in the attic rooms of her predecessor. In 1750 he permitted her to descend to the ground floor in the same part of the palace. Here, he gave her much more prestigious rooms once belonging to his royal cousins, the Toulouse family, rooms that were linked by a private staircase to his small apartments overhead. Both apartments survive, much altered. After the marquise's death here in 1764, her ground-floor rooms were thought good enough for Madame Adélaïde, the king's daughter.

At her death Madame de Pompadour owned eight pairs of harem trousers. It is tempting to suppose that she sometimes appeared in them when she and the king were together in private.[42] In 1754 she had had herself painted as a sultana.[43] On one level, this play with the Orient was harmless fantasy. In eighteenth-century France the Turkish world was exotic, rather than threatening. Few were still alive who could remember the year 1683, when the sultan's armies came close to capturing Vienna. There was a growing fashion for *turquerie*. In the next reign, ladies at Marie-Antoinette's carnival balls wore costumes *à la sultane* or *à la turque*. The queen's brother-in-law, the comte d'Artois, had a suite of three "Turkish rooms" in his apartment in the south wing. Although the apartment no longer exists, fragments of the paneling survive, painted with turbaned males, crescent moons, and scenes from the harem.[44]

Madame de Pompadour may have used *turquerie* to press home a more serious point. By 1754, with the marquise now a friend and no longer a lover, Louis XV had begun a series of liaisons with unmarried girls. Travelers' descriptions of Constantinople had introduced educated French people to the intricate structure of the sultan's harem, presided over by the sultana valide, or queen mother. A shrewd manipulator of her image, as her painted portraits show, the marquise may have sought to remind the court that it was she who occupied the senior position in what was fast becoming a royal seraglio.[45]

The best known of these girls, depicted naked by the court painter Boucher, was the sixteen-year-old Marie-Louise O'Murphy, the pretty daughter of a Parisian shoemaker of Irish extraction. There were others: between 1754 and 1765 Louis, now middle-aged, fathered seven illegitimate children by five different mothers.

Louis XVI's future minister, Saint-Priest, remembered as a young man seeing sedan chairs, their curtains closed, arriving "under a small arch where a secret door was opened leading by the backstairs to a bedroom which the King could reach from his apartment. This little chamber had a window from which the beauty could see the king getting into his coach."

This description points to the covered passage that once existed just east of the king's guardroom, on the north side of the Royal Court. It led to his inner courtyards. The bedroom seems to have overlooked the guardroom door from which the king emerged to climb into his waiting coach. The courtiers called this room "the trap, because it snares young birds." It was widely rumored that one of the king's head valets, Lebel, acted as pimp for his master.[46]

In 1755 the king bought a small house in the rue Mériadec, in the Parc-aux-Cerfs quarter of the town, southeast of the palace. It had stables and kitchens and living accommodations for one or at most two people on the first floor. Around 1900 the then head of the palace museum, Pierre de Nolhac, was shown around this house by its tenant at the time, an Englishwoman. Upstairs Nolhac was intrigued by one eighteenth-century feature in particular, a dumbwaiter permitting discreet meals without servants.

Supervised by one Madame Bertrand, this house was where Lebel, according to Saint-Priest, often kept "one or two young girls for the pleasures of his master." It is not clear whether Louis XV ever came to this house: to leave the palace unnoticed he certainly would have needed accomplices, as in his early trysts with Madame de La Tournelle. Nolhac espied an old garden door—it still exists—and wondered whether this side entrance might once have been used surreptitiously by the king of France.[47]

In 1768, the year of the queen's death, the fifty-eight-year-old king was already seeing Jeanne Bécu, a twenty-five-year-old beauty of humble origins who had met with success in Paris as a high-class prostitute. The next year Jeanne was presented at court as comtesse du Barry—a good example of the rules of presentation being waived by the monarch when he chose. Jeanne was far from overawed by the royal dignity. This quality no doubt had its charm for the aging king, who once let her perch on his armchair at a meeting of the council.[48]

As with her predecessors, the king wanted his new mistress near him. In 1770 she moved into a luxurious apartment based around the rooms once occupied by Madame de Mailly. Existing occupants were dislodged and new works carried out, including a privy built out onto the Parc-aux-Cerfs directly above the king's bed. Conscious of her status as official mistress, Jeanne demanded gilding throughout the apartment. Lack of funds forced her to scale back her pretensions.[49]

In no time at all Jeanne had been transformed into a grande dame of Versailles. Croÿ was astonished to see her one morning in the king's official study with two duchesses in attendance, like ladies-in-waiting. "This was really remarkable." He took in too that the numerous family of the monarch kept to the other side of the room. They did not approve of the mistress.[50]

Louis XV's womanizing damaged him deeply in the eyes of his subjects. In the 1740s a rash of anonymous tracts condemned the king's successive liaisons with the sisters, which in eighteenth-century eyes smacked of incest as well as adultery. The police traced the author of one of these works back to a servant at Versailles itself.

It is clear that some of the upper servants at Versailles disapproved of what they heard and saw of the court. Nicolle du Hausset, Madame de Pompadour's tirewoman, was convent-educated and had been forced into domestic service by hard times. She once struck up conversation with the prince de Croÿ when he was paying his court to her mistress. She told him with surprising frankness of her "boredom" with the "terrible" world of the court and of "her astonishment at seeing great lords, who could have been kings on their grand estates, playing the valet in her antechamber." To his credit Croÿ, instead of taking offense, was impressed by "so much good sense."[51]

The author of the tract in question was Marie Bonafon, a twenty-eight-year-old tirewoman of the princesse de Montauban, herself a lady-in-waiting of Marie Leczinska. As with Madame du Hausset, her surroundings at Versailles had given her food for thought. She later told her interrogators that her ideas had come from "what people were saying in public" about the king and Madame de Châteauroux.[52]

For the rest of the reign the temperature of public opinion rose steadily. It was fanned by French fears that the king was neglecting his duties while women ran the kingdom. There was concern too that the king by his affairs would make God angry with France. He was after all a semi-sacred figure, his divine right to rule made manifest in the royal touch.

After refusing to exercise these powers in 1739, he never again performed the royal touch. To do so he would first have had to cleanse himself of his sins through confession and communion. But this in turn would have meant breaking with his mistresses, something Louis was not prepared to do.[53]

In the provinces the abbé de Véri came across a nun who could recite by heart a sixty-line lampoon at Madame de Pompadour's expense which ended with the shocking words "In these places [i.e., the court] everything is vile: King, minister, mistress." Jeanne du Barry's origins were a further shock to the French system: "Who'd ever think that, without shame, / Louis would give up the helm / To such a bitch . . . ?"[54]

Orientalist imagery now came back to haunt the monarchy. In a time when underage prostitution was widespread in France, people were less concerned than we would be today for the well-being of the girls in Parc-aux-Cerfs. Indeed, their lot as royal mistresses could seem enviable. They were well looked after, and some were found respectable, even noble, husbands.[55]

Public chat in the Parisian cafés and among the newsmongers was far more concerned about what these dalliances said about the middle-aged king. For the author of *The Private Life of Louis XV,* a bestseller published in 1781, Louis was the "sultan" whose "benumbed senses" were serviced at a cost of millions to the state by the "seraglio" of Parc-aux-Cerfs. These salacious exaggerations stuck like mud. In 1793, when Madame du Barry was on trial for her life, the indictment remembered Louis XV to the jurors as "this Sardanapalus of modern times."[56]

Public concern about the political influence of women at Versailles surfaced on a number of occasions between 1682 and 1789. Today historians might say that this sort of influence was "institutionalized" in a monarchy such as France's. In effect, the king ruled from home. At Versailles the spatial divide between his workplace and his domestic quarters was nonexistent. The official study, meeting place of the royal council but also frequented by the royal mistress, symbolized this absence of boundaries. Versailles gave women with close access to the king the chance to influence him.

Rumors of this kind of influence first surfaced after Louis XIV married his second wife, the marquise de Maintenon. This was done in such secrecy that twenty-six years later, in 1709, his sister-in-law was still not entirely certain "that the king is married." One clue was the increasingly regal behavior of the marquise. The duchess of Burgundy, the king's granddaughter-in-law and "first lady" of Versailles in the absence of a queen or a dauphine, once fell ill in the marquise's rooms. The princess was about to be lifted onto the marquise's bed when the marquise had her deposited instead on some hastily arranged cushions. To those in the know, the marquise's game was obvious: etiquette forbade anyone from lying on the queen of France's bed except the king.[57]

Claims of damaging female influence on male monarchs are difficult to assess: they often served as covert attacks on royal policy, quite apart from what now would be called their implicit or explicit sexism. But it is beyond doubt that Louis XIV rearranged his working day around Madame de Maintenon in a way that could hardly capture better the essence of household government. To understand what follows, a dose of palace topography is necessary.

Louis XIV had arranged an apartment for Madame de Maintenon in 1682, when the court moved to Versailles. It ended up occupying six first-floor windows on the south side of the Royal Court, and its main entrance was off the landing at the top of the Queen's Staircase, opposite the door into the king's guardroom. After crossing two antechambers, the visitor entered one of those agreeable angle rooms at Versailles. This was the marquise's cabinet, in effect her living room, where she had her fireside armchair.

On one side of this fireplace was an alcove hung with crimson damask, containing her bed and a door to the tiny chamber of her faithful Ninon, the housekeeper. On the other side, five steps led to a much larger room in the adjacent Old Wing. The marquise used this for private concerts and theatricals.

Saint-Simon describes how the king came here more or less every day after dinner to work with his ministers. In the cabinet he had his own armchair and table, with a folding stool on the other side for the minister. The marquise sat silently on the king's right working at her tapestry, saying nothing but hearing everything. Sometimes she would have her supper served and be put to bed in the alcove while Louis continued working with a minister.

These arrangements were unnerving (to say the least) for the ministers, who had no idea what she would say about them after they left. Unsurprisingly they felt obliged, as Madame puts it, "to seek by a thousand servilities to curry her favor."[58] These rooms became a hub of the palace to rival the king's. The marquise too was solicited for audiences by people, high and low, who waited at her door to catch her on her way out.[59] Important arrivals at Versailles, like the duke of Burgundy on his return from the front, went straight to the marquise's because the king was there. To mark the birth of the duke's son in July 1704, Bontemps, the king's head valet, arranged for musicians to sing celebratory verses under the balcony of the marquise's corner cabinet, "where the king was."[60]

As the reign wore on, it was not just Saint-Simon who believed that the marquise interfered in affairs of state. *The Tatler,* in an issue of 1709, gives the view from London. Madame de Maintenon is portrayed presumptuously writing on France's behalf to Torcy, Louis XIV's peace emissary to The Hague: "If you have any Passion for your unhappy Country, or any Affection for your distress'd Master, come home with Peace!"[61]

The truth is harder to gauge. But Voltaire in the eighteenth century heard the anecdote told by the same Torcy of a scene in Madame de Maintenon's rooms in 1701. The exiled James II of England had just died. Louis XIV's council had resolved not to recognize his son, the Old Pretender, as England's rightful king. Then James II's widow came to Versailles to plead with Louis XIV to reverse his decision. Despite the certain offense that this action would give to England's actual king, William of Orange, Madame de Maintenon supported her and the king was won over. Torcy used to say afterward that he did not include this episode in his memoirs "because it did not do honor to his master that two women had made him change a decision taken in his council."[62]

Louis XV certainly delegated to his mistresses the business of fielding requests for royal graces and favors. Madame de Pompadour became a kind of "minister of the court." It suited the king for his courtiers to believe that she had a great influence over him. She acted in effect as a screen. People like Croÿ, a shrewd judge of what he called "the system of the court," started to make their way to her rooms for her morning toilette. There, one morning he saw the grand chamberlain of France, the duc de Bouillon, grovel with gratitude. These things should be done, he felt, with more dignity.[63]

Madame du Barry's apartment likewise became a court powerhouse. By May 1770, Croÿ noted on a visit to Versailles that, "little by little, more and more people were going to the countess's." Her reception room, the corner room of Madame de Mailly's old apartment, was furnished with an array of seats: four chairs, thirteen armchairs, and a large settee, all in the latest style. Like the Mailly sisters, Jeanne turned to her family to help her in her new role.

The duc du Châtelet describes a visit to this apartment to enlist Jeanne's support for the affairs of his disgraced friend Choiseul. During the interview, they were interrupted by Jeanne's sister-in-law, Mademoiselle Choin du Barry, who came in and "whispered something in her ear." Jeanne had installed her in a next-door lodging. It transpired that a messenger from the all-powerful duc d'Aiguillon, Choiseul's archenemy, was waiting in the antechamber. "Good, tell him I won't be long," Jeanne replied, now visibly keen to finish with du Châtelet. At eleven that same evening, another family member, her nephew, brought a message to du Châtelet in his palace lodging: the countess had had a word with the king. Louis XV told her that while he would be pleased in general to see du Châtelet at the court, he did not wish to talk to him directly about Choiseul's affairs. It was this discouraging outcome that then prompted Choiseul to write his letter to the king.[64]

Courtiers adapted their techniques to winning over powerful women. The duc de Nivernais, a friend of Madame de Pompadour, advised against patronizing them: "It would be maladroit to seem to fear of tiring them or to want to spare them dry and complex details." According to Besenval, d'Aiguillon captivated Jeanne du Barry by the "infallible method with women" of being a good listener.[65]

In the following reign, the uxorious Louis XVI ensured that there were no more royal mistresses. But the royal households remained full of women. The total embedding of their influence in the court system is shown by the papers abandoned in her Versailles apartment at the Revolution by the comtesse de Coëtlogon. Eugénie had been one of sixteen ladies-in-waiting of the comtesse d'Artois, a minor royal with little or no "credit." Even so, the papers show that the countess received an "overwhelming avalanche of requests, supplications and demands" during her years at Versailles.[66]

Under Louis XVI the rule of women was now supposed by many people to be incarnate in Marie-Antoinette and her female friends. Marie-Antoinette's political influence should not be exaggerated, at least not in the first decade or so of her husband's reign. But to distract his wife from affairs of state, Louis XVI and Maurepas, his first minister, had tacitly delegated to her essentially the same role—"minister of the court"—as Louis XV had bestowed on the marquise de Pompadour.

But Marie-Antoinette's withdrawal into private life made her less accessible to courtiers, unlike the marquise. The result was to empower the female friends for whom the queen had found places in the royal household. Courtiers seeking access to her instead approached one in particular, her closest confidante, Gabrielle de Polignac, governess of the royal children. Gentle and malleable, but also shrewd, Gabrielle excelled at the kind of unchallenging conversation that Marie-Antoinette preferred. "Homer was blind and played the oboe" is recorded as one of her sallies.

In these concentric circles of influence, Gabrielle in turn was said to be guided by her lover, Vaudreuil, and by her more clever sister-in-law, the comtesse Diane de Polignac. In turn, Gabrielle had secured household posts for these two as well—Vaudreuil as grand falconer and Diane, despite being the unmarried mother of an illegitimate child, as governess of the young Madame Élisabeth, Louis XVI's virtuous sister. In the 1780s the apartments of these women in the south wing became centers of the court.[67]

As governess, Gabrielle was paid by Louis XVI to entertain on the court's behalf, just as Madame de Marsan had done under Louis XV. In her official apartment at the far end of the wing Gabrielle gave suppers three times a week, served by her own kitchens in the Grand Commons.

On Sunday afternoons between four and six she received all the courtiers who came to Versailles from Paris. If the queen's footmen were waiting in Gabrielle's antechamber, courtiers knew that Marie-Antoinette was inside. Bombelles describes the sight of the governess in her fireside armchair presiding over one of these receptions, with the queen—inside her own palace—seated next to her "like a visitor."[68]

In December 1786 the government's financial troubles prompted Louis XVI to take the drastic step of convening an assembly of the kingdom's notables. This met at Versailles the following February, when Louis opened the plenary session in a converted storehouse in the town belonging to the royal Entertainments Office. The British ambassador was among those who heard his speech from the throne, "deliver'd under much apparent agitation."

The notables then divided into seven boards of twenty-two members, who fanned out across the palace to discuss national reform in the apartments of their respective chairs, each a royal prince. The presence of these committees electrified a building where until now state affairs had rarely been discussed in the open outside the royal council.

Debate was heated, openly pitching courtier against prince. A former captain of the king's bodyguard, the maréchal de Beauvau, was bold enough to request more facts about the royal finances. To close down this unwelcome line of questioning, the comte d'Artois had to threaten to report him to the king.[69]

After the notables rejected his reform proposals, Louis XVI fell into a depressive state from which he never really reemerged. This state of mind may explain his decision in spring 1788 to triple the size of the privy next to his bedchamber, redecorate it lavishly, install a fireplace, and in effect transform it into a luxurious hideaway. This "almost inexplicable expense" as the finances continued to deteriorate baffled Pierre de Nolhac, the great nineteenth-century historian of Versailles.[70]

Marie-Antoinette now became more active politically. Saint-Priest remembered seeing her attend several meetings of the council of state during the winter of 1788, something "I believe without parallel in the history of the monarchy except when a queen was regent."[71]

That winter Bombelles heard a seditious prediction from a young nobleman in the salons of Versailles that "the royalty of our Bourbons is touching its term." The palace was unusually quiet. In mid-February 1789, Bombelles passed a delightful evening in the near-empty salon of Gabrielle de Polignac. This room was a large wooden extension, which she had been allowed to build onto the terrace overlooking the Orangery so as to have more space for her official receptions—another eighteenth-century addition that upset the pristine lines of Mansart's façades.

Bombelles accompanied Marie-Antoinette on a new invention, the pianoforte. The queen enjoyed the singing so much that she sent for some opera scores from her rooms. Gabrielle's daughter joined in for the duos. Then Bombelles played a waltz and Marie-Antoinette danced with the chevalier de Roll. For the pianist, only one thing spoiled a soirée at which he had shone: "I would have liked at least *some* spectators." On the eve of the Revolution, the life was already ebbing out of the great palace.[72]

## 10.

# "The royal zoo"

AS THE eighteenth century progressed the financial woes of the French monarchy took their toll on the fabric of Versailles. In 1770 the magnificent outbuildings erected by Mansart were in danger from years of neglect, according to Pluyette, the royal architect in charge of their upkeep. He warned that the stables were so full of rotten wood that they would have to be abandoned unless urgent work was carried out.[1]

In the gardens the waterworks had fallen into disrepair. The anonymous *Private Life of Louis XV* depicts the huge crowds at the marriage of the dauphin and Marie-Antoinette in 1770 taking up positions to view the fireworks display amid dry basins, a canal full of filth, and toppled statues that no one had bothered to reerect.[2]

On the town side, visitors reported broken windows and brickwork described as "shabby" or "black." A small detail suggests the attitudes to routine upkeep at Versailles on the eve of the Revolution. The window-cleaning records of the Royal Buildings Office show that in the mid-1780s no one bothered to clean the five central windows beneath the Hall of Mirrors because the ground-floor rooms behind them were temporarily unoccupied.[3]

Under Louis XVI the unfinished Gabriel wing was a building site until 1780, when the exterior was completed. The work had required the demolition of a section of the gilt railing separating the Ministers' Court from the Royal Court. But the plan to restore this railing was never carried out before the Revolution. Instead, the gap continued to be closed with a temporary palisade. Nearby three makeshift huts were built as provisional homes for objects displaced from the demolished building. One housed the clock that used to surmount its roof.[4]

Under Louis XIV some of the merchants with royal warrants were allowed to set up their wooden booths against the retaining wall of the Ministers' Court. The booths reappeared after 1722. Sightseers from abroad, Blondel complained a few decades later, were shocked by these "ridiculous" structures, which "accord so little with the majesty of the place."[5] They captured perfectly the atmosphere of "magnificence and negligence," which was how Benjamin Franklin summed up Versailles in the late eighteenth century.[6]

By 1789 the town at the palace gates had mushroomed into the sixth largest in the realm, with a population of seventy thousand, mainly nobility, small tradesfolk, and servants. There was little commerce. "Only the court and all the people drawn to it provided a living for this immense population." The symbol of this relationship was a Versailles institution known literally as the water waiter *(serdeau)*.[7]

The water waiter was an ancient position in the royal kitchens. At Versailles the incumbent was charged with clearing the tables after royal meals. The profligate style of eating at the French court meant that many dishes brought to the royal table were cleared away more or less untouched. From these leftovers the water waiter hosted a table for the gentlemen servants in one of the dining rooms of the Grand Commons. But even then there was plenty left. The kitchen boys sold the remainder to local women, who in turn resold it at a profit from booths that used to line the rue de la Chancellerie, running down from the place d'Armes. Townsfolk came here to buy freshly cooked game or fish at good prices. Drawing their nutriment from the palace, they were parasites in the most literal sense.[8]

The status of Versailles as a royal town did little to shield its inhabitants from the social ills of the time. Winters were often harsh, and none was worse than that of 1709, which heaped misery on the local poor. Madame, Louis XIV's sister-in-law, heard the terrible story of a woman caught stealing a loaf of bread. When she pleaded poverty, a suspicious policeman accompanied her back to her home, where he found three shivering children, clad only in rags. "Where is your fa- ther?" he asked the eldest. "Behind the door" came the reply. Indeed he was: he had hanged himself in despair.[9]

Harsh weather meant poor harvests and hikes in food prices. In August 1740 Luynes described a riot at Versailles prompted by the rising price of grain. Bread was the rock of the poor man's diet, and a price hike of only a few sous meant real hardship for poorly paid workers. On this occasion local women erupted at the sight of Parisian bakers loading up sacks of grain at the town's grain market, on the same site as today's food halls: prices here were lower than in Paris because Louis XIV had made Versailles a free market in 1669 in order to ensure the provisioning of the court. Around two thousand people attacked the bakers with stones and stole some of the sacks. Ten or so bakers were wounded before the military police were called in.[10]

The privileged members of the court saw the destitute as part of God's will. Christianity also taught them charity. The king himself set the example. In 1672 he set up a religious house staffed by nuns to care for construction workers who fell sick from the illnesses that plagued the building site of Versailles. Under Louis XV this became the Royal Infirmary, a hospital for the care of the local poor and members of the king's household. Poor patients ate off pewter, the royal bodyguards off silver plate, laden with choice cuts from the water waiter.[11]

Good works were the particular province of the court ladies, whose piety made them as concerned for souls as stomachs. After a service in the parish church of Notre Dame Madame de Pontchartrain, wife of Louis XIV's chancellor, stopping in the street to interview a beggar girl, arranged for her admission into a local poorhouse. Her main worry was that, with such a pretty face, the girl would be driven into prostitution.[12]

These were the "known" poor of the parish, the familiar faces outside the church. They pricked more noble consciences than the droves of beggars attracted to Versailles by the presence of the court. In the eighteenth century, when they were blamed for the nocturnal muggings that plagued the town, their presence prompted an order to the well-to-do to close their gates at seven in the evening to prevent vagabonds from sleeping rough in outbuildings.

From Louis XIV on, a series of royal ordinances spectacularly failed to keep these beggars away. They even haunted the palace. In 1787 an English visitor, Arthur Young, was struck by "the blackguard figures that were walking uncontrolled about the palace and even in [the king's] bedchamber, whose rags betrayed them to be in the last stage of poverty."[13]

Versailles had its own equivalent of the friction found today between "town and gown" in certain university towns. The courtiers saw the townsfolk as a bad lot. The noble Hézecques was struck by what he saw as their ingratitude in 1789. More than in any other corner of the kingdom, the "fire of the Revolution" inflamed the residents of this court city.[14]

But it is not hard to sympathize with the town. Imbued with aristocratic arrogance and military swagger, the courtiers of the sword nobility could be brutal in dealings with people deemed their inferiors: the anecdotal evidence suggests an undeniable tendency, at least in the eighteenth century.

In 1749 two or three royal pages—in general, a constant source of trouble between court and town—indecently accosted the wife of a *charcutier*. The husband was joined by his butcher father-in-law, and between them, they saw her harassers off. But the pages returned with twenty-five or so comrades armed with large sticks. A regular street battle ensued, with both sides taking serious casualties.[15]

Police records point to more of the same from the reign of Louis XVI, when there seems to have been a constant undercurrent of violence in the streets. An impatient officer of the bodyguard beats an office boy with his cane; an officer from the royal kitchens strikes a townswoman across the face—again with a cane—when she resists his advances; an equerry of Madame Sophie, the king's aunt, uses the flat of his sword to beat her chairman after her sedan chair receives a jolt.[16]

It is not hard to understand why the townsfolk cheered and shouted "Long live the nation" from the rooftops as they watched the court vanish down the avenue de Paris on October 6, 1789, even though it took their livelihoods with it.[17]

As the seat of a monarch who did not just reign but also ruled, the palace of Versailles was a magnet for protest. One weapon was the written word. In every reign anonymous writings would suddenly appear in the grounds or the palace itself. The culprits were rarely caught.

In 1706 the duchess of Burgundy was the subject of rude verses daubed on a balustrade and some statue bases in the garden. In 1709, at the height of France's sufferings during the War of the Spanish Succession, one of Louis XIV's senior court officials, François VII, duc de La Rochefoucauld, received a death threat against Louis XIV at his official residence at Versailles. Inverting the eulogists' praise for the monarch as a new Augustus, the anonymous letter lauded Brutus, the "tyrant-killer" who had sought to restore the Roman republic by assassinating the dictator Caesar.[18]

In 1750 papers insulting Louis XV were found lying on mantelpieces and floors inside the palace, or were even thrown on the table as he dined. Yet others, said to be "very insolent and treating the king as a tyrant," were dropped the next year into the cradle of his grandson, the duke of Burgundy. In 1778 an entire collection of handwritten songs was thrown into the Bull's Eye, attacking Marie-Antoinette "and all the ladies prominent by their rank or their court posts."[19]

In the eighteenth century protest marches were not unknown, but gauging their seriousness is not always easy. In 1774 a rise in grain prices triggered a wave of disorders in France. In May, peasants from the surrounding region converged on Versailles. The newly acceded Louis XVI promptly dispatched his bodyguards to restore order. Parisian chroniclers claimed that the protesters invaded the courtyards of the palace and compelled the young king to make an appearance on the balcony of his ancestor's bedchamber and order a price drop. By now there was a ready readership in Paris and elsewhere for exaggerated stories of the royal government's woes. In fact, a letter from Louis XVI himself shows that the riots at Versailles were confined to the area around the town market.[20]

In January 1786, two thousand hungry workers from the Auvergne arrived at Versailles. Their aim was peaceful protest; they carried no arms, not even sticks. But their arrival coincided with one of the queen's balls, for which a sumptuous but vulnerable tent had been erected on the parterre in front of the south wing. Taking no chances, Louis XVI approved the closing of the grilles in the forecourts and had the household cavalry saddle their horses. Bombelles, for one, was surprised at these precautions against such a "risible revolt." He noted in his journal that "people danced with the greatest gaiety" at the ball.[21]

A generation earlier, a middle-aged Louis XV had been stabbed by an apparent loner from provincial Arras named Robert Damiens. This was by far the most serious act of political protest at Versailles prior to the events of 1789. Under interrogation it emerged that, like many French people at the time, Damiens objected to the king's authoritarian treatment of the magistrates of the Parlement of Paris, who were widely seen in eighteenth-century France as defenders of liberty against royal absolutism.

The attack, in January 1757, sent shockwaves through Europe. It happened on a moonlit night in the Royal Court. Louis had just come down his private staircase and was emerging from its guardroom to get into his carriage to drive to Trianon. Damiens was waiting for him close by, apparently in the same passageway through which the girls from the Parc-aux-Cerfs were being carried in their sedan chairs.

As Louis looked down for the steps from the guardroom to the courtyard, Damiens pushed through the bodyguards and struck him a blow between the ribs. In the flickering torchlight, amid the crowd that always formed when the sovereign left his palace, no one saw at first what had happened. An equerry or footman seized Damiens almost immediately, but this was because he was wearing his hat in the king's presence. Then a lightly wounded Louis looked up and saw his assailant. "Duc d'Ayen, I am wounded," he told the captain of his bodyguards, who was walking behind him as usual.

After giving orders for Damiens not to be harmed, Louis turned back into the palace and ascended his staircase unaided to his first-floor quarters. Here, there was bedlam, as always happened when royalty departed from its minutely regulated schedule. On this occasion everyone and everything, sheets included, were in readiness for the king's arrival at Trianon.

The bodyguards dragged Damiens into the adjacent guardroom. Here, they strip-searched him, retrieved the weapon, and interrogated him. A senior minister, Machault, the Keeper of the Seals, hurriedly arrived. Disregarding the king's order in the panic of the moment, he had Damiens tortured there and then to probe the vital question of accomplices. Inside the guardroom bodyguards applied hot irons to the feet of their captive. But Damiens said nothing. After several hours he was transferred to the town jail, where sixty-four soldiers were felt necessary to guard him. Eventually he was sent to Paris for trial.

The next day Dufort de Cheverny saw the weapon resting on the mantelpiece in the king's official study. It was a penknife. Croÿ, who spoke to Damiens in his jail cell, judged him a madman who only meant to give the king a shock, not kill him. As it was winter, Louis was wearing a thick shirt and waistcoat, which had helped to parry the blow.

On this occasion old Landsmath rushed over from the Kennel and calmed the fears of the wounded king as he lay in his bedchamber. "Sire, tell all these weeping women to leave," he said, indicating the dauphine and the king's daughters. "I need to talk to you alone." He told the king that his wound was nothing. He bared his own chest, showing four or five large scars: "These are real wounds; I've had them for thirty years."

He then handed the king his chamber pot and told him "in the briefest way possible to make use of it." Louis obeyed him. "It's nothing. You can joke about it." But what if the blade had been dipped in poison? In the mid-eighteenth century this was a reasonable worry at Versailles. Tasters still tested each dish when the sovereigns ate publicly. Any sudden death of a prominent person routinely gave rise to rumors. Madame de Châteauroux, Louis XV's mistress, was widely believed to have died from handling papers impregnated with poison. Again, Landsmath reassured the king: poisoned blades were the stuff of old wives' tales; anyway, the king's thick clothes would have wiped it off. Reassured, the king "passed a very good night."

After a few days in bed, Louis made a full recovery, although an enduring gloom settled over the court for much of the year, with no more concerts in the queen's rooms or plays.[22] Things went less well for Damiens. Found guilty in Paris, he was condemned to drawing, quartering and burning at the stake in the main square of the capital. As in the way of these gruesome spectacles, a huge crowd turned out to watch his suffering.[23]

～

Afterward Louis could not resist teasing the duc d'Ayen: "You must allow, Monsieur, that I am well guarded!" When the remark reached the ears of the other officers, they nearly died of shame, as well they might. The bodyguards had failed in their first duty, protecting the king in his own palace.[24]

Before Louis XVI's cutbacks, this personal bodyguard of four hundred or so picked men formed the cream of the household troops. All these soldiers lent Versailles a decidedly military air, one that is hard to imagine today. When the monarch was in residence the routine sights and sounds of the palace included the dazzling uniforms of the bodyguards and the Hundred Swiss; the daily drums and fifes when the king went to mass; the salutes for passing royalty and princes; and the archaic cry of "Hhay hha Mier" (Hey I'm here) as the bodyguards of the Scots company—formed in the fifteenth century and originally composed of actual Scotsmen—locked up the Royal Court at night.[25] Each evening troops rolled out their camp beds in the guardrooms and state apartments, surrounding themselves with the screens that came into use after Queen Marie Leczinska once saw a guard asleep in "an immodest posture." Sometimes there were superb parades on the place d'Armes, when the mounted monarch presented a new commanding officer to the Swiss or French Guards formed up in a square.[26]

The guards imposed themselves on the townscape, too. The grandiose portals of former barracks survive on the rue Royale and the avenue de Paris, where the splendid sculpture of No. 6, the old quarters of the king's gendarmes, remains a delight to the eye. Most conspicuous of all in their day were the barracks, long since gone, on the south side of the place d'Armes which Louis XV erected on the cheap for the French Guards. Timber-built, the complex imitated a group of tents, right down to the striped ticking rendered in paint. This building was demolished in 1831, over forty years after the French Guards had left Versailles for good.[27]

The first Bourbon, Henri IV, fell to the assassin's knife. All too aware of recent family history, not to mention his personal memories of the civil war, Louis XIV was extremely security-conscious. In the Louvre he never passed from one apartment to another "without guards being placed in the corridors, on the stairs and in the communicating passages." One of the undoubted attractions of Versailles for Louis XIV was that he felt safer there than in his capital.[28]

The next two kings maintained some of this tight security. Whenever he walked in the gardens at Versailles, Louis XV was followed by twelve bodyguards and twelve Swiss. After the attack by Damiens, who was a former manservant, courtiers' lackeys were no longer allowed to enter the various royal guardrooms off the Queen's Staircase. From then on a row of guards completely surrounded the royal coach while the king climbed in.[29]

Louis XVI maintained this last usage. But in general "anything military was kept at a distance from the court" during his reign. In the name of economy Louis agreed to savage cuts to his brilliant retinue of household troops. Marie-Antoinette was of a like mind: "At last, no more red uniforms in the Hall of Mirrors," she is supposed to have said when the last of the gendarmes were disbanded in 1787.

As queen, Marie-Antoinette with her love of informality and privacy dispensed with the queen's traditional outdoor guard. She drove herself to the Petit Trianon, where she walked in the grounds on her own. In the formal gardens of Versailles her retinue remained minimal. In 1784, when Madame d'Oberkirch encountered her in the grove of Apollo, the queen was followed by just a footman.[30]

Chosen for their height and looks, the bodyguards, originating in the fifteenth century, were essentially ceremonial troops by this date. The captain-in-waiting, always from the highest nobility, served the king in full court dress, with only a black cane to signify his office. The bodyguards may have been an impressive sight, but in an age of professional soldiers, they were an anachronism. Well-mannered, proud, sure of their courage, but undisciplined and disdaining tactics, they resembled knights of the Round Table in the view of Saint-Priest, one of Louis XVI's ministers.

For all these reasons, royal guards made ideal ladies' men. There are numerous stories of smitten women at Versailles, like the marquise de La Suze, who had such a penchant for handsome Swiss officers that Louis XVI's courtiers nicknamed her "the Thirteen Cantons" (after the units that made up the federal state of Switzerland). Marie-Antoinette relied on guards officers as dancers and broke with tradition by admitting them to her balls, where they could be seen eating their supper with the very prince that they were supposed to guard. Bombelles, for one, disapproved of this contradiction of "all the sage principles which Louis XIV established for the guard of our kings." But it was typical of the more laissez-faire attitude to security under Louis XVI.[31]

The military household, what was left of it after cuts, was far from immune to the revolutionary ideas of 1789. The French Guards were the first to revolt. On July 14 their main garrison in Paris joined in the popular attack on the Bastille. Not long after, the detachment seconded to Versailles abandoned its traditional posts in the Ministers' Court, either of its own volition or because Louis XVI had no wish to be guarded by disloyal troops.

As the year wore on, the loyalty of even the bodyguards wavered. After the deputies of the Estates-General unilaterally turned themselves into a National Assembly on June 20, it was to this revolutionary body that the bodyguards took certain grievances. As Saint-Priest put it, they had joined everyone else, the king's footmen included, who "thought they had the right to attack the government and the ministers."[32]

It was on these troops that the royal family was obliged to rely for its personal safety on October 5, when women from Paris marched on Versailles to protest, yet again, the price of bread. This was after an extraordinary five months in French history during which the crown was stripped of most of its traditional powers. By October Louis was a constitutional monarch. But he still lived in an absolute monarch's palace.

The sparks that triggered the French Revolution lit an explosive mix of grievances and dreams. Somewhere in this combustible recipe was Versailles itself: as the symbol and working center of a political and social system that many French people now saw as anachronistic and corrupt, and as the residence of a group of individuals whom the public had come to regard as the personal embodiment of France's ills.

Louis XIV's Versailles had been an exercise, on a scale unparalleled in Europe before or since, in what now might be called royal "spin." But by 1789 the image projected by the palace was all wrong: in terms of presentation, Versailles had become a millstone around the monarchy's neck—so much had French attitudes evolved in the intervening century.

In the decade before the Revolution, Mercier captured the national pride still felt by many ordinary French people in the magnificence of the monarchy's principal seat. "A Parisian bourgeois says in all seriousness to an Englishman, 'What is your king? He is badly lodged: to be pitied, in fact. Look at ours. He lives at Versailles.' "[33]

But not all the French were so enthusiastic. A minority opinion going back to Saint-Simon had always been critical of the architecture of the palace. Voltaire added his weighty voice in 1748: the town façades were "in the poorest, the worst, taste."[34] But this image problem went far beyond aesthetics. Mercier was among those enlightened Frenchmen who saw in Versailles a symbol of royal tyranny in its huge cost, its regimenting of nature, and its ceaseless lauding of Louis XIV in paint and stone. A generation earlier, the marquis d'Argenson thought that the palace had signaled the arrival on French soil of "oriental regal extravagance." A king of France had followed the wrong ancient model: the opulent Darius of Persia, not the (supposedly) austere Alexander the Great.[35]

This negative stereotype of Versailles emerges in an incident witnessed by Madame Campan in July 1789, just after the fall of the Bastille. Three men walking on the terrace stopped beneath the state rooms. One of them shouted at the top of his voice: "Up there is the throne which is about to topple!" They were looking up at the windows of the Salon of Apollo, Louis XIV's throne room. They were unaware that the sovereign never used it for audiences with his French subjects—let alone that Louis XIV used to make a point of sitting informally on the steps of its dais during Apartment.[36]

The image of the despot, fair or not, in turn rubbed off on the court. Mercier was the latest in a long line when he poked fun at the courtiers of Versailles "so small before the sun": people who die of despair in the Bull's Eye when the usher fails to include them in the king's supper list, and who spend the better part of their lives standing in antechambers.[37]

This critique extended to what was seen, with justification, as the extravagance of the court. The reign of Louis XVI had ushered in hopes of reform just as public hostility to court expenditure was becoming more noticeable. The insistence of court grandees on the traditional perks at Louis XV's death attracted criticism. Only the then grand master of the wardrobe, the duc d'Estissac, won praise: entitled to Louis XV's apparel, he had nobly disdained these "profits of valets."[38] The Grand Stables in particular attracted public censure. In 1775 anonymous tracts accused the then grand equerry, the prince de Lambesc, of taking 120 of the king's horses for his personal use. Under Lambesc, numbers of personnel and horses rose inexorably. Did Louis XVI need two thousand horses when Louis XIV had managed with seven hundred?

Louis XVI and his ministers were well aware of these problems and tried, with limited success, to attack court expenditure. The king himself took on the comtesse de Brionne, Lambesc's mother. When she objected to proposed cuts in 1780, Louis brusquely interrupted her: "Madame, why are you interfering? This is none of your business."[39]

Critics also claimed that Versailles isolated the king from his people. After 1682, the French monarch showed himself far less frequently to his people, above all, the people of Paris. The Parisians saw so little of him that they came to believe, rightly or not, that the point of Versailles was to make their monarch invisible. Yet the capital was the proper residence of the king of France in the view of many French people.

The marquis d'Argenson, briefly one of Louis XV's ministers, believed that the relocation of the court away from the capital allowed courtiers to exercise too much influence on the king. "This ascendancy of the court has come about since there is a capital expressly for the court—Versailles." The Parisian writer Barbier had suspected as much in 1720, when the rumors of Louis XV's impending return to Versailles first started to circulate: "*They* will do what they like," he wrote, meaning the royal entourage. After Louis XVI was forcibly brought back to the capital on October 6, 1789, the patriotic playwright André Chénier used the Parisian stage to tell him that he should now rule of his own accord: "Be King of France, not Despot of Versailles."[40]

At Versailles the king and his ministers were relatively immune from popular expressions of discontent. If the monarch anticipated a frosty reception from his people, he could simply avoid Paris altogether, as Louis XV had taken to doing by 1750. Versailles could not see Paris, nor Paris, Versailles. By contrast, Madame de Pompadour's new house at nearby Bellevue, on the heights above the Sèvres bridge, commanded an exceptional view overlooking the Seine basin and Paris. In the days of her unpopularity, a distant crowd gathering on the plain of Grenelle below, in the vicinity of today's Eiffel Tower, was enough to intimidate her into canceling planned illuminations of the house in Louis XV's honor.[41]

Another consequence of the twelve short miles between Versailles and the capital was that Versailles was easily turned into a legend, and not necessarily one that flattered the monarchy. Visitors returned home to the provinces and made up stories about what they had seen. The most damaging were the Arabian Nights tales of extravagance, "credited without reservation by persons otherwise rational."[42]

By 1789 these fantasies swirled above all around Marie-Antoinette. Madame Campan tells the story of the provincial deputies to the Estates-General who all asked to see her country house, the Petit Trianon, widely rumored to contain a room studded with precious stones. Here, the kernel of truth seems to have been the use of diamonds, during Louis XV's reign, to decorate ballrooms and stage sets in the royal palaces, including Versailles.[43]

In 1789 the call for the king to return to his capital was in the air. The Third Estate of Paris had demanded as much in the written grievances that its elected deputies took to Versailles for the Estates-General. After the fall of the Bastille, the idea that the king would be more politically malleable if removed to Paris started to gain ground, at first among the political radicals, then more broadly among the Parisians.

This mood in Paris was fueled by the perception that Versailles had never been the rightful home of the monarchy in the first place. In mid-September a retired soldier was heard to say in public that at Versailles the king merely had a château, but in Paris he had a "Louvre," meaning a royal palace. He went on to say that the king should be brought back to Paris, and that he would willingly go and get him.[44]

For the opening of the Estates-General on May 5, the Entertainments Office put all the pageantry of the court of France on display to dazzle the assembled deputies. The show began with a magnificent procession from the older parish church of Notre Dame across the place d'Armes to the newer parish church of Saint-Louis, built by Louis XV to cater to the growing population of the Parc-aux-Cerfs quarter. The streets, as usual on these occasions, were hung with the tapestries of the crown.

The town was filled with the deputies of the Third Estate. As the month proceeded, Bombelles observed that these deputies were by no means as respectful of the king and his palace as Bombelles would have liked. Hostility to the court rose to the surface. Some deputies insulted the duchesse d'Uzès on the garden terrace. One evening in the new theater in the Gabriel wing, two deputies leapfrogged a barrier to sit themselves down uninvited in the large box reserved for the ministers. Yet others, spectators at the public supper of Louis and Marie-Antoinette on the warm evening of May 24, told the king to his face that he should find a better use for his money than paying for court spectacles.

The stately routines of the court continued regardless. On Whitsunday there was the usual chapter, procession, and service for the knights of the Holy Ghost. The ordeal of collecting in the chapel fell to the marquise de Maillé, admired by the courtiers for her "grand air and pretty figure."

In the first week of June the political temperature heated up. The progress of the Estates-General was frustrated by a lack of royal guidance. But the deputies of the Third Estate found the king inaccessible thanks to a family crisis: the dauphin was dying at Meudon. The mood of the Third Estate was somber: "His son is much less ill than the state," one of them said in public. In the early hours of the next day, the boy died.

The court now went into prolonged mourning. On June 7, standing against the balustrade in her state bedchamber, surrounded by a black-clad household, Marie-Antoinette struggled to keep her composure as the presented ladies filed past her to offer their condolences. In Paris the theaters closed: a political mistake in Dufort's view, since this would have been a good time to distract the people with "circuses"—a reference to the "bread and circuses" with which the Roman emperors allegedly sedated the urban plebs.[45]

Life at Versailles had resumed some of its ceremonial normality on June 11, when the annual procession of Corpus Christi day took place. As always, the king, the royal family, and the court traveled by coach to the parish church of Notre Dame. Here, they formed up to follow the Host under its *baldaquin* (canopy) back to the palace via the place d'Armes. In the Ministers' Court the procession snaked through the ranks of kneeling French and Swiss Guards, paused at the chapel, then returned to Notre Dame for the usual high mass.[46]

The Paris insurrection leading to the fall of the Bastille on July 14 took the court by surprise. It completely changed the mood at Versailles. The day after, the people invaded the palace forecourts. With no regal paraphernalia, indeed no escort except his two brothers, Louis had just been on foot to the National Assembly to assure its members of his benevolence and to announce the withdrawal of the extra troops who had been summoned to protect Versailles. These were camped out in the Orangery under the command of the maréchal de Broglie, whose preparations had given the palace and grounds the atmosphere of a military headquarters.[47]

Elated by this capitulation, the deputies escorted the king back to the palace. A huge crowd gathered, and it took Louis three hours to cross the place d'Armes and the forecourts. During this enforced "walkabout" the ordinary public approached him, not always affably. A woman asked if he really meant what he had just told the Assembly. Household troops were insulted: "Be off, valets of despotism. The king no longer needs your services."[48]

Sensing its power, the crowd demanded an appearance by the royal family on the balcony of Louis XIV's bedchamber. Marie-Antoinette knew better than to be seen with the new dauphin's governess, Gabrielle de Polignac, identified (like her mistress) with the reactionary party. Instead, she sent Madame Campan to fetch the boy, a "sad commission." Gabrielle, who saw all too clearly the implications, was reduced to tears.

Madame Campan then went down and mingled with the crowd. This action took courage, since the head tirewoman was a well-known member of Marie-Antoinette's entourage. She heard threats against the people's enemies: the queen, Gabrielle, Artois. A veiled woman grabbed her: "Tell your queen to let her husband and our good Estates-General get on with the job of making the people happy." A man whom she took for a market porter, his hat pulled down over his eyes, told her that the days of the people's deputies addressing the throne on bended knee were over. Later, Marie-Antoinette had Madame Campan repeat these details to the king.[49]

That evening all the royal family, the aunts included, met in agitated conclave in the queen's state bedroom: in hindsight, the last time they would be united. Hours later, hard on the heels of the departed troops, the comte d'Artois and the Polignacs left the palace for the frontier on the express orders of the sovereigns.[50]

With the several hundred persons comprising the various Artois households and the Polignac entourage gone, the palace had never felt emptier. When Marie-Antoinette sent for some friends, padlocks were found on their doors. Arriving at eleven one evening in late July, Saint-Priest found the buildings of the Ministers' Court plunged in darkness, as if the king were not in residence.[51]

In August the queen told Gabrielle by letter that she was learning perforce "to recognize those who are truly attached and those who are not." The palace was now divided politically. She and the king felt, and indeed were, watched by their own servants. The comtesse d'Escars, wife of the king's chief maître d'hôtel, feared for her safety in her husband's lodging on the town side of the south wing, since it was "well-known for aristocracy."[52]

Constitutional politics found a welcome on the other side of the palace. In their first-floor lodging on the garden side of the north wing, the governor of the palace, a member of the Noailles family, and his wife, the princesse de Poix, welcomed "patriot" deputies in their salon. In the attic lodging of the grand master of the wardrobe, over the king's state apartments, Arthur Young, a well-connected English traveler, heard talk hostile to Louis XVI that no one checked, least of all his host, the duc de La Rochefoucauld-Liancourt, a well-known liberal.[53]

This split echoed that of the town itself. The neighborhood of the markets was nicknamed the Patriots' Quarter because the concentration of working people made it a hotbed of extreme views. The residents on the south side of town, home to the ministries and many holders of court posts who lived in lodgings, were more moderate in their views. The radicals called this the Aristocrats' Quarter.[54]

It is sometimes said that the attack on the palace in the early hours of October 6 took Louis XVI by surprise. It is true that the royal family expected to winter at Versailles as usual. That summer, work began on Marie-Antoinette's ground-floor bathroom and on the apartment of the new governess who had replaced Gabrielle, Madame de Tourzel. The king ordered two stoves to combat the dreadful cold in the chapel.[55]

But the king and queen were well aware of the menace in the air. They no longer felt safe even inside their own palace. In recent years they had been used to supping together in the apartment of the comte and comtesse de Provence at the extremity of the south wing. Each prince or princess ate a meal cooked in their own kitchen and reheated in the countess's. The countess, struggling with alcoholism, offered a kind of "specialty of the house": a soup made from the wild birds caught with nets in the grounds of her country house at Montreuil, on the avenue de Paris.[56] From July, for safety's sake these reunions were switched to the queen's private rooms in the central block, near the guardrooms and the royal children lodged on the ground floor below.[57]

The Paris march on Versailles on October 5, a Monday, was prompted by the king's refusal to sanction pressing measures voted by the National Assembly, including the abolition of feudalism. To break this deadlock, the political operators in the Assembly at Versailles, working with the revolutionary government that had been running Paris since the fall of the Bastille, stirred up the working people of the capital and persuaded them to lose a day's pay to bring king and court back to Paris.[58]

The trigger was popular anger at a banquet given by the officers of the bodyguard in the palace opera the previous Thursday. These officers had a tradition of clubbing together to fête special occasions at Versailles. On October 1 they gave a fraternal banquet, according to military custom, to the officers of the newly arrived Flanders regiment, summoned to Versailles to replace the defected French Guards.

The king had given permission for the use of the opera. The diners sat at a horseshoe-shaped table on the stage, a military band played in the pit, and courtiers filled the boxes to watch. Sitting in one of them, Madame Campan professed to be "astonished" when the royals made their appearance. But the fact that they had brought with them the new dauphin, the king's younger son, points to a calculated act by Louis and Marie-Antoinette to inspire the officers with loyalty to the dynasty.

By this time the wine had already overexcited the officers and prompted ill-considered talk. Marie-Antoinette, with a mother's natural misgivings, allowed a Swiss officer to carry off the little dauphin and present him to the diners. In the queen's honor, the band struck up an air by her favorite composer, Grétry. The men joined in, singing, "O Richard, oh my king / The universe abandons you."

There may have been no trampling of the tricolor cockade, the symbol of the Revolution, as was afterward claimed. But the men escorted the king and the royal family back to their apartments and danced under the royal windows. A soldier from the Flanders regiment even scaled the balcony of Louis XVI's bedroom to shout, "Long live the king!" In the charged atmosphere since the fall of the Bastille, the whole occasion reeked of political incorrectness. In Paris the next day, popular opinion condemned the banquet as an orgy.[59]

Four days later, about six or seven thousand women, respectable citizens as well as the howling fishwives of legend, set out for Versailles. Several hours behind them followed the new National Guard, a Parisian militia formed after the fall of the Bastille. Numbering well over twenty thousand, this force was led by an aristocratic liberal, the marquis de La Fayette, whose wife was a Noailles.

When news of the approaching women reached Versailles in the afternoon, the royal bodyguards closed the gates of the forecourts. A messenger brought the king back from the hunt in the woods of Meudon.

Another warned the queen, finding her, according to Madame Campan, sitting alone in her grotto at Trianon "given over to sorrowful reflections." Another tradition places her, "almost alone," in the palace at this moment of crisis.[60]

Inside the palace, the royal family could not decide whether to stay or leave. The many factors that Louis had to weigh included the "incalculable misfortunes" that could befall the abandoned palace.[61] When he finally did decide to leave, mid-evening, the crowd would not allow the carriages to reach the palace.[62]

The crowd had bivouacked under rainy skies on the place d'Armes. Some had found the carcass of a horse and roasted the flesh around a fire. Between ten and midnight the Paris National Guard under La Fayette arrived. This force included former French Guards, the same who had defected en masse after the fall of the Bastille. La Fayette had agreed to try to secure the return of their old posts guarding the outside of the palace. Louis XVI fatefully consented, and the guard of the Ministers' Court was transferred from the bodyguards to troops of dubious loyalty.

Traditionally the posts of the French Guards, responsible for the southern half of the Ministers' Court, included, as well as several in the gardens, the gate from that court into the Princes' Court, the small courtyard between the south wing and the Old Wing. The French Guards had long been in the habit of leaving this gate open, to save the trouble of locking and unlocking it for each new patrol. This laxity, strange though it may seem to us, was typical of the easygoing attitudes to security at Louis XVI's Versailles. That night was no different: the gate was left open as of old; so, for the same reason, was the nearby gate from the rue de la Surintendance into the Ministers' Court. This last gate allowed the patrols, by means of the street running between the Grand Commons and the south ministers' wing—today's rue Pierre de Nolhac—to pass easily between their posts in the palace and grounds and their barracks on the south side of the place d'Armes.

Around daybreak, when it was light enough for these unguarded posts to be visible, a group of three or four hundred women, along with men dressed as women, launched an organized attack on the palace.

They seem to have gained access to the Ministers' Court through the open gate from the rue de la Surintendance. The French Guards did nothing to hinder them; nor, it seems, did the Swiss Guards who had the watch of the northern half of the Ministers' Court, where the Royal Court was vulnerable at its weak point, the temporary palisade of 1771. Some of the band entered the Princes' Court by its open gate, then reached the Royal Court by means of the passage inside the terminal colonnade of the Old Wing. The bodyguards on duty at the locked gates to the Royal Court found themselves outflanked.[63]

Jérôme L'héritier, a seventeen-year-old cabinetmaker in the vanguard, fell on the Marble Court, breaking his head open. He had probably slipped on the marble, wet from the previous night's rain. The crowd believed that he had been shot by the bodyguards. In fact, this was unlikely. The evening before Louis XVI, ever pacific, had relayed express orders to the bodyguards not to fire, not to beat anyone, and not even to defend themselves. Hézecques recalled that the bodyguards inside the palace that night had even unloaded their firearms. They were armed only with swords.[64]

The angered crowd attacked the bodyguards in the Royal Court. One was finished off by a fellow who rested his foot on the guard's chest before beheading him with a hatchet. His killers rubbed the blood of their second victim, the twenty-nine-year-old Rouph de Varicourt, on their arms and face, like war paint.

Led by people who knew their way around this most accessible of palaces, the crowd surged up the Queen's Staircase. Two soldiers from the Hundred Swiss were beaten back. Some bodyguards made a stand on the top landing, but took refuge when an advancing figure announced that he had come for the king's heart and the queen's entrails.

At this point the crowd was mainly interested in the queen. From the top landing they followed the retreating bodyguards into the queen's guardroom and the antechamber beyond, breaking down the doors. Half-dressed, Marie-Antoinette fled with her two women by the door of her bedroom alcove to seek refuge with the king. Madame Auguié, the head tirewoman in service that evening, gave her account of what happened to her sister, Madame Campan. Her version refutes the claim of other accounts that the assailants entered the queen's bedroom, trashing the furnishings and driving blades into the queen's sheets. As Campan points out, had they got this far, the bodyguards admitted by her sister minutes earlier would never have survived, which they did.[65]

Marie-Antoinette was frightened. With assailants in the Marble Court below, she did not use the king's passage, which also gave access to her rooms on the ground floor: an obvious target, she may have thought, for a mob intent on harming her. Opting for the most direct route, she headed for the Bull's Eye, presumably in the full knowledge that her back door had been locked or bolted from the other side since 1779. A furious banging ensued until a servant in the Bull's Eye heard and opened up. A terrified Marie-Antoinette was in floods of tears: "My friends, my friends, save me!"[66]

According to one tradition, Axel de Fersen was in the palace that night tête-à-tête with the queen, either in the bedchamber or one of the private rooms behind the alcove, escaping the invaders by jumping out a window. After Waterloo, Napoleon told this story to his companions in captivity on Saint Helena. He in turn had learned it in conversation with Madame Campan, who survived the Revolution and went on to open a girl's school, where she taught the emperor's stepdaughter. In her memoirs, published under the Bourbon restoration, when Louis XVI and Marie-Antoinette were revered by royalists as martyrs, Madame Campan was extremely discreet in her references to Fersen.[67]

The king too was the target of the night's violence. Those who had searched in vain for the queen joined in the attack on the sovereign's guardroom, forcing its door. Inside, the bodyguards fell back on the Bull's Eye, barricading themselves in with the royal furniture. Had they known the way, the attackers could have mounted a two-pronged assault on the king's rooms, since his private staircase on the north side of the Royal Court, leading straight to his bedroom, was undefended at this moment.[68]

Salvation was at hand in the person of La Fayette, who arrived from his lodgings in the Hôtel de Noailles, the town house of his wife's family. He sent in the National Guard. The former French Guards, at last come to do their duty, pushed the attackers back down into the courtyards at bayonet point. After an anxious half hour listening from the

Bull's Eye, the bodyguards opened up to their rescuers. Order was now reestablished in the palace.

As the crowds and the National Guard filled the forecourts, the royal family regrouped in Louis XVI's bedchamber and exchanged stories. At the far end of the south wing the comte and comtesse de Provence had slept through the whole alarm. Not so in the ground-floor rooms beneath the state apartments belonging to the king's aunts. Here Madame Adélaïde, who was popularly believed to be giving the king bad advice, had been found by her lady-in-waiting sitting in a shuttered room in the broad daylight. According to Madame de Boigne, every one of her windows had been broken by missiles.[69]

The shout now went up, "The king to the balcony!" The king, queen, and their immediate entourage made several appearances before the crowd from Louis XIV's bedchamber. Then the crowd called for the queen on her own, without children. Bravely she obeyed, hands crossed on her breast, dropping a gracious curtsy and provoking the unexpected cry of "Long live the queen!" Next came the cry "To Paris!" A reluctant Louis XVI at last accepted the inevitable. In a final appearance on the balcony to announce his departure he addressed the crowd with sufficient authority and majesty to alarm one of the ringleaders, who saw too many onlookers "stupefied" by the royal words.[70]

Sometime during this eventful morning Mercy, the Austrian ambassador, had arrived from Paris for the usual Tuesday audience. Clearly uncertain what to expect, he took the precaution of entering the palace inconspicuously from the extremity of the north wing, using the covered passages, now destroyed, that once linked an entrance in the park to Gabriel's opera house. Traversing the first-floor gallery, he arrived in the state apartments, now patrolled by National Guardsmen. Sensing that something was seriously wrong, he turned back, afraid of being recognized as one of the queen's close advisers.[71]

Meanwhile, the royal family was doing some hasty packing. The procession that set off around two in the afternoon was like a parody of the old "voyages" of the court to Fontainebleau or Compiègne. This time the bodyguards were present in the grisly form of two severed heads held aloft on pikes. The royal carriage was followed by more than two thousand vehicles carrying the court, the ministers, deputies, sacks of flour, and royal belongings, the king fearing the pillage of the palace in his absence.[72]

By leaving quietly, Louis saved his palace. There was some minor harm to doors and locks. Perhaps it was at this time that the damage was done to the fine mahogany chairs in the princesse de Lamballe's rooms on the ground floor of the south wing. But the interior was essentially unscathed. While the Revolution unfolded around him in Paris, Louis continued to worry about his ancestral home. From the Tuileries, he gave his last order for works at Versailles in November of that same year: an iron grille to bar the approach to his private staircase.[73]

In the seventeenth century, collections of rare or savage animals were a prestigious feature of a royal residence, not least as a symbolic means of expressing royal dominion over nature. One of the young Louis XIV's first additions to his father's château at Versailles had been a *ménagerie,* or zoo. Commissioned from the architect Le Vau, the complex included a chapel, a grotto fitted out with pretty rooms for visiting royalty, a dairy, and a fan-shaped arrangement of seven pens for the animals. A favorite retreat of the duchess of Burgundy, Louis XIV's granddaughter-in-law, it went out of fashion in the eighteenth century, but was kept stocked for sightseers: in 1750 residents included two tigers, two or three lions, and a camel. The site now forms part of a walled farmhouse and is mostly demolished, apart from two patched-up pavilions that once formed part of the duchess's dairy.[74]

After the events of October 1789, and even more so after the failed attempt of the sovereigns to escape from Paris in the summer of 1791, the invective of the revolutionaries reached a boiling point. Now it was the turn of the royal family, imprisoned in the Tuileries, to be lampooned as a costly zoo. "The public has inspected the ferocious beasts in their respective cages in the park at Versailles; they can watch more comfortably and without going to much trouble, a number of quadrupeds gathered at the Louvre. We will list the most remarkable of these ferocious beasts." Descriptions then follow of each royal "animal."[75]

In August 1792 the revolutionaries attacked the Tuileries and imprisoned the royal family in the medieval fortress of the Temple. After declaring a republic, they put, first Louis, then Marie-Antoinette, on trial. Both were beheaded. When they finally came for the contents of the palace in August 1793, the revolutionaries arrived as the new rulers of France, with a full set of keys.

# II.

# *After the Deluge*

AFTER THE royal family left for Paris on October 6, 1789, the Royal Buildings Office kept Versailles in readiness for a brightening of the political skies. In January 1791, ten commissioners were sent to Versailles to report on the state of the palace. In the state rooms the furnishings had been removed, but mirrors, tapestries, and paintings were still in place. In the queen's private rooms the paintwork and gilding were fresh; later that year they would be renewed again.

After the fall of the Tuileries on August 10, 1792, the municipal authorities of Versailles placed seals on the palace to prevent any unauthorized entry and to protect its remaining contents. Following the abolition of the monarchy, the revolutionaries were initially unsure what to do with what was now a huge white elephant. Then, in 1793, the republican government undertook to maintain all the old royal palaces at state expense. This decision staved off the real threat that Versailles might be demolished for its building materials, as later happened to Marly.

Even so, the Republic sold off parts of the royal domain, including the Grand Canal, which was drained and made over to pasture, and the Petit Trianon, which a lemonade maker turned into an inn. All the palace railings were torn up for scrap metal. Teams of craftsmen were sent in to efface the royal insignia from the royal apartments and the chapel. A plan to install a national library in the former palace, followed by one for a fine-arts museum, prompted the first alterations to the royal apartments in the central block: on the ground floor, certain entresols, partitions, chimneypieces, and mirrors were removed.[1]

At war with Austria and England, the fledgling French republic was badly in need of funds. In August 1793, "in the presence of the representatives of the people," a series of sales began at Versailles in the former rooms of the princesse de Lamballe, gruesomely massacred in Paris the previous September. The printed announcement sought to tempt the public by appealing to the homemaker, not the collector:

*Many furnishings, such as damask and silk sheets; horsehair mattresses; cushions; feather-beds, covers; curtains of different fabrics; chests of drawers, secrétaires, desks and tables of different woods with upper parts of marble; settees, armchairs, chairs and bergères upholstered in damask, Utrecht velvet, moquette and tapestry; firedogs; candelabra; porcelain; faience; mirrors and other objects.*[2]

These sales dispersed the great bulk of the contents of the palace, including superb royal furniture auctioned at knockdown prices. The demand in France for royal memorabilia being at rock bottom, many of these objects found their way into the castles of Germany and the stately homes of England, helped by the waiving of export taxes by the Republic.

After crowning himself emperor of the French, Napoleon incorporated Versailles into the imperial domain and toyed with the idea of establishing his grandiose court in the old royal palace. He patched up the dilapidated fabric, leaving his insignia on the garden façade, where it can still be seen. He restored the Petit Trianon, which became a favorite residence of his second empress, Marie-Antoinette's Habsburg great-niece. More alterations ate away at the old topography of the royal palace. One loss from these years was a hub of the old court: Louis XIV's much adapted Comedy Room. This was now demolished and the space restored as an open passageway into the gardens.

Napoleon also revived the Grand Project of Louis XV and Louis XVI. He had architects draw up new plans for a spectacular remodeling of the Paris façades. He planned to refurbish the central block in the Empire style. New hangings were commissioned from the silk workers at Lyon. But work had scarcely begun when Napoleon was ousted from power in 1814.

Louis XVIII, the former comte de Provence, now returned to France as a constitutional monarch. With more reason than Napoleon, he too contemplated installing himself at Versailles, where he had been born and lived until 1789. In the end, lack of funds and politics got in the way: Versailles had too many absolutist associations. But Louis XVIII had not forgotten his grandfather's Grand Project. To match Gabriel's wing, he demolished the terminal pavilion of the so-called Old Wing opposite and rebuilt it in the same ponderous classical style.

Versailles on the whole still remained much as Louis XVI had left it. The radical change came after 1830, when Louis-Philippe, head of the Orléans line of the royal family, made himself king of the French by a kind of coup against his cousins of the senior branch. To promote his rule as legitimate, he turned Versailles into a patriotic museum. The aim was to create a symbol of unity that would bring together a politically fractured France in the memory of national glories.

He conceived these glories chiefly in terms of feats of arms. This allowed him to accommodate the overpowering memory of Napoleon and to include his own military career as a young man, when he fought with distinction in the Revolutionary army. Rooms were renamed to reflect their martial displays: the Marshals' Room, the Admirals' Room, the Room of the Crusades. . . .

The centerpiece of the museum was a Gallery of Battles, which can still be visited. Here, vast canvases commissioned from contemporary painters depict the triumphs of French arms from early medieval times up to and including Napoleon. To appease the royalists, victories still within living memory from the reigns of Louis XV and Louis XVI—such as the siege of Yorktown—were included. At the far end of the gallery comes the climax as the viewer steps into a room created out of the lodgings once occupied by the royal governess. Here, a series of paintings depicts the tumultuous scenes in Paris that had "called" Louis-Philippe to the throne in 1830.

When the new museum opened to great fanfare in 1837, the few visitors old enough to remember the old Versailles found it more or less totally transformed. The two great wings had been gutted of their former apartments and turned into display areas. Where once there had been two floors of lodgings, including those of the comte d'Artois with their little Turkish rooms, the south wing now housed the Gallery of Battles. Old staircases like the Princes' Staircase had been altered out of all recognition or suppressed altogether, and new ones built. Of the state apartments, only the Hall of Mirrors and its flanking salons of War and Peace survived intact. Other rooms were given modern paneling into which rows of historical paintings of uniform size were fitted.

The Salon of Apollo was deprived of its superb chimneypiece, made of a rare marble described by Félibien as "green, brown and red with spots and veins of emerald green."[3] In the Gabriel wing, the last vestiges of Marie-Antoinette's wooden theater vanished. The aspect of the galleries in the wings was transformed by blocking up the doors and windows of the old princely apartments and by installing floor-length windows in the previously open-air arcades. In what used to be Marie-Antoinette's private domain, attic rooms were demolished. The floor of her second-floor billiard room was raised by three feet. Shorn by Louis-Philippe of their stairway, her entresols can now be seen only from a ladder.[4]

With the collapse of his regime in 1848, Louis-Philippe's museum fell out of fashion. Half a century later, as nostalgia for the former royal palace became a permissible sentiment in France, the king's drastic conversion of Versailles was condemned as the work of a barbarian. But in the 1830s few French people could have cared much about, say, the former bedchamber of the decapitated queen. The rococo Louis XV style, in which many of the private apartments were decorated, was regarded at the time as "gothic."

Louis-Philippe had many old canvases enlarged or reduced to fit into their uniform frames. His ancestor Louis XIV did the same when he ordered works by Italian masters to be "enlarged as required" for the Bull's Eye antechamber.[5] Louis-Philippe had saved the fabric and given it a contemporary purpose. In hindsight, this is his great and lasting achievement at Versailles.

In 1870 the Second Empire of Napoleon III declared war on Prussia. This error of military judgment by Napoleon's nephew cost him his throne and triggered an invasion of France by the Prussians later in the same year. While the Prussian army besieged the capital, the Prussian king and his chancellor, Bismarck, made their headquarters at Versailles. In the Hall of Mirrors, beneath Le Brun's painting of Louis XIV crossing the Rhine in triumph, Wilhelm I was enthroned as emperor of Germany.

The enduring taste of this bitter pill helps to explain why, in 1919, the French government proposed to their victorious allies that the defeated Germans should be brought back to the Hall of Mirrors to sign the peace that closed the First World War. On a Louis XV desk in the center of the gallery, the tearful German delegates placed their signatures on the treaty that humiliated their country and paved the way for the Second World War two decades later.[6]

In 1872, after the victorious Prussians, newly incorporated in the German Empire, had withdrawn, France's provisional government emerged from its exile at Tours and installed itself at Versailles in a national atmosphere of political turmoil. In the capital working Parisians were in open revolt, stung in part by the humiliation of the peace terms. The French army was sent in to quell them, with much bloodshed.

At Versailles the provisional organs of government took up residence in Louis-Philippe's museum. Here, the political action centered on the improvised meeting place of the National Assembly in Gabriel's opera house. Stenciled signs from this era can still be made out on the stonework of the two wings. When members finally agreed on a constitution for France in 1876, they decided on a new second chamber. This would need its own auditorium. A site was chosen in the middle of the south wing, where Mansart's Commons Staircase, demolished by Louis-Philippe, had once stood.

In 1879 the politicians of the Third Republic steeled themselves and returned to Paris, leaving a lasting legacy at Versailles. On rare occasions France's two chambers still meet jointly in the south wing, where they debate beneath a vast painting depicting the opening of the Estates-General in 1789. Six parliamentary officials, the quaestors, continue to enjoy "grace-and-favor" lodgings in the palace, to the irritation of the museum service, pressed for space.[7]

For some French people, the capitulation of France to the new Germany in 1870 marked "the end of the greatness of France."[8] After this defeat France's mood swung away from militarism as a basis for national identity. People were ready to look back nostalgically on a golden age when Louis XIV's France enjoyed a dominance in Europe based not just on French arms but also French culture. Versailles was the crowning symbol of this triumphant moment in French history.

In the museum a young curator called Pierre de Nolhac caught the changing atmosphere. Today few visitors to Versailles have heard of him—he is largely forgotten even by the French. But it was thanks to his perseverance as conservator between 1892 and 1919 that today's Versailles is no longer a paean to old French battles but a restored version of the royal palace. The erudite Nolhac was the first scholar to reconstruct the history of Versailles from the papers of those who built, altered, and maintained the royal palace. Formidably knowledgeable about the place and its onetime residents, he was said to keep the truth about Marie-Antoinette's alleged adultery in a drawer of his desk.[9]

Nolhac's task was never easy. In his youth the French had completely forgotten about the artists who created the Versailles of Louis XIV. Nolhac also had to deal with the ambivalence of France's politicians and ordinary citizens regarding the memory of the ousted monarchy. He once overheard a schoolmaster brusquely remind his charges that the lovely sculptures in the park came from "the sweat of the people."[10]

Since Nolhac retired after the First World War, the palace has undergone an astonishing rebirth under a succession of conservators who have continued to develop his version of a restored Versailles. Buffed and spruced, today's Versailles bears witness to how official French attitudes to the monarchy have turned full circle since the Revolution. With massive state funding, its curators aim to re-create the palace as it looked on the eve of Louis XVI's final departure. The restoration of Marie-Antoinette's bedchamber to its appearance on the last night that she slept there is a monument to this endeavor.

In 1978, three years after the restored bedchamber was reopened to the public, Breton separatists let off a bomb in the palace. No serious damage was done. But the French reaction is revealing. The mayor of Versailles described the attack as a "profanation"—strong language, the same as was used under Louis XVI by an usher admonishing a disre-spectful courtier: "Monsieur, you are profaning the king's bedroom." Versailles has once again become a place of cult.[11]

For the world at large, the legacy of Versailles can be summed up in three mythic figures. One is the generic French aristocrat, embodiment of the decadence that a revolution was needed to lance. He was im-mortalized by Charles Dickens in the foppish Monseigneur of *A Tale of Two Cities,* "one of the great lords in power at the Court," who "could swallow a great many things with ease, and was by some few sullen minds supposed to be rather rapidly swallowing France."[12]

Fascination with Marie-Antoinette hinges on the complex feelings of empathy that her life arouses, especially among women. Napoleon III's empress, Eugénie, was convinced (wrongly) that she was heading for a fate similar to Louis XVI's queen. She was a devotee, holding the first Marie-Antoinette retrospective at Petit Trianon in 1867.[13] The empress was ahead of her time in France, where the rehabilitation of the queen's memory among a republican citizenry could be claimed as "something quite new" in 1955.[14]

Not so in England, where rich nineteenth-century collectors like Ferdinand de Rothschild and Lord Hertford had been swooping on the fine furniture that once adorned her apartments at Versailles. In Eng-land the emotional charge from her memory is best captured, not by films or documentaries or biographies, but by a curious little book called *An Adventure.* This is an account by two spinster academics from Oxford of their sighting of the queen's ghost at Trianon on August 10, 1901: a lady in an old-fashioned dress and "a shady white hat," sitting on the lawn as if sketching on an afternoon of "unnatural stillness and oppressiveness."[15]

Ever since *An Adventure* was published, attempts have been made to come up with a solution to the mysterious events it describes. The sin-cerity of Annie Moberly and Eleanor Jourdain, the authors, seems be-yond doubt. There are those who, peppering their discussion with words like *cryptethesia* and *metavigil,* wish to argue for an unusual form of paranormal experience.[16] In the era of gender studies, others have seen a tale of suppressed sexuality: almost unknown to themselves, the authors are said to have made "wishful use of a supernatural third party to triangulate, and therefore legitimate, their lesbian relationship."[17]

The prudent may wish to keep open minds. Even a member of the professional staff attached to the museum of Versailles has found himself "in the presence of phenomena which I have not been able to explain to myself" while working inside the palace. The words are those of Henri Racinais, whose scholarly account of the private domain of Louis XV and Louis XVI was published in 1950.[18]

The third figure is Louis XIV himself. For the French, the Sun King is a monarch in whom they can, and do, take great historical pride. In other parts of Europe, he is remembered as the "neighbor from hell." To stand under the painted ceiling of the William and Mary refectory at Greenwich Hospital, celebrating English triumphs over Louis, or in the Grand Place of Brussels, which the local burghers rebuilt after it was reduced to rubble by Louis' artillerymen, is to be reminded that the creator of Versailles was also a hated enemy. As for his style of monarchy, after the Revolution there have been few who still admire it. One exception was the crackpot Ludwig II of Bavaria. His political tribute to his hero was the replica of Versailles, which he began to build in 1878 at Herrenchiemsee, a lake at the foot of the Alps.

Today Louis captures the popular imagination above all for Versailles itself. Thanks to his palace he has joined the pharaohs and other rulers in history whose monuments give off an imposing aura of riches and power. In the seventeenth century, French people saw magnificence as a particularly suitable attribute for the king of France.[19] Those who believe in national characteristics can point to the French government's enduring fondness for architectural statements like the Centre Pompidou or the "great university" on the plateau of Saclay, west of Paris, contemplated by French president Nicolas Sarkozy in 2007.[20]

An enduring image of opulence explains the attraction of Versailles as a marketing tool. Its gardens are used for photographic shoots with glamorous models by the Paris designer Karl Lagerfeld. The interior is a venue for private functions, like the sumptuous wedding feast thrown by an Indian steel tycoon, Lakshmi Mittal, in 2004.[21] The palace where Louis XIV once sought to dazzle the envoys of Asia is now available for hire as an international luxury brand.

Nowhere is the appeal of Versailles stronger than across the Atlantic. It may seem contradictory that the Land of the Free should feel close ties with Versailles, the former seat of an absolute monarchy. American feelings for Versailles are rooted historically in the support that Louis XVI gave to the rebels in the American War of Independence. French warships helped to win the decisive victory at Yorktown.

In 1783 all the belligerents signed an armistice at Versailles, followed by a peace treaty between the English and the newly emerged United States, signed in Paris. The French government, from Louis XVI himself to the staff at the ministry of foreign affairs, was deeply involved in these negotiations. Louis was so pleased with the outcome that he had the silk curtains on the doors of his new council room at Compiègne decorated with scenes from the engagements at "Yorcktonn," "Brimstomhill," and "Pensacola."[22] A century and a half later the townsfolk of Versailles commemorated France's brokering role in this momentous peace by changing the name of the street on which the former ministry of foreign affairs—now the municipal library—still stands from rue de la Surintendance to rue de l'Indépendance américaine.

By this date, 1935, local feelings for the United States had been warmed further by an astonishingly generous gift from the American magnate John D. Rockefeller Jr. Between 1923 and 1932 the son of the founder of Standard Oil gave millions of petrodollars to France to use in repairing three great national monuments: the cathedral at Rheims and the palaces at Fontainebleau and Versailles. A massive program of works set out to repair the years of neglect experienced during the First World War. The roof, the masonry, and the exterior woodwork of the main palace could all be renewed. It is no exaggeration to say that American money saved Versailles.[23]

~

In 1789 as in 1715, the departure of the court for Paris had a devastating effect on the town of Versailles. It lost half its population as well as its old identity as a court city. This past era remained just a memory embodied by impoverished old retainers and aristocrats who managed to lie low, as Madame d'Angivilliers did. She adroitly gave the local revolutionaries a bust of their hero, Marat; later she placed an image of Napoleon on her mantelpiece. At the height of the Revolution, Versailles was a dangerous place for royalist sympathizers. In September 1792 a revolutionary mob massacred forty-four prisoners at the foot of the steps of the Orangery, including the last grand baker of France, the duc de Brissac.

Under the kings, Versailles had been the responsibility of the palace governor. The townsfolk had no corporate identity of their own and no real means of representing their collective interests. Symptomatic of this subordinate status was the physical division of the town. Its two main quarters, Saint-Louis to the south and Notre Dame to the north, were kept apart by the trio of royal avenues fanning out from the place d'Armes and by the annexes of the palace that filled the spaces between them. It was only in the early nineteenth century that a new transverse axis—today's avenue du Général de Gaulle is based on it—allowed traffic to pass directly from one side of town to the other.

This new thoroughfare expressed the growing confidence of nineteenth-century Versailles, a town that had become the head of one of the *départements,* the new units of administration into which the revolutionaries had divided France in 1790. Its mayors raised public buildings to express this new identity, if necessary at the expense of the old royal palace. In 1867 Mansart's moribund Kennel complex made way for the Prefecture. Opposite rose the Palais de Justice, on the site of the grand huntsman's residence.

The inhabitants of nineteenth-century Versailles did not forget that their town was the cradle of the French Revolution. In the 1870s the provisional government in the palace debated France's constitution. For a brief moment a restoration of the monarchy seemed possible in the person of Louis XVI's great-nephew, the comte de Chambord. But the town electorate remained staunchly republican.[24]

Despite being home to the former royal palace and benefiting economically from the crowds that came to enjoy the gardens, if not Louis-Philippe's neglected museum, the then mayor approved a new town hall that seems deliberately to defy the old royal regulations limiting the height of buildings in the town. This enormous and exaggeratedly tall building in Renaissance style, inaugurated in 1900, occupies an elevated site on the avenue de Paris, well within sight of the windows of the palace. Over its three portals the words LIBERTÉ, FRATERNITÉ, ÉGALITÉ blaze out in large gilt letters as if throwing a gauntlet toward the old royal residence.

To build this municipal pile, another building by Mansart was demolished. This was the official residence of the grand master of the royal household. It was probably here, rather than in the palace, that the grand master's "table of honor" offered hospitality at royal expense to a select group of twelve diners.[25] All that survives of its splendor is some old paneling, redeployed in the new town hall, and the faded fleurs-de-lys still just about visible in the stonework of the railings on the avenue du Général de Gaulle.

No sooner had royalty abandoned the palace than the Romantics discovered it. As early as 1796 a visitor of Swiss origin, Charles de Constant, had this to say:

> *The taste and elegance of the [king's] Small Apartments are perfect; there one still breathes a perfumed air recalling the voluptuousness and ambrosia enjoyed there in former days. But the silence and the solitude of this place, the sad and gloomy air of its guardians, the contrast between the sights of yesterday and those of today, impose on the soul a sadness, an inescapable melancholy. I believed myself surrounded by shadows.*[26]

In the nineteenth century, French writers saw Versailles as a ghost town. Shorn of its purpose, the former royal palace was compared with Venice, another onetime center of power now "tottering under the weight of its cloak of sculpture."[27]

Today this air of melancholy is hard to recapture in the burnished palace, especially amid the forty thousand or so daily visitors at peak times. It is only in the byways of Louis XIV's Versailles that the old sense of decay sometimes still lingers. Mansart's Grand Commons has always dominated the southern part of the palace complex since its completion in 1684. In 1832 the building was deemed suitable for conversion into a military hospital, which it remained for well over 150 years. Only after 1995 were patients and medical staff finally moved out of their seventeenth-century premises.

For a few years around the turn of the millennium the emptied building stood in limbo. Window glass unchanged since the time of Louis XIV looked out onto a neglected courtyard in which weeds sprouted. On the ground floor, vaulted ceilings and huge chimney breasts betrayed a time when these rooms, long before they became hospital wards, were royal kitchens. But from 2007 it has been "all change" at the Grand Commons too: the building is to be restored and used by the museums service of Versailles. The archaeologists moved in first, uncovering traces of the forgotten village of Versailles, which Louis XIV's palace had obliterated.

What of the future? In 1771 the Parisian Jean-Sébastien Mercier, burning with dislike of aristocrats and the court, imagined a French paradise set in the year 2440, by which time Versailles would have been reduced to rubble. The young writer saw the ruins of Versailles as a lesson "to all sovereigns that those who abuse a momentary hold on power only reveal their weaknesses to the generations which follow."[28] As with many French people of his generation, politics blinded Mercier to the claims of Versailles as a monument to France's culture.

Nowadays Versailles faces the threat of global warming. In 1999 a terrible storm battered the park. One fatality was a mighty beech tree planted by Marie-Antoinette over two centuries earlier in her garden at the Petit Trianon. Elsewhere in the park, new trees were planted to replace the casualties. But a succession of freakishly dry summers has left many saplings withered. While gardeners wrestle with these problems, Versailles is once again a place of cult, and cult buildings, lovingly tended, can last for centuries. Mercier may yet be proved wrong.

One rainy evening in September 2007 a hundred or so devotees of this cult gathered for a private view at Versailles.[29] The occasion was an exhibition of original treasures sold off during the Revolution and returned to the palace over the previous century, from musical instruments—a pair of drums with their original painted inscription, KING'S CHAPEL—to the chest of drawers from Louis XVI's first-floor library. Seized by the Nazis from the Rothschilds of Vienna, this masterpiece of marble, gilt bronze, and rare woods had been returned to the Rothschild heirs in 1998. It was bought the following year for Versailles thanks mainly to a generous French benefactress.

Guests filed slowly past the exhibits laid out in the cramped spaces of the Small Apartments. They were overwhelmingly French, of all ages, a father with his daughter, young couples; some came from Paris, others were local. They included professionals still carrying their brief-cases, chic women, men in suits, one or two people in jeans. A husband and wife debated the technical term for a particular form of royal chair with an elbow pad on the top of its back; a middle-aged Frenchwoman nodded in recognition of an engraving of wedding celebrations for Louis XV's son. Others talked animatedly with their backs to the objects in the best tradition of an opening-night crowd.

Prosperous, knowledgeable about Versailles, these guests somehow divined too that champagne was on offer a short walk across the Marble Court in the vestibule beneath the Hall of Mirrors. They clearly felt at home in the palace. In a way, nothing could convey better than this soirée the legacy of 1789. Excluded from these rooms in the days of the monarchy, the French bourgeoisie has now made Versailles its own.

# NOTES

PREFACE

1. Verlet, *Le château de Versailles,* 675.

I. BUILDERS OF THE LABYRINTH

1. Hézecques, *Souvenirs,* 145.

2. H. G., "Notes d'un voyageur anglais à Versailles en 1838," *Revue de l'histoire de Versailles et Seine-et-Oise* 25–26 (1923–1924), 372–75.

3. Le Guillou, "Le château neuf," 163, citing E. Soulié, *Notice du Musée Impérial de Versailles* (1859).

4. Le Guillou, "Les châteaux de Louis XIII," 167 n. 21.

5. *Mercure galant,* cited by Tiberghien, *Versailles,* 33.

6. Le Guillou, "Le château neuf," 126, citing P. Clément, *Lettres, instructions et mémoires de Colbert* (1868, vol. 5, no. 23).

7. Kimball, *The Creation of the Rococo Style,* 42 with fig. 12; Marie, *Mansart à Versailles,* 2:314–15.

8. Nolhac, *Versailles. Résidence de Louis XIV,* 97, citing the memoirs of Sourches.

9. Verlet, *Le château de Versailles,* 149; Labatut, *Les ducs,* 302.

10. Princesse Palatine, *Lettres,* 321.

11. Tiberghien, *Versailles,* 20, citing a letter of Racine; Déon, *Louis XIV par lui-même,* 267.

12. Tiberghien, *Versailles,* citing the memoirs of Antoine Du Bois the elder, Louis XIV's *porte-arquebuse.*

13. Verlet, *Le château de Versailles,* 195–202.

14. Evrard, "Les eaux de Versailles," 589–60.

15. Princesse Palatine, *Lettres,* 268–69; Michel, *"Le château de Versailles,"* 94 with 101, n. 3.

16. Nolhac, *Versailles au XVIIIe siècle,* 43; Marie, *Mansart à Versailles,* 2:637–43.

17. Marie, *Naissance de Versailles,* 1:61; Dulaure, *Nouvelle description,* 1:259.

18. Edmunds, *Piety,* 111 (chapel). The unfinished state of the theater in 1688 is apparent from the painting of Versailles in that year by Jean Baptiste Martin.

19. Nolhac, *Versailles. Résidence de Louis XIV,* 289–93.

20. Baillie, "Etiquette," 189; Nolhac, *Versailles. Résidence de Louis XIV,* 290, citing Mansart's record of Louis XIV's orders (doors); Verlet, *Le château de Versailles,* 211–12.

21. Déon, *Louis XIV par lui-même,* 148, citing the memoirs of the maréchal de Villars.

22. Maral, *La chapelle royale,* 392, *Te Deums* for Quesnoy and Bouchain in October 1712.

23. Edmunds, *Piety,* 127, citing the bishop of Metz in 1710.

24. Saint-Simon, *Historical Memoirs,* 2:441.

25. Pitou, "The Players' Return," 7–8.

26. Marie, *Versailles au temps de Louis XIV,* 26–27.

27. Buvat, *Journal,* 2:381.

28. Antoine, *Louis XV,* 102.

29. Ibid., 196.

30. Papillon de La Ferté, *Journal,* 125.

31. A list of occasions appears in Beaussant, *Les plaisirs de Versailles,* 441–43.

32. Correspondence cited by Newton, *La petite cour,* 90–91.

33. Blondel, *L'architecture française,* 4:133.

34. Marie, *Mansart à Versailles,* 2:643 (plans); Nolhac, *Versailles au XVIIIe siècle,* 90–93 (du Barry).

35. Nolhac, *Versailles au XVIIIe siècle,* 352–58.

36. Ibid., 232, citing an annotated plan of the architect Le Roy.

37. Campan, *Mémoires,* 223–24.

2. "ROME IN ONE PALACE"

1. Besenval, *Mémoires,* 45.

2. Ssu-ma Ch'ien, *Han-shu,* translated by H. Dubs (1962), 1:118f. Cited by Hans van Ess in Spawforth, *The Court and Court Society,* 238.

3. Le Guillou, "Les châteaux de Louis XIII," 151, citing *Archives départementales des Yvelines,* 1: 32 F (inventory of 1630).

4. Déon, *Louis XIV par lui-même,* 43.

5. Voltaire, *Le siècle de Louis XIV,* 349.

6. Milanovic, *Du Louvre à Versailles,* 22 (warrant of appointment).

7. Sabatier, "La gloire du roi," 527–31.

8. Louis XIV, *Mémoires,* 136.

9. Sabatier, *Versailles,* 111, citing Félibien's description.

10. Saint-Simon, *Historical Memoirs,* 1:66.
11. Sabatier, *Versailles,* 261, citing the official record of the Academy of Inscriptions for 1994.
12. Bluche, *Louis XIV,* 370–71.
13. For the following remarks, I am indebted to Cornette ("L'histoire au travail") and Drévillon (*L'impôt du sang*).
14. Saint-Simon, *Historical Memoirs,* 1:387.
15. Mercier, *Tableau de Paris,* 4:146–52.
16. Princesse Palatine, *Lettres,* 223–24 (letter of March 18, 1698).
17. Drévillon, *L'impôt du sang,* 278, citing the *livre de raison* of Étienne Borelly.
18. Blondel, *L'architecture française,* 4:123.
19. Marie, *Mansart à Versailles,* 2:482–90.
20. Le Monnier, introduction to *Procès-verbaux,* xxxvii, xxxviii, n. 1.
21. Compare McGowan, *The Vision of Rome,* 167–73, figs. 38 and 40.
22. Levron, *Versailles,* plate v. The engraving is in the Biblioteca Estense in Modena.
23. Edmunds, *Piety,* 132–33.
24. Burke, *The Fabrication of Louis XIV,* 157.
25. *Mercure galant,* May 1682, cited by Edmunds, *Piety,* 96.
26. Maral, *La chapelle royale,* 34 ("complexe presque monastique").
27. Louis XIV, *Mémoires,* 454.
28. Edmunds, *Piety,* fig. 109 (photograph).
29. Sabatier, *Versailles,* fig. 151; see pp. 394–96 and 399–400 for a perceptive discussion.
30. Bonney, "Vindication of the Fronde?"; Crouzet, "Postscript," 230.
31. Nolhac, *Versailles au XVIIIe siècle,* 336, citing Dargenville, *Voyage pittoresque des environs de Versailles.*
32. Sévigné, *Lettres,* 5:492 (October 12, 1678); Tiberghien, *Versailles,* 149, 161, 165–68.
33. *Gazette d'Amsterdam,* July 5, 12, and 26, 1668. O. Lefèbvre d'Ormesson, *Journal* for July 1668 cited by Apostolidès, *Le roi-machine,* 10.
34. Cited by Tiberghien, *Versailles,* 256.
35. Bonney's "Vindication of the Fronde?" now supersedes all earlier discussions. See also Hézecques, *Souvenirs,* 141–42; Tiberghien, *Versailles,* 252–57.
36. Perrin, "Un Versailles inédit."
37. Norton, ed., *Saint-Simon at Versailles,* 223.
38. Mercier, *Tableau de Paris,* 4:146–52.
39. Cited by Duindam, *Vienna and Versailles,* 167 n. 140.
40. Sabatier, *Versailles,* 436.
41. See Batiffol, *Versailles et ses Habitants,* ch. 1 for the details.

### 3. A GILDED CAGE?

1. The breakdown is that of Beaussant in *Les plaisirs de Versailles,* 252.
2. Girault de Coursac, *Louis XVI et Marie-Antoinette,* 205, citing the dauphin's accounts book (Archives Nationales, Museum).
3. Table in Mansel, *The Court of France,* 197; Duindam, *Vienna and Versailles,* 61 (*Almanach Royal* for 1789).
4. Figure cited by Duindam, *Vienna and Versailles,* 56.
5. Levron, *Versailles,* 94–95 (census); Newton, *L'espace du roi,* 26 (364 lodgings).
6. Bombelles, *Journal,* 1:173.
7. Fleury, *Les derniers jours de Versailles,* 54–55, citing Archives Nationales, series O$^1$ 354 192; Duindam, *Vienna and Versailles,* 54–56 (on the unquantifiable "lower fringes of commissioned labor").
8. Mansel, *The Court of France,* 11 (ex-king of Poland).
9. Luynes, *Mémoires,* 1:151 (duke of Medina-Celi).
10. Newton, *La petite cour,* 31.
11. Boigne, *Mémoires,* 34.
12. Hézecques, *Souvenirs,* 152.
13. Reproduced in Saule, "Tables à Versailles," 450.
14. Ibid., 44 (route).
15. Walpole, *Horace Walpole's Correspondence,* 10:291–92.
16. Black, *France and the Grand Tour,* 142.
17. Massounie, *L'architecture des écuries royales,* 72, 78.
18. Hézecques, *Souvenirs,* 121.
19. Lemoine, "Les écuries du roi"; Beaussant, *Les plaisirs de Versailles,* 335–37 (music).
20. Luynes, *Mémoires,* 11:30.
21. Duma, *Les Bourbon-Penthièvre,* 122, citing Archives Nationales G5 164 (the 1737 accounts).
22. Dufort de Cheverny, *Mémoires,* 1:144.
23. Campan, *Mémoires,* 457–58.
24. Elias, *The Court Society,* 201, citing Delloye's 1843 edition of the *Mémoires,* vol. 8, ch. 229, p. 71.
25. Luynes, *Mémoires,* 11:434.
26. Hézecques, *Souvenirs,* 133.
27. Bergin, "The Royal Confessor."
28. Letter of July 7, 1719, cited by Newton, *La petite cour,* 17.
29. Luynes, *Mémoires,* 10:240–41.
30. Newton, *La petite cour,* 354, 361.
31. Salvadori, *La chasse,* 255; for the ritual, see McManners, *Church and Society,* 1:375, 380.

32. Hézecques, *Souvenirs*, 212.

33. Da Vinha, *Les valets de chambre*, 58.

34. Ibid., 181–82.

35. Antoine, *Louis XV*, 449.

36. Bombelles, *Journal*, 1:248–49.

37. Doyle, *Venality*, 78.

38. Bombelles, *Journal*, 1:248–49.

39. Hézecques, *Souvenirs*, 8.

40. Ibid., 115–16.

41. Ibid., 75.

42. Ibid., 125.

43. Tilly, *Mémoires*, 81–95. The lodging of Madame de Tavannes at this date (around 1778) was in the attics on the town side of the south wing: Newton, *L'espace du roi*, 317.

44. Mercy, *Correspondance secrète*, vol. 2, letter to Maria Theresa of September 17, 1776.

45. Luynes, *Mémoires*, 3:189.

46. Illustration in Saule, "Tables à Versailles," 40.

47. Bombelles, *Journal*, 1:160, 164–65.

48. Croÿ, *Journal inédit*, 4:286.

49. Duindam, *Vienna and Versailles*, 100, citing a memorandum by Necker, Louis XVI's finance minister.

50. Lever, *Correspondance de Marie-Antoinette*, 258–59.

51. Horowski, "Such a Great Advantage," 165, citing Archives Nationales 273 A.P. 188.

52. Newton, *L'espace du roi*, 17.

53. Cited by Norton, *Saint-Simon at Versailles*, 223.

54. Choiseul, *Mémoires*, 9.

55. Isherwood, *Music*, 41–43, 258, citing various texts.

56. Brancas, *Histoire*, 34–35.

57. Déon, *Louis XIV par lui-même*, 70.

58. Sévigné, *Lettres*, 7:217–18 (February 12, 1683).

59. Horowski, "Such a Great Advantage," 172 n. 123, citing Sévigné, 6:182–83.

60. Elias, *The Court Society*, 197, citing Saint-Simon, *Mémoires*, edited by Delloye, 2:82.

61. Ibid., 129, citing Saint-Simon, *Mémoires*, edited by Delloye, 1:167.

62. Labatut, *Les ducs*, 207, citing d'Antin's memoirs.

63. Hézecques, *Souvenirs*, 266.

64. Princesse Palatine, *Lettres*, 442 (letter of March 26, 1711).

65. Cited by Verlet, *Le château de Versailles*, 267.

66. Béguin, *Les princes de Condé,* esp. chs. 9–10.
67. Elias, *The Court Society,* 197, citing Saint-Simon, *Mémoires,* edited by Delloye, 2:85.

4. "HOW RIGHT TO INSIST ON CEREMONY . . ."

1. Cited by Le Roy Ladurie, *Saint-Simon,* 65.
2. Campan, *Mémoires,* 90.
3. Saint-Priest, *Mémoires,* 1:92.
4. Saint-Simon, *Historical Memoirs,* 1:118–23.
5. Ibid., 2:148.
6. Labatut, *Les ducs,* 203–4.
7. Baillie, "Etiquette," 191 n. 1, citing Mlle de Montpensier, *Mémoires,* edited by Petitot and Monmergue (Paris, 1825), 42:275.
8. Norton, *Saint-Simon at Versailles,* 229.
9. Saint-Simon, *Historical Memoirs,* 2:173.
10. Luynes, *Mémoires,* 2:289–90 (December 17, 1738).
11. Ibid., 1:64–65.
12. Ibid., 7:88, cited by Brocher in *Le rang et l'étiquette.*
13. Hézecques, *Souvenirs,* 176.
14. Mercy, *Correspondance secrète,* 2:457, 2:535–39; Chantal Thomas in Genlis, *De l'esprit des étiquettes,* 12–16 (challenging the view of Elias).
15. Verlet, *Le mobilier royal français,* 3:49–50, 3:229.
16. Campan, *Mémoires,* 54–55.
17. La Tour du Pin, *Recollections,* 89.
18. Saint-Simon, *Historical Memoirs,* 1:118.
19. Visconti, *Mémoires,* 27–28.
20. Bombelles, *Journal,* 1:24 (entry for January 30, 1784).
21. Da Vinha, *Les valets de chambre,* 49–50, citing Molière, *Oeuvres complètes,* edited by G. Couton (1971), 1:87.
22. Sévigné, *Lettres,* 4:544 (letter of July 29, 1676).
23. Trabouillet, *L'état de la France,* 1:265.
24. Duindam, *Vienna and Versailles,* 45–46 with notes.
25. Croÿ, *Journal inédit,* 1:86.
26. Genlis, *De l'esprit des étiquettes,* 35–36.
27. Princess Daschkoff, cited by Saule, "Tables à Versailles," 50.
28. Norton, *Saint-Simon at Versailles,* 208.
29. Hézecques, *Souvenirs,* 197.
30. La Tour du Pin, *Recollections,* 50.
31. Campan, *Mémoires,* 92. Public meals: Marie, *Mansart à Versailles,* 2:322–32; Saule, "Tables à Versailles,"; Strong, *Feast,* ch. 5 passim.

32. Illustrated in the exhibition catalogue *L'homme paré* (Paris, 2005), 5.

33. Croÿ, *Journal inédit,* 1: 439–41; Maral, *La chapelle royale,* 233–51.

34. Argenson, *Journal,* 2:117.

35. Saint-Simon, *Historical Memoirs,* 2:281–82.

36. Black, *France and the Grand Tour,* 23–24, citing James Brogden.

37. McManners, *Church and Society,* 1:43.

38. See Petitfils, *Louis XVI,* 252: "profondément croyant."

39. Luynes, *Mémoires,* 5:20.

40. Tourzel, *Mémoires,* 387.

41. Luynes, *Mémoires,* 2:218–19.

42. Luynes, *Mémoires,* 14:396.

43. Hézecques, *Souvenirs,* 187.

44. Maral, *La chapelle royale,* 283–86; Duindam, *Vienna and Versailles,* 137–40; Antoine, *Louis XV,* 486–87; Bloch, *The Royal Touch,* 223–26.

45. Salmon, *Pomp and Power,* 101–3 no. 42.

46. Dufort de Cheverny, *Mémoires,* 1:83, 1:221.

47. Luynes, *Mémoires,* 5:135.

48. Luynes, *Mémoires,* 1:293–94.

49. For these paragraphs I am heavily indebted to Castelluccio's article "La Galerie des Glaces."

50. Bombelles, *Journal,* 1:253, entry for August 15, 1783.

51. As pointed out by Baillie, "Etiquette," 191.

52. Luynes, *Mémoires,* 11:202.

53. Lévis, *Souvenirs-Portraits,* 81.

54. Antoine, *Louis XV,* 536; Nolhac, *Versailles,* 130–62, 160–62 for the new décor.

55. See Luynes, *Mémoires,* 15:196; Hézecques, *Mémoires,* 206–9; Petitfils, *Louis XVI,* 586–87 (1788).

56. Croÿ, *Journal inédit,* 3:83–92.

57. Luynes, *Mémoires,* 14:23, 14:29.

58. Saint-Simon, *Historical Memoirs,* 2:217.

59. Luynes, *Mémoires,* 14:23, 8: 151–52.

60. Luynes, *Mémoires,* 8:151.

61. [Michaud], *Biographie universelle,* 23:29. For further details on court mourning, see Chrisman-Campbell, "Mourning and *La Mode.*"

62. Genlis, *De l'esprit des étiquettes,* 103–4.

63. For details see Meyer, "Les obsèques," and Maral, *La chapelle royale,* 217–20.

64. Hézecques, *Souvenirs,* 170–71.

65. Saint-Priest, *Mémoires,* 1:4.

66. Argenson, *Journal,* 1:182.

67. Luynes, *Mémoires,* 5:93–98.

68. Hézecques, *Souvenirs,* 5–6.

69. La Tour du Pin, *Recollections,* 49.

70. Véri, *Journal,* 1:241.

71. Boigne, *Mémoires,* 42.

72. Croÿ, *Journal inédit,* 4:285.

73. Ibid., 4:188.

74. Hézecques, *Souvenirs,* 188.

75. Véri, *Journal,* 1:241.

76. Bluche, *Louis XIV,* 349–50.

77. Véri, *Journal,* 1:131 (July 14, 1774).

78. Chastenay, *Mémoires,* 29.

79. Lévis, *Souvenirs-Portraits,* 280.

80. Oberkirch, *Mémoires,* 461.

81. Genlis, *De l'esprit des étiquettes,* 330.

82. Campan, *Mémoires,* 189–90.

83. Ibid., 477–78.

84. Bombelles, *Journal,* 1:243 (entry for July 7, 1783). See Mansel, *Dressed to Rule,* 63–66.

## 5. FOLLOW THE KING!

1. Choiseul, *Mémoires,* 92; Véri, *Journal,* 1:42–45.

2. Ranum, *Richelieu,* 25.

3. Saint-Simon, *Historical Memoirs,* 3:46.

4. Bombelles, *Journal,* 1:43.

5. Chastenay, *Mémoires,* 3.

6. Dufort de Cheverny, *Mémoires,* 1:93.

7. Princesse Palatine, *Lettres,* 394 (October 28, 1708).

8. Croÿ, *Journal inédit,* 2:341–43.

9. Dion, *Emmanuel de Croÿ,* 88.

10. Croÿ, *Journal inédit,* 2:125, 2:128, 2:145–46, 2:151, 2:155, 2:172–73.

11. Campan, *Mémoires,* 524.

12. Luynes, *Mémoires,* 10:238, 14:390.

13. Saint-Priest, *Mémoires,* 1:115–66. For further details, not without an edge, see Boigne, *Mémoires,* 76–80.

14. Labatut, *Les ducs,* 310, 319.

15. Croÿ, *Journal inédit,* 1:421, 1:257.

16. Luynes, *Mémoires,* 2:30–31.

17. Duma, *Les Bourbon-Penthièvre,* 14, 39, 428–29, 453–56.

18. Saint-Simon, *Historical Memoirs,* 1:4.

19. Oberkirch, *Mémoires,* 459.
20. Sapori, *Rose Bertin,* 141–43.
21. Luynes, *Mémoires,* 7:139, 8:143, 8:454, 14:376.
22. Hézecques, *Souvenirs,* 180–81.
23. Luynes, *Mémoires,* 13:247.
24. Solnon, *La Cour de France,* 537–38.
25. *Abrégé historique.*
26. Cited by Royon, "La noblesse de province."
27. Luynes, *Mémoires,* 14:320.
28. Luynes, *Mémoires,* 2:66–67; Da Vinha, *Les valets de chambre,* 322–24 (Louis XIV).
29. Baillie, "Etiquette," 171–72.
30. Choiseul, *Mémoires,* 291–93. Besenval, *Mémoires,* 141–57.
31. Saint-Simon, *Historical Memoirs,* 1:501.
32. Princesse Palatine, *Lettres,* 472 (March 19, 1712).
33. Saint-Simon, *Historical Memoirs,* 3:445.
34. Ibid., 1:184.
35. Ibid., 1:504, 1:507–8, 2:23–28.
36. Campan, *Mémoires,* 450.
37. Saint-Simon, *Historical Memoirs,* 1:432.
38. Blondel, *L'architecture française,* 4:131.
39. Cited by Nolhac, *Versailles. Résidence de Louis XIV,* 33.
40. Saint-Simon, *Historical Memoirs,* 1:151.
41. Mauricheau-Beaupré, *Versailles,* 9. The first-floor stone cornice can still be seen in what is now Room 90 of the north wing.
42. Hézecques, *Souvenirs,* 145.
43. Saint-Simon, *Historical Memoirs,* 1:398; Luynes, *Mémoires,* 8:95; Hézecques, *Souvenirs,* 158.
44. Saint-Simon, *Historical Memoirs,* 1:38.
45. Ibid., 1:288.
46. Ibid., 1:396.
47. Lévis, *Souvenirs-Portraits,* 332–33. By "your staircase" Provence, in a letter to Lévis describing these maneuvers, meant the one marked on Newton, *L'espace du roi,* fig. 20, as debouching at attic level in front of AP91, the lodging occupied by members of the Lévis family from 1772 to 1789: Newton, *L'espace du roi,* 285, 545.
48. Newton, *L'espace du roi,* 415–16.
49. Saint-Priest, *Mémoires,* 1:231.
50. Croÿ, *Journal inédit* 1:229, 1:326.
51. Ibid., 1:323.

52. Ibid., 2:90.
53. La Tour du Pin, *Recollections*, 85.
54. Croÿ, *Journal inédit*, 1:426.
55. Newton, *L'espace du roi*, 435 and 459–60, citing, respectively, Archives Nationales O¹ 1810 II 92 and 1802 128.
56. Le Roi, *Histoire de Versailles*, 2:166.
57. Croÿ, *Journal inédit*, 2:89, 4:141.
58. Now on display in the municipal library of Versailles, formerly the ministry of foreign affairs.
59. Pinot-Duclos, *Considérations*, 62–63.
60. Luynes *Mémoires*, 1:256–57. His father was the duke of Berwick, son of James II and Arabella Churchill.
61. Delpy, "Un chef de service."
62. Watson, *Digest*, 1: 16, 6, 3.
63. Da Vinha, *Les valets de chambre*, 28.
64. Mossiker, *The Queen's Necklace*, 122, citing eyewitness testimony from the unpublished dossier of the Necklace trial.
65. Perrin, "Un Versailles inédit."
66. See the *Almanach de Versailles* for 1788, 245.
67. Da Vinha, *Les valets de chambre*, 28.
68. Saint-Priest, *Mémoires*, 1:226.
69. Tilly, *Mémoires*, 208–17.
70. Levron, *Les courtisans*, 99–105; Delafosse, "Affairistes."
71. Levron, *Les inconnus*, 205–17.
72. Dufort de Cheverny, *Mémoires*, 1:93.
73. Saint-Simon, *Historical Memoirs*, 1:411.
74. Horowski, "Such a Great Advantage," 171 n. 122, citing Picciola, *Le comte de Maurepas*, 73.
75. Thomas, *The Wicked Queen*, 57–58.
76. Saint-Simon, *Historical Memoirs*, 3:292.
77. Bombelles, *Journal*, 1:45; Lévis, *Souvenirs-Portraits*, 128–29.
78. Lévis, *Souvenirs-Portraits*, 91–92.
79. Tilly, *Mémoires*, 77.
80. Levron, *Les courtisans*, 91.
81. Besenval, *Mémoires*, 370, in his larger discussion of "The Society of Kings" (368–75).
82. Boigne, *Mémoires*, 67–68.
83. J. de Witte in Véri, *Journal*, 2:xiii, citing the *Journal intime* of the chevalier de Corberon.

6. "all the pleasures"

1. Verlet, *Le château de Versailles,* 149.
2. Luynes, *Mémoires,* 12:190.
3. Ibid., 1:132.
4. Verlet, *Le château de Versailles,* 374–75.
5. Studied by Pitou, "The Players' Return to Versailles."
6. Luynes, *Mémoires,* 2:62.
7. Papillon de La Ferté, *Journal,* 45.
8. See, for example, Marie, *Mansart à Versailles,* 1:278, citing Dangeau's *Journal* for November 23, 1685. Compare Beaussant, *Les plaisirs de Versailles,* 393.
9. See the papers in Rubin, *The Sun King.*
10. Cited by Foster, "Dancing the Body Politic," 168 n. 13.
11. Saint-Simon, *Historical Memoirs,* 2:249; Bombelles, *Journal,* 2:32; Chastenay, *Mémoires,* 31.
12. Bombelles, *Journal,* vol. 2, entry for February 27, 1786; Boigne, *Mémoires,* 38–39.
13. Saint-Simon, *Historical Memoirs,* 1:17.
14. Beaussant, *Les plaisirs de Versailles,* 143–44, citing Luynes.
15. Marie, *Mansart à Versailles,* 2:454–55; Beaussant, *Les plaisirs de Versailles,* 402 (illustration).
16. Marie, *Mansart à Versailles,* 2:455.
17. Argenson, *Journal,* 1:141–42.
18. Luynes, *Mémoires,* 2:334–44.
19. Chastenay, *Mémoires,* 21.
20. Boigne, *Mémoires,* 39–40. The magistrate's name was de Lavie.
21. Besenval, *Mémoires,* 234.
22. Luynes, *Mémoires,* 6:354.
23. Saint-Simon, *Historical Memoirs,* 3:290–91.
24. McManners, *Church and Society,* 2:269, 2:271.
25. Newton, *L'espace du roi,* 325.
26. Dufort de Cheverny, *Mémoires,* 1:123.
27. Sévigné, *Lettres,* 4:544.
28. Saint-Simon, *Historical Memoirs,* 3:203.
29. Hézecques, *Souvenirs,* 227.
30. Verlet, *Le mobilier royal français,* 4:150–55.
31. Marie, *Mansart à Versailles,* 2:452–53.
32. Oberkirch, *Mémoires,* 463.
33. Mercy, *Correspondance secrète,* vol. 3, letter of January 17, 1780.

34. Boigne, *Mémoires,* 42–43; Girault de Coursac, *Louis XVI,* 430–33; 803–4.
35. Saint-Simon, *Historical Memoirs,* 1:203.
36. Princesse Palatine, *Lettres,* 271–72 (February 11, 1700).
37. Bombelles, *Journal,* 1:298 (entry for January 15, 1784).
38. [Bachaumont], *Choix des mémoires secrets,* 1:159.
39. Girault de Coursac, *Louis XVI,* 175.
40. Princesse Palatine, *Lettres,* 399; Walpole, *Horace Walpole's Correspondence,* 7:266.
41. Saint-Simon, *Historical Memoirs,* 1:23–24.
42. Tiberghien, *Versailles,* 22–23.
43. Dangeau, *Journal,* 6:122.
44. Luynes, *Mémoires,* 2:8.
45. Fleury, *Les derniers jours de Versailles,* 191.
46. Dangeau, *Journal,* 6:15.
47. Luynes, *Mémoires,* 9:66.
48. Hézecques, *Souvenirs,* 252–53.
49. Verlet, *Le château de Versailles,* 46–47; Salvatori, *La chasse,* 204; Mansel, *Dressed to Rule,* 56.
50. Luynes, *Mémoires,* 1:317–18, 2:225.
51. Genlis, *Mémoires,* 144.
52. Isherwood, *Music,* 306.
53. Black, *France and the Grand Tour,* 23.
54. Beaussant, *Les plaisirs de Versailles,* 302; Maral, *La chapelle royale,* 34.
55. Letter of February 1, 1764, cited by Beaussant, *Les plaisirs de Versailles,* 159.
56. Ibid., 293.
57. Maral, *La chapelle royale,* 39.
58. Besenval, *Mémoires,* 101; compare Luynes, *Mémoires,* 6:85; Argenson, *Journal,* 2:133–34.
59. Baulez, "La tribune"; Walpole, *Horace Walpole's Correspondence,* 10:291–92.
60. Luynes, *Mémoires,* 2:164.
61. Lemoine, "Les logements de Saint-Simon," 20, 26–27; Luynes, *Mémoires,* 1:289.
62. Document cited by Newton, *L'espace du roi,* 216.
63. Croÿ, *Journal inédit,* 1:206, 2:50, 2:58.
64. Croÿ, *Journal inédit,* 2: 95, 99, 122. He distinguishes the two princesses de Carignan as "de Paris" (the grandmother, a bastard of the duke of Savoy, with a lodging at Versailles) and "de Turin" (the mother, a princess of Hesse, whose daughters included the future princesse de Lamballe).
65. Luynes, *Mémoires,* 5:166.
66. Luynes, cited by Dufourcq, *Musique,* 148.

67. Genlis, *De l'esprit des étiquettes,* 111–12.
68. Saint-Simon, *Historical Memoirs,* 1:40.
69. Newton, *L'espace du roi,* 137–38.
70. Besenval, *Mémoires,* 69; Luynes, *Mémoires,* 16:185; Newton, *L'espace du roi,* 111–12 (rooms).
71. Brancas, *Histoire,* 33.
72. Besenval, *Mémoires,* 57–67; Lévis, *Souvenirs-Portraits,* 100–104; Genlis, *Mémoires,* 150–51; Newton, *L'espace du roi,* 351–53 (rooms).
73. Véri, *Journal,* 1:42–45.
74. Newton, *L'espace du roi,* 220, citing Archives Nationales O$^1$ 1798 521.
75. Dufort de Cheverny, *Mémoires,* 1:331–32.
76. Oberkirch, *Mémoires,* 298; Besenval, *Mémoires,* 289–90; Luynes, *Mémoires,* 8:33 (presentation); 15:78–79 (theft); Croÿ, *Journal inédit,* 4:295; Girault de Coursac, *Louis XVI,* 220–22 (machinations).
77. Besenval, *Mémoires,* 544 n. 130.
78. Boigne, *Mémoires,* 34–35, 64; Lévis, *Souvenirs-Portraits,* 126–29; Lilti, *Le monde des salons,* 75; Newton, *L'espace du roi,* 475 (lodgings).

7. COMFORTS, OR LACK OF THEM

1. The stenciled numbers still to be seen above some attic doors prior to the 1970s (Stratmann-Döhler, "Les logements des courtisans," 175) date from the nineteenth century, as Roland Bossard pointed out to me.
2. Boigne, *Mémoires,* 87; Hézecques, *Souvenirs,* 146.
3. Saint Simon, *Historical Memoirs,* 2:250.
4. Ibid., 1:134; Marie, *Mansart à Versailles,* 1:256.
5. Dufort de Cheverny, *Mémoires,* 1:255; Antoine, *Louis XV,* 684–85.
6. Hézecques, *Souvenirs,* 78.
7. See Newton, *L'espace du roi,* 28–39, 99 (citing Archives Nationales O$^1$ 1796 641: Princes' Court full of carriages in 1758). This chapter as a whole could not have been written without William Newton's meticulous and ground-breaking research on courtiers' accommodations at Versailles in two outstanding studies: *L'espace du roi* and *La petite cour.*
8. Saint-Simon, *Historical Memoirs,* 2:453.
9. Cited by Lagny, "L'hôtel de Saint-Simon."
10. Labatut, *Les ducs,* 301, citing Archives Nationales M.C., 8:896, November 8, 1712.
11. Saint-Simon, *Historical Memoirs,* 3:69, 3:79–80; Horowski, "*Such a Great Advantage,*" 132–33.
12. Saint-Simon, *Historical Memoirs,* 2:312–16; Lemoine, "Les logements de Saint-Simon," 27–28.

13. Newton, *La petite cour,* 35–36, 563–69; Evrard, "Les moeurs à Versailles," 95–97.

14. Saint-Simon, *Historical Memoirs,* 1:202–3.

15. Visconti, *Mémoires,* 61; Hézecques, *Mémoires,* 214; Saint-Simon, *Historical Memoirs,* 3:456.

16. Newton, *La petite cour,* 559.

17. Ibid., 559.

18. Newton, *L'espace du roi,* 181, 207, 288.

19. Luynes, *Mémoires,* 6:366 n. 1; Nolhac, *Versailles au XVIIIe siècle,* 205; Newton, *L'espace du roi,* 201, 397; compare 302; Bombelles, *Journal,* 1:173.

20. Newton, *L'espace du roi,* 283, 299; Levron, *Les inconnus,* 245 (comtesse de Coëtlogon); Moussoir, "Les Gardes-Françaises," 13.

21. Newton, *L'espace du roi,* 346, 474; Racinais, *Un Versailles inconnu,* 125–26.

22. Hézecques, *Souvenirs,* 214–16.

23. Newton, *L'espace du roi,* 217; Le Guillou, "Le 'côté du Roi,'" 134.

24. Visconti, *Mémoires,* 65; Vigarello, *Concepts of Cleanliness,* 68.

25. Newton, *La petite cour,* 278–79.

26. Verlet, *Le château de Versailles,* 88–91; Marie, *Mansart à Versailles,* 2:581–86.

27. Trabouillet, *L'état de la France,* 125.

28. Marie, *Versailles au temps de Louis XV,* 64–67; Campan, *The Private Life,* 66 (Marie-Antoinette: fuller text than Campan, *Mémoires,* 96).

29. Newton, *L'espace du roi,* 217, 255–56, 259, 357.

30. Moussoir, "Les Gardes-Françaises," 13–14.

31. Verlet, *Le mobilier royal français,* 4:37–39; Salmon, *Madame de Pompadour,* 329; Racinais, *Un Versailles inconnu,* 125–26.

32. Norton, *Saint-Simon at Versailles,* 168–69.

33. Blondel, *L'architecture française,* 97–98; Marie, *Versailles au temps de Louis XV,* 206–9.

34. Newton, *L'espace du roi,* 208; compare 418.

35. Girault de Coursac, *Louis XVI,* 205.

36. Racinais, *Un Versailles inconnu,* 25–26; Luynes, *Mémoires,* 10:53 (pump).

37. Baulez, "L'appartement," 50, citing the inventory of the duchess's rooms.

38. Argenson, *Journal,* 1:309–10; Luynes, *Mémoires,* 5:11, 5:18.

39. Newton, *L'espace du roi,* 272.

40. Ibid., 357.

41. Luynes, *Mémoires,* 11:336; Bombelles, *Journal,* 2:28.

42. Boigne, *Mémoires,* 34.

43. Lemoine, "Les logements de Saint-Simon," 35 fig. 5.

44. Newton, *L'espace du roi,* 102; 206.
45. Saint-Simon, *Historical Memoirs,* 1:416; Princesse Palatine, *Lettres,* 396.
46. Newton, *L'espace du roi,* 224, 345.
47. Lévis, *Souvenirs-Portraits,* 103.
48. See, for example, Newton, *L'espace du roi,* 213, 285, 286, 305; Reyniers, "Contribution" (invention).
49. Newton, *L'espace du roi,* 294.
50. *The Spectator,* no. 2, Friday, March 2, 1711.
51. Princesse Palatine, *Lettres,* 321.
52. For *barbes pendantes* or *tombantes,* see Boigne, *Mémoires,* 36; Hézecques, *Souvenirs,* 195.
53. As shown in the superb 2005–6 exhibition *L'homme paré* in the Musée des arts décoratifs, Paris. Some of the clothes on display there are illustrated in the accompanying special edition of the series "Connaissance des arts," *L'homme paré* (Paris, 2005). But even excellent photographs hardly do justice to the exquisite detailing (buttons, embroidery) or the texture and color of fabrics shot through with gold and silver thread.
54. Bombelles, *Journal,* 2:188–89, cited by Lilti, *Le monde des salons,* 152–53.
55. Campan, *Mémoires,* 88. In general Sapori, *Rose Bertin,* especially 25–31.
56. Newton, *L'espace du roi,* 87, 161–62, 287–88.
57. Forster, *The House of Saulx-Tavanes,* 123–26.
58. Dufort de Cheverny, *Mémoires,* 1:125.
59. Saint-Simon, *Historical Memoirs,* 1:96–97.
60. Inventory at death cited by Helge Seifert in Salmon, *Madame de Pompadour,* 31.
61. Argenson, *Journal,* 2:166.
62. Oberkirch, *Mémoires,* 245.
63. According to Chaussinand-Nogaret, *The French Nobility,* 53.
64. Saule, "Tables à Versailles," 63.
65. Papillon de La Ferté, *Journal,* 147.
66. Bombelles, *Journal,* 1:142–43 n. 33; 1:231, 1:337, 2:180–81.
67. Saint-Simon, *Historical Memoirs,* 2:78.
68. Luynes, *Mémoires,* 8:112–13; Saint-Priest, *Mémoires,* 2:69.
69. Luynes, *Mémoires,* 3:336.
70. Newton, *L'espace du roi,* 155–56, citing the memoirs of the comte de Liedekerke-Beaufort.
71. Saint-Simon, *Historical Memoirs,* 2:162, 2:349.
72. Levron, *Les inconnus,* ch. 15.
73. Newton, *L'espace du roi,* 284; Luynes, *Mémoires,* 13:234–35, 13:247–48.

74. Newton, *L'espace du roi,* 372, 375.
75. Cited ibid., 138.
76. Ibid., 288–89, citing a letter from the Princesse Palatine.
77. Luynes, *Mémoires,* 10:224–25.


8. BEHIND CLOSED DOORS
 1. Hézecques, *Souvenirs,* 151.
 2. Luynes, *Mémoires,* 15:397.
 3. Girault de Coursac, *Louis XVI,* 87, 109–10 (with a different interpretation of the episode).
 4. Luynes, *Mémoires,* 7:89.
 5. Verlet, *Le mobilier royal français,* 2:65–75.
 6. Norton, *Saint-Simon at Versailles,* 34; Saint-Simon, *Historical Memoirs,* 2:39–41.
 7. Da Vinha, *Les valets de chambre,* 319–20.
 8. Piganiol de La Force, *Nouvelle description des châteaux et parcs de Versailles et Marly,* cited by Marie, *Mansart à Versailles,* 2:395.
 9. The 1727 edition of the guidebook by J. C. Nemeitz, cited by Sabatier, *Versailles,* 437.
 10. Cited by Marie, *Mansart à Versailles,* 2:371, whose detailed account of these rooms on pages 363–434 is followed here.
 11. Princesse Palatine, *Lettres,* 273.
 12. Argenson, *Journal,* 1:175.
 13. Saint-Simon, *Historical Memoirs,* 1:414.
 14. Newton, *L'espace du roi,* 137, 171, 185, 250, 252, 356, 422; Massounie, *L'architecture des écuries royales,* 110, 113.
 15. Tilly, *Mémoires,* 210.
 16. Luynes, *Mémoires,* 5:93–98; Baulez, "L'appartement," 52.
 17. On Cucé's rooms, see Newton, *L'espace du roi,* 390; on his library, see Chaussinand-Nogaret, *French Nobility,* 75–76.
 18. Bombelles, *Journal,* 1:76, 1:81.
 19. A point made by Le Guillou, "Le 'côté du Roi,'" 131–32.
 20. Verlet, *Le mobilier royal français,* 3:62–66, 3:106–9.
 21. Luynes, *Mémoires,* 6:479 (June 1745).
 22. Antoine, *Louis XV,* 533; Hézecques, *Souvenirs,* 154–55.
 23. Dufort de Cheverny, *Mémoires,* 2:90–91.
 24. Antoine, *Louis XV,* 446–52, 533–35.
 25. Louis XV, *Lettres,* 62.
 26. Croÿ, *Journal inédit,* 2:90; Campan, *Mémoires,* 23.
 27. Argenson, *Journal,* 1:99.

28. Luynes, *Mémoires,* 1:194.

29. Argenson, *Journal,* 1:175.

30. Verlet, *Le château de Versailles,* 475–76.

31. Saule, "Tables," 58; Noël-Waldteufel, "Manger à la cour," 77–78.

32. Ibid., 58–59; Luynes, *Mémoires,* 5:93–98.

33. Cited by Hours, *Louis XV,* 116.

34. Croÿ, *Journal inédit,* 1:83, 195; Le Roi, *Histoire de Versailles,* 1:93 (Fortisson's, since demolished).

35. Hours, *Louis XV,* 115–20.

36. Saint-Simon, *Historical Memoirs,* 2:168, 2:172–80, 2:237–39.

37. Campbell, *Power and Politics,* 115, citing the correspondence of the marquis de Silly with the duc de Richelieu.

38. Luynes, *Mémoires,* 6:166.

39. Bombelles, *Journal,* 1:235–36.

40. Boigne, *Mémoires,* 53.

41. Le Guillou, "Le 'côté du Roi,' " 112; Oberkirch, *Mémoires,* 461, 463.

42. For details, see Le Guillou, "Le 'côté du Roi.' "

43. Campan, *The Private Life,* 88, citing the eyewitness account (1792) of Jean-Louis Soulavie.

44. Oberkirch, *Mémoires,* 218.

45. Hézecques, *Souvenirs,* 315.

46. Besenval, *Mémoires,* 302–3.

47. Le Guillou, "Le 'côté du Roi,' " 108, citing Archives Nationales O¹ 1800³ 391; Campan, *Mémoires,* 293.

48. Campan, *Mémoires,* 185; Besenval, *Mémoires,* 461.

49. Verlet, *Le château de Versailles,* 641–42.

50. Hézecques, *Souvenirs,* 243–44; Choffé, "Le jardin champêtre," 67–68 (illustrations). Today the grotto has been charmingly restored.

51. Cited by Jallut, "Château de Versailles."

52. Cabanès, *La princesse de Lamballe intime,* 442.

53. Huisman and Jallut, *Marie Antoinette,* 158.

54. Luynes, *Mémoires,* 1:138, 5:384; Solnon, *La Cour de France,* 490–96.

55. Bombelles, *Journal,* 1:138, 1:240, 1:247–48; 2:16; Mercy, *Correspondance secrète,* 2:535–39.

56. Furet and Richet, *La Révolution française,* 45.

57. Baillie, "Etiquette," 184.

58. Thomas, *The Wicked Queen,* 216–27, a translation of the *Bord(el) r(oyal).* The action of this anonymous printed pamphlet is set "à Versailles, dans l'appartement de la Reine." The dramatic date falls between July 16 and October 5, 1789.

59. Lévis, *Souvenirs-Portraits*, 66.
60. Jallut, "Château de Versailles," 300; Huisman and Jallut, *Marie Antoinette*, 160. Accepted by Newton, *L'espace du roi*, 128; Petitfils, *Louis XVI*, 289.
61. Bombelles, *Journal*, 1:193.
62. Genlis, *De l'esprit des étiquettes*, 61; Campan, *Mémoires*, 93.
63. Tilly, *Mémoires*, 352.
64. Campan, *Mémoires*, 164–65. The author is audibly defensive.
65. Besenval, *Mémoires*, 378.
66. Besenval, *Mémoires*, 379; Campan, *Mémoires*, 245. The version of events, by the cardinal himself, appears in the memoirs of Georgel, his factotum; it sounds too good to be true: Mossiker, *The Queen's Necklace*, 275.
67. Croÿ, *Journal inédit*, 3:224, cited by Girault de Coursac, *Louis XVI*, 349–60 (sorting fact from myth); Le Guillou, "Le 'côté du Roi,'" plan 1, nos. 22–25, and plan 9, nos. 23–25. See Genlis, *De l'esprit des étiquettes*, 60–61.
68. Genlis, *De l'esprit des étiquettes*, 60.
69. Boigne, *Mémoires*, 57; Genlis, *De l'esprit des étiquettes*, 117.
70. Bombelles, *Journal*, I:262–63. This passage discusses rumors at Versailles of the queen's partiality for Fersen in an entry for September 24, 1783. In the historical record these rumors first emerge in a letter of the Swedish ambassador dating from April 10, 1779: Creutz, *La Suède*, no. 146.
71. Lever, *Correspondance*, 25.
72. Boigne, *Mémoires*, 44–45.
73. Attempts have been made to play down the eyewitness comments of Saint-Priest in his memoirs: see, most recently, Girault de Coursac, *Louis XVI*, 701–8. But it is not easy to believe that this former royal minister, writing his memoirs in old age, for the eyes of his family alone rather than for publication (Saint-Priest, *Mémoires*, 1:1), and long after the queen and Fersen had both died in tragic circumstances, would have gone to the trouble of inventing his portrait of their relationship. Saint-Priest also says that the relationship was sufficiently "known" in 1789 for Fersen's presence at the Tuileries awaiting the arrival of the king and queen in Paris on October 6, following the attack on Versailles, to seem potentially injurious to the royal interest and even personally dangerous to the king and queen; after a tête-à-tête with Montmorin, another minister, Saint-Priest advised Fersen to leave, which he did (Saint-Priest, *Mémoires*, 2:22; compare 2:90). As for Louis XVI's attitude, at least as reported by Saint-Priest, it was perfectly in tune with the mores of "good society" *(la bonne compagnie)* in late-eighteenth-century France. Marie-Antoinette "had put the king on the footing of a great discretion with respect to herself. When he saw someone, he withdrew, and she did not have to fear on his part any surprise" (Saint-Priest, *Mémoires*, 2:91–92).

### 9. A GARDEN WITH FLOWERS

1. Pierre de Brantôme, cited by Solnon, *La Cour de France,* 21.
2. Sévigné, *Lettres,* 5:546.
3. Luynes, *Mémoires,* 9:500–501.
4. Saint-Simon, *Historical Memoirs,* 1:503.
5. De la Chesnaye-Desbois and Badier, *Dictionnaire,* 14:982–84.
6. Ibid., 14:988.
7. Luynes, *Mémoires,* 5:92; Mercy, *Correspondance secrète,* vol. 2 (letter of September 17, 1776).
8. Levron, *Les inconnus,* ch. 7.
9. Princesse Palatine, *Lettres,* 153–54, 188; Saint-Simon, *Mémoires,* 1:256 with n. 2.
10. Baillie, "Etiquette," 191 with n. 2, citing Luynes, *Mémoires,* 8:152.
11. Mercier, *Tableau de Paris,* 4:153–54; Luynes, *Mémoires,* 1:357, 3:282.
12. Hézecques, *Souvenirs,* 157.
13. Walpole, *Horace Walpole's Correspondence,* 7:266; Blondel, *L'architecture française,* 4:101; Marie, *Mansart à Versailles,* 1:184–85.
14. Mercier, *Tableau de Paris,* 4:146–52.
15. Newton, *L'espace du roi,* 247, citing Archives Nationales O$^1$ 1801 187; Verlet, *Le château de Versailles,* 537.
16. Beaussant, *Les plaisirs de Versailles,* 156; Papillon de La Ferté, *Journal,* 68–69.
17. Campan, *Mémoires,* 132. For these paragraphs I am heavily indebted to Beaussant, *Les plaisirs de Versailles,* especially 211–46, 474–81.
18. Stanislas Leczinski's instructions to his daughter cited by Antoine, *Louis XV,* 459.
19. Walpole, *Horace Walpole's Correspondence,* 7, section 5, 90 (letter of Madame du Deffand to Walpole, December 6, 1778).
20. Luynes, *Mémoires,* 10:321, 325; Barbier, *Chronique,* 2:383 (mourning).
21. Newton, *L'espace du roi,* 222, citing the memoirs of Sourches.
22. Dufourcq, *Musique,* 148–49, 147–48; Luynes, *Mémoires,* 10:326.
23. Luynes, *Mémoires,* 11:240, 11:246.
24. Lever, *Correspondance,* 45 (Maria Theresa to Marie-Antoinette, May 4, 1770).
25. Mercy, *Correspondance secrète,* 2:323.
26. Le Guillou, "Le 'côté du Roi,'" 97–98; Girault de Coursac, *Louis XVI,* 139–40, citing Turin, *Letteri Ministri Francia, Mazzo 222,* dispatch no. 188, 502.
27. Véri, *Journal,* 2:19; Bombelles, *Journal,* 1:185.
28. Burke, *The Fabrication of Louis XIV,* 139, 142 with fig. 61.
29. Marais, *Journal,* 2:319.
30. Ibid., 319–22, entry for July 31, 1722.

31. Evrard, "Les moeurs à Versailles," 200–202.
32. Labourdette, "Conseils," 92.
33. Note the remarks of Nolhac, *Versailles au XVIIIe siècle,* 103.
34. Le Guillou, "La création des cabinets," 141.
35. Brancas, *Histoire,* 15.
36. Dufort de Cheverny, *Mémoires,* 1:394–95.
37. Rogister, "Le petit groupe."
38. Brancas, *Histoire,* 63.
39. At full speed: Richelieu, *Mémoires,* 61–62.
40. Baulez, "L'appartement."
41. Beaussant, *Les plaisirs de Versailles,* 165–89, 414–22.
42. H. Siefert in Salmon, *Madame de Pompadour,* 32.
43. Ibid., 179 nos. 49–50.
44. Gruber, *Les grandes fêtes,* 205 and fig. 98; Constans and Salmon, *Splendors of Versailles,* 196–97; Kisluk-Grosheide, "Versailles," 85–86; Têtart-Vittu, "Grandes robes," 150–51 and fig. 5.
45. Stein, "Madame de Pompadour"; Xavier Salmon in *Madame de Pompadour,* 179–81.
46. Saint-Priest, *Mémoires,* 1:98; Argenson, *Journal,* 2:216.
47. Nolhac, *La résurrection de Versailles,* 177–79.
48. Campan, *Mémoires,* 36.
49. Racinais, *Un Versailles inconnu,* 116–28.
50. Croÿ, *Journal inédit,* 3:64.
51. Croÿ, *Journal inédit,* 1:359.
52. Darnton, "An Early Information Society."
53. Duindam, *Vienna and Versailles,* 139.
54. Véri, *Journal,* 1:191; Guicciardi, "Between the Licit and the Illicit," citing E. Raunié, *Chansonnier historique* (Paris: 1879–82), 8:252–53.
55. Antoine, *Louis XV,* 501–10.
56. [Mouffle d'Angerville], *La vie privée de Louis XV,* 3:12–13; Laski, *The Trial,* 172, citing *Procès verbal de la séance du 16 frimaire,* Archives Nationales W[1] 300.
57. Princesse Palatine, *Lettres,* 399; Argenson cited by Brocher, *Le rang,* 190.
58. Princesse Palatine, *Lettres,* 104.
59. See Newton, *L'espace du roi,* 163–64, citing a letter of Madame de Maintenon ("always pressed").
60. Marie, *Mansart à Versailles,* 2:568–79 for plans and details of the marquise's rooms; Dufourcq, *Musique,* citing the journal of Sources for July 26, 1704.
61. *The Tatler,* no. 19, Tuesday, May 24, 1709 (vol 1. 155–56 in the version edited by D. F. Bond).

62. Voltaire, *Le siècle de Louis XIV,* 196–97.

63. Croÿ, *Journal inédit,* 1:86, 2:139.

64. Choiseul, *Mémoires,* 265–66.

65. Croÿ, *Journal inédit,* 2:439; Nivernais, *Lettres,* 149–50; Besenval, *Mémoires,* 216.

66. Levron, *Les inconnus,* 239.

67. Campan, *Mémoires,* 128.

68. Bombelles, *Journal,* 1:173.

69. Browning, *Despatches from Paris,* 1:175, 1:181–82, 2:109.

70. Price, *The Fall of the French Monarchy,* 25–26; Le Guillou, "Le 'côté du Roi,'" 131–32.

71. Saint-Priest, *Mémoires,* 1:218.

72. Lévis, *Souvenirs-Portraits,* 156; Bombelles, *Journal,* 2:239, 2:284.

10. "THE ROYAL ZOO"

1. Massounie, *L'architecture,* 80–81, 113.

2. [Mouffle d'Angerville], *La vie privée de Louis XV,* 4:133; compare Blondel, *L'architecture française,* 4:111.

3. Le Guillou, "L'appartement," 209–10.

4. Heitzmann and Didier, "La grille," 31–33.

5. Levron, *Les inconnus,* ch. 12; Blondel, *L'architecture française,* 4:114.

6. Hibbert, *Versailles,* 145, citing a letter of Franklin; compare Walpole, *Horace Walpole's Correspondence,* 13:167.

7. Hézecques, *Souvenirs,* 147–48.

8. Saule, "Tables à Versailles," 64; Houth, *Versailles aux trois visages,* 340.

9. Princesse Palatine, *Lettres,* 400.

10. Luynes, *Mémoires,* 3:242–43; Le Roi, *Histoire de Versailles,* 1:289–93.

11. Houth, *Versailles aux trois visages,* 284–85, 308–10.

12. Saint-Simon, *Historical Memoirs,* 2:327–28.

13. Cited by Baillie, "Etiquette," 183, n. 2; Evrard, "Les moeurs à Versailles," 198–200; Le Roi, *Histoire de Versailles,* 399–400; Houth, *Versailles aux trois visages,* 306–308.

14. Hézecques, *Souvenirs,* 147–48; compare Bombelles, *Journal,* 2:238.

15. Luynes, *Mémoires,* 9:417–18.

16. Evrard, "Les moeurs à Versailles," 104–8.

17. Tourzel, *Mémoires,* 29.

18. Saint-Simon, *Historical Memoirs,* 1:294, 1:438.

19. Argenson, *Journal,* 2:101, 2:109, 2:156–57; Campan, *Mémoires,* 168.

20. Le Roi, *Histoire de Versailles,* 1:293–98; Petitfils, *Louis XVI,* 195–203.

21. Beaussant, *Les plaisirs de Versailles,* 474 (tent); Bombelles, *Journal,* 2:104.

22. Pitou, "The Players' Return," 143.

23. Croÿ, *Journal inédit,* 1:364, 1:368, 1:384; Luynes, *Mémoires,* 15:355ff; Hézecques, *Mémoires,* 158; Dufort de Cheverny, *Mémoires,* 1:210; Rogister, "From Louis XIV to Louis XVI," 161 (on the guardroom); Campan, *Mémoires,* 456–57 (Landsmath).

24. Argenson, *Journal,* 2:369–71.

25. Saule, *La journée de Louis XIV,* 18, citing the *État de la France* for 1698, 1:417.

26. Hézecques, *Souvenirs,* 131. Parades: see, for example, Luynes, *Mémoires,* 14:322–23 (reception of comte d'Eu as colonel-general of the Swiss).

27. Le Roi, *Histoire de Versailles,* 1:414, 2:3; Moussoir, "Les Gardes-Françaises," (with illustration).

28. Baillie, "Etiquette," 184 n. 4, citing a Venetian dispatch of 1683.

29. Oberkirch, *Mémoires,* 218; Luynes, *Mémoires,* 15:397; Hézecques, *Souvenirs,* 133.

30. Campan, *Mémoires,* 136–37; Bombelles, *Journal,* 1:329; Oberkirch, *Mémoires,* 422.

31. Hézecques, *Souvenirs,* 130; Boigne, *Mémoires,* 35; Saint-Priest, *Mémoires,* 1:19; Besenval, *Mémoires,* 20; Bombelles, *Journal,* 1:303.

32. Hézecques, *Souvenirs,* 133–34, 137–38; Saint-Priest, *Mémoires,* 1:247.

33. Mercier, *Tableau de Paris,* 4:146–52.

34. Voltaire, *Oeuvres complètes,* 15:237, cited by Michel, "Le château de Versailles," 98.

35. Argenson, *Journal,* 1:293, 1:335.

36. Campan, *Mémoires,* 270.

37. Mercier, *Tableau de Paris,* 5:146–52.

38. Véri, *Journal,* 2:106–7.

39. Lemoine, "Les écuries du roi."

40. Argenson, *Journal,* 1:121–22; 2:60; Verlet, *Le château de Versailles,* 652, citing Barbier's *Journal;* Thompson, *The French Revolution,* 115, citing Chénier's play *Charles IX, or the School of Kings.*

41. Argenson, *Journal,* 2:109, 2:119.

42. Popkin, *The Panorama of Paris,* 167–68.

43. Campan, *Mémoires,* 261; Papillon de La Ferté, *Journal,* 30, 35, 38, 42.

44. Rudé, *The Crowd,* 71, citing Archives Nationales Y 18767.

45. Bombelles, *Journal,* 2:292, 2:304–8, 2:325–28, 2:331; Dufort de Cheverny, *Mémoires,* 2:117.

46. Bombelles, *Journal,* 2:333; Hézecques, *Souvenirs,* 193.

47. Besenval, *Mémoires,* 498.

48. Fleury, *Les derniers jours,* 181.

49. Campan, *Mémoires,* 267–70.

50. Price, *The Fall of the French Monarchy,* 92–96, quoting from an unpublished memoir by the marquis de Sérent, governor of the Artois princes.

51. Saint-Priest, *Mémoires,* 1:237; Campan, *Mémoires,* 276.

52. Lever, *Correspondance,* 494; Newton, *L'espace du roi,* 240, citing L. F. des Cars, *Mémoires,* 2:84.

53. Saint-Priest, *Mémoires,* 1:237, 1:246.

54. Le Roi, *Histoire de Versailles,* 2:22.

55. Le Guillou, "L'appartement," 212–16; Verlet, *Le château de Versailles,* 537.

56. Hézecques, *Souvenirs,* 58. Note Campan, *Mémoires,* 270: "Le roi n'ignorait pas toutes ces menaces populaires."

57. Verlet, *Le château de Versailles,* 649 (citing no source).

58. Rudé, *The Crowd,* ch. 5.

59. La Tour du Pin, *Recollections,* 91–92; Campan, *Mémoires,* 286–89; Beaussant, *Les plaisirs de Versailles,* 237–48.

60. Campan, *Mémoires,* 289–90; Chastenay, *Mémoires,* 99.

61. Hézecques, *Souvenirs,* 309 (threat to palace).

62. Chastenay, *Mémoires,* 101.

63. Heitzmann and Didier, "La grille," 34.

64. Hézecques, *Souvenirs,* 312.

65. Campan, *Mémoires,* 293–94.

66. This version of events, told to Madame Campan (*Mémoires,* 293) by her sister Madame Auguié, who was there, is preferred here to the tradition (see, for example, La Tour du Pin, 104) that the queen escaped via the king's passage.

67. Cabanès, *La princesse de Lamballe intime,* 432–36 and 446, n. 39, citing comte de Las Cases, *Mémorial de Sainte Hélène* (Paris, 1823), 7:395ff.

68. Saint-Priest, *Mémoires,* 2:88.

69. Boigne, *Mémoires,* 90.

70. Girault de Coursac, *Louis XVI,* 852, citing the autograph account of Fournier "the American" in the Archives Nationales.

71. Lever, *Correspondance,* 494 n. 2. For this entrance see Bombelles, *Journal,* 2:199; Hézecques, *Souvenirs,* 315.

72. Fleury, *Les derniers jours,* 219. Except where otherwise stated, this account of the October days is based on Leclercq, *Les journées d'octobre.*

73. Verlet, *Le mobilier royal français,* 2:150–51 citing Archives Nationales O$^1$3426$^8$; Le Guillou, "Le 'côté du Roi,'" 136.

74. Luynes, *Mémoires,* 10:317.

75. Thomas, *The Wicked Queen,* 239–46, includes a translation of *Description de la ménagerie royale d'animaux vivans établie aux Tuileries,* by F. Dantalle.

*Notes*

II. AFTER THE DELUGE

1. For details, see Jallut, "Les petits appartements."
2. Reproduced by Gaehtgens, *Versailles,* 49.
3. Cited by Barbier, "De Versailles à Fontainebleau," 39–40.
4. Jallut, "Les petits appartements."
5. Nolhac, *Versailles. Résidence de Louis XIV,* citing the king's own orders.
6. Ferrand, *Ils ont sauvé Versailles,* 234–41.
7. Olivier de Rohan in Nolhac, *La résurrection de Versailles,* iv.
8. Taylor, *The Assassin's Cloak,* 65, citing the Brothers Goncourt.
9. Cabanès, *La princesse de Lamballe intime,* 442.
10. Nolhac, *La résurrection de Versailles,* 102.
11. Ferrand, *Ils ont sauvé Versailles,* 302–3; Boigne, *Mémoires,* 68.
12. Charles Dickens, *A Tale of Two Cities* (London: Chapman and Hall, 1890), 417.
13. Ferrand, *Ils ont sauvé Versailles,* 163–64.
14. Charlotte Mosley, ed., *The Letters of Nancy Mitford* (London, 1993), 410 (letter of November 19, 1955).
15. Morison and Lamont, *An Adventure,* 8–9.
16. Sénelier, *Le mystère,* 170.
17. Castle, "Marie-Antoinette Obsession," 233, n. 44.
18. Correspondence between Racinais and Jean Sénelier in 1967 and 1977, quoted by Sénelier, *Le mystère du Petit Trianon,* 133.
19. Milovanovic, *Du Louvre à Versailles,* 180.
20. See the interview reported in *Le Figaro* for September 17, 2007 (page 28).
21. *The Times* of London, June 26, 2004.
22. [Starcky], *Louis XVI,* 99–105, nos. 14C, E, F.
23. Ferrand, *Ils ont sauvé Versailles,* 248–51.
24. Dauphin, "Versailles," 92–94.
25. As suggested by Marie, *Versailles au temps de Louis XV,* 76.
26. Cited by Gaehtgens, *Versailles,* 49.
27. Houth, *Versailles aux trois visages,* 14, quoting Théophile Gautier.
28. Michel, "Le château de Versailles" 98, citing Mercier's *L'An 2440.*
29. The exhibition *Cent ans, cent objets,* September 18–November 18, 2007.

# SOURCES

The bibliography for Versailles is huge. This list confines itself to the principal sources consulted, including the books and articles cited in the references.

*Abrégé historique des chevaliers et officiers commandeurs de l'Ordre du Saint-Esprit depuis son institution jusqu'à la révolution de 1789 suivi de la liste des personnes admises aux honneurs de la cour.* Geneva, 1873.

Adhémar, comtesse d'. *Souvenirs sur Marie Antoinette, archiduchesse d'Autriche, reine de France, et sur la cour de Versailles.* 4 vols. Paris, 1836.

Antoine, Michel. *Louis XV.* Paris, 1989.

Apostolidès, Jean-Marie. *Le roi-machine.* Paris, 1981.

Argenson [René-Louis, marquis d']. *Journal and Memoirs of the Marquis d'Argenson.* Translated by Katharine P. Wormeley. 2 vols. Boston, 1909.

Ariès, P., and G. Duby, eds. *A History of Private Life.* Vol. 3, *Passions of the Renaissance,* edited by Roger Chartier, translated by A. Goldhammer. Cambridge, Mass., 1989.

[Bachaumont, L. Petit de]. *Choix des mémoires secrets pour servir à l'histoire de la république des lettres.* 2 vols. London, 1788.

Baillie, Hugh Murray. "Etiquette and the Planning of the State Apartments in Baroque Palaces." *Archaeologica* 101 (1967): 169–99.

Barbet, L.-A. *Les grandes eaux de Versailles.* Paris, 1907.

Barbier, Edmond Jean François. *Chronique de la Régence et du règne de Louis XV, 1718–1763.* 8 vols. Paris, 1866–77.

Barbier, Muriel. "De Versailles à Fontainebleau. Devenir d'une cheminée sous la Monarchie de Juillet." *Versalia* 7 (2004): 38–41.

Batiffol, Louis. *Versailles et ses Habitants en 1789.* Versailles, 1890.

Baulez, Christian. "L'appartement de la duchesse de Châteauroux au château de Versailles." *Versalia* 7 (2004): 42–54.

————. "La tribune de la marquise de Pompadour à la chapelle du château de Versailles." In *Madame de Pompadour et les arts,* edited by Xavier Salmon, 86–87. Paris, 2002.

Beaussant, Philippe. *Les plaisirs de Versailles.* With Patricia Bouchenot-Déchin. Paris, 1996.

Béguin, Katia. *Les princes de Condé. Rebelles, courtisans et mécènes dans la France du grand siècle.* Paris, 1999.

Bély, Lucien. *Espions et ambassadeurs au temps de Louis XIV.* Paris, 1990.

Benoît, Jérémie. *Napoléon et Versailles.* An exhibition catalogue. Paris, 2005.

Bergin, Joseph. "The Royal Confessor and His Rivals in Seventeenth-Century France." *French History* 21 (2007): 187–204.

Besenval [Pierre-Victor, baron de Besenval]. *Mémoires du baron de Besenval sur la cour de France.* Edited by Ghislain de Diesbach. Paris, 1987.

Black, Jeremy. *France and the Grand Tour.* Basingstoke, 2003.

Blanning, Tim. *The Culture of Power and the Power of Culture.* Oxford, 2002.

Bloch, Marc. *The Royal Touch.* Translated by J. E. Anderson. New York, 1989.

Blondel, Jacques-François. *L'architecture française.* 4 vols. Paris, 1752–56.

Bluche, François. *Louis XIV.* Translated by Mark Greenglass. Oxford, 1990 (French original, 1984).

Boigne [Adèle, comtesse de Boigne]. *Mémoires de la comtesse de Boigne, née Osmond.* Edited by Jean-Claude Berchet. Vol. 1. Paris, 1999.

Bombelles, marquis de. *Journal.* Edited by J. Grassion, F. Durif, and J. Charon-Bordas. 4 vols. Geneva, 1978–98.

Bonney, Richard. "Vindication of the Fronde? The Cost of Louis XIV's Versailles Building Programme." *French History* 21 (2007): 205–25.

Brancas, Madame de [Marie-Angélique Fremyn de Moras, duchesse de]. *Histoire de Madame de Châteauroux.* Paris, 2005.

Brocher, Henri. *Le rang et l'étiquette sous l'ancien régime. A la cour de Louis XIV.* Paris, 1934.

Browning, Oscar, ed. *Despatches from Paris 1784–1790.* 2 vols. London, 1910.

Burke, Peter. *The Fabrication of Louis XIV.* Cambridge, 1992.

Burrows, Simon. *Blackmail, Scandal and Revolution.* Manchester, 2006.

Buvat, Jean. *Journal de la Régence (1715–1723).* Edited by É. Campardon. 2 vols. Paris, 1865.

Cabanès, Docteur. *La princesse de Lamballe intime.* Paris, n.d.

Campan, Jeanne Louise Henriette. *The Private Life of Marie Antoinette.* London, 1887.

Campan [Jeanne Louise Henriette Genet, Madame Campan]. *Mémoires de Madame Campan.* Edited by Jean Chalon. Paris, 1988.

Campbell, Peter R. *Power and Politics in Old Regime France 1720–1745*. London and New York, 1996.

Castelluccio, Stéphane. "La Galerie des Glaces: Les réceptions d'ambassadeurs." *Versalia* 9 (2006): 24–52.

Castle, Terry. "Marie-Antoinette Obsession." In *Marie-Antoinette: Writings on the Body of a Queen,* edited by Dena Goodman, 199–238. London, 2003.

Chastenay, Madame de. *Mémoires 1771–1815*. Edited by Guy Chaussinand-Nogaret. Paris, 1987.

Chaussinand-Nogaret, Guy. *The French Nobility in the Eighteenth Century*. Translated by William Doyle. Cambridge, 1985 (French edition, 1976).

Choffé, Laurent. "Le jardin champêtre de Trianon: L'alliance du pittoresque à la botanique." *Versalia* 7 (2004): 56–69.

Choiseul [Étienne-François, duc de]. *Mémoires du duc de Choiseul*. Edited by Jean-Pierre Guicciardi. Paris, 1987.

Chrisman-Campbell, Kimberly. "Mourning and *La Mode* at the Court of Louis XVI." *Costume* 39 (2005): 64–78.

Constans, Claire, and Xavier Salmon, eds. *Splendors of Versailles*. An exhibition catalogue. Mississippi Commission for International Cultural Exchange and Musée National des Châteaux de Versailles et de Trianon. New York, 1998.

Cornette, Joël. "L'histoire au travail. Le nouveau 'Siècle de Louis XIV': Un bilan historiographique depuis vingt ans (1980–2000)." *Histoire, Économie et Société* 19 (2000): 561–620.

Coward, D. A. "Attitudes to Homosexuality in Eighteenth-Century France." *Journal of European Studies* 10 (1980): 231–55.

Creutz, comte de. *La Suède et les Lumières: Lettres de France d'un Ambassadeur à son Roi (1771–1783)*. Edited by Marianne Molander Beyer. Paris, 2006.

Crouzet, Denis. "Postscript." *French History* 21 (2007): 226–30.

Croÿ, Emmanuel, duc de. *Journal inédit,* edited by vicomte de Grouchy and P. Cottin, 4 vols. Paris, 1907.

Dangeau [Philippe de Courcillon, marquis de Dangeau]. *Journal de la Cour du Roi Soleil*. Vol. 6, *La Prise de Namur*. Paleo, Clermont-Ferrand.

Darnton, Robert. "An Early Information Society: News and Media in Eighteenth Century Paris." *American Historical Review* 105 (2000), http://www.historycooperative.org/joumals/ahr/105.1/ah000001.html (accessed March 10, 2006).

Dauphin, Noëlle. "Versailles, le château et la ville." *Histoire urbaine* 9 (2004): 79–96.

Da Vinha, Mathieu. *Les valets de chambre de Louis XIV*. Paris, 2004.

De la Chesnaye-Desbois, A., and Badier. *Dictionnaire de la noblesse.* 19 vols. 3rd edition. Paris, 1868–76 (Krauss reprint, 1969).

Delafosse, Marcel. "Affairistes et solliciteurs sous Louis XIV." *Revue de l'Histoire de Versailles et de Seine-et-Oise* 57 (1968–69): 61–69.

Delpy, A. "Un chef de service au Département du Duc de La Vrillière." *Revue de l'Histoire de Versailles et Seine-et-Oise* 8 (1906): 173–92 and 232–47.

Déon, Michel, ed. *Louis XIV par lui-même.* Paris, 1991.

Dewald, Jonathan. *Aristocratic Experience and the Origins of Modern Culture: France 1570–1715.* Berkeley, 1993.

Dion, Marie-Pierre. *Emmanuel de Croÿ (1718–1784).* Brussels, 1987.

Doyle, William. *Venality: The Sale of Offices in Eighteenth-Century France.* Oxford, 1996.

Doyle, William, ed. *Old Regime France, 1648–1788.* Oxford, 2001.

Drévillon, Hervé. *L'impôt du sang.* Paris, 2005.

Dufort de Cheverny, comte de. *Mémoires.* Edited by Pierre-André Weber. 2 vols. Paris, 1970.

Dufourcq, Norbert. *Musique de la cour de Louis XIV et de Louis XV d'après les Mémoires de Sourches et Luynes 1681–1758.* Paris, 1970.

Duindam, Jeroen. *Vienna and Versailles.* Cambridge, 2003.

Dulaure, J. A. *Nouvelle description des environs de Paris.* 2 vols. Paris, 1786.

Duma, Jean. *Les Bourbon-Penthièvre (1678–1793).* Paris, 1995.

Dunlop, Ian. *Versailles.* 2nd edition. London, 1970.

Edmunds, Martha Mel Stumberg. *Piety and Politics: Imagining Divine Kingship in Louis XIV's Chapel at Versailles.* Newark and London, 2002.

Elias, Norbert. *The Court Society.* Translated by Edmund Jephcott. Oxford, 1983.

Evrard, Fernand. "Les eaux de Versailles." *Annales de Géographie* 42 (1933): 583–600.

———. "Les moeurs à Versailles sous Louis XVI." *Revue de l'histoire de Versailles et de Seine-et-Oise* 30 (1928): 85–113 and 178–204.

Ferrand, Franck. *Ils ont sauvé Versailles.* Paris, 2003.

Flandrin, J. L. *Families in Former Times: Kinship, Household and Sexuality.* Translated by Richard Southern. Cambridge, 1979 (French original, 1976).

Fleury, Vicomte. *Les derniers jours de Versailles.* Paris, 1929.

Forster, Robert. *The House of Saulx-Tavanes: Versailles and Burgundy 1730–1830.* Baltimore, 1971.

Foster, Susan Leigh. "Dancing the Body Politic: Manner and Mimesis in Eighteenth-Century Ballet." In *From the Royal to the Republican Body: Incorporating the Political in Seventeenth- and Eighteenth-Century France,* edited by Sara E. Melzer and Kathryn Norberg, 162–81. Berkeley, 1998.

Fraser, Antonia. *Marie-Antoinette.* London, 2001.

Fromageot, P. "Les hôtelleries et cabarets de l'ancien Versailles." *Revue de l'histoire de Versailles et de Seine-et-Oise* 8 (1906): 24–46, 217–31.

Furet, François, and Denis Richet. *La Révolution française*. Paris, 1973.

G., H., "Notes d'un voyageur anglais à Versailles en 1838." *Revue de l'histoire de Versailles et de Seine-et-Oise* 25–26 (1923–24), 372–75.

Gaehtgens, Thomas W. *Versailles. De la résidence royale au musée historique*. Anvers, 1984.

Garrioch, David. *The Making of Revolutionary Paris*. Berkeley, 2002.

Genlis [Stéphanie Félicité Ducrest, comtesse de]. *De l'esprit des étiquettes*. With a preface by Chantal Thomas. 1996.

———. *Mémoires de Madame de Genlis*. Edited by Didier Masseau. Paris, 2004.

Girault de Coursac, Paul, and Pierrette de Coursac. *Louis XVI et Marie-Antoinette*. Paris, 1990.

Girouard, Mark. *Life in the French Country House*. London, 2000.

Goodman, Dena. *The Portraits of Madame de Pompadour: Celebrating the Femme Savante*. Berkeley, 2000.

Gordon, Daniel. *Sovereignty and Sociability in French Thought, 1670–1789*. Princeton, 1994.

Goubert, Pierre. *Louis XIV et vingt millions de français*. Revised ed. Paris, 1991.

Goubert, Pierre. *The Ancien Régime. French Society 1600–1750*. Translated by Steve Cox. London, 1997 (1st English edition, 1973; French original, 1969).

Grivel, Marianne. "Le cabinet du roi." *Revue de la Bibliothèque Nationale* 5 (1985): 36–57.

Gruber, Alain-Charles. *Les grandes fêtes et leurs décors à l'époque de Louis XVI*. Geneva, 1972.

Guicciardi, Jean-Pierre. "Between the Licit and the Illicit: The Sexuality of the King." In *"'Tis Nature's Fault": Unauthorized Sexuality During the Enlightenment*, edited by Robert P. Maccubbin. 88–97. Cambridge, 1985.

Hardman, John. *Louis XVI*. New Haven and London, 1993.

———. *Louis XVI: The Silent King*. London, 2000.

Hartle, Robert Wyman. "Louis XIV and the Mirror of Antiquity." In *The Sun King: Louis XIV and the New World*, edited by S. G. Reinhardt. 106–17. New Orleans, 1984.

Haskell, Francis, and Nicholas Penny. *Taste and the Antique: The Lure of Classical Sculpture, 1500–1900*. New Haven and London, 1981.

Heitzmann, Annick, and Frédéric Didier. "La grille et la cour royales." *Versalia* 10 (2007): 26–43.

Hézecques, Félix, comte de France d'. *Souvenirs d'un page de la cour de Louis XVI*. Brionne, n.d.

Hibbert, Christopher. *Versailles*. New York, 1972.

Himmelfarb, Hélène. "Versailles: functions et légendes." In *La Nation,* vol. 2 of *Les lieux de mémoire,* edited by Pierre Nora, 235–92. Paris, 1986.

Horowski, Leonhard. "'Such a Great Advantage for My Son': Office-Holding and Career Mechanisms at the Court of France, 1661–1789." *The Court Historian* 8 (2003): 125–76.

Hours, Bernard. *Louis XV et sa cour.* Paris, 2002.

Houth, Émile, and Madeleine Houth. *Versailles aux trois visages.* Versailles, 1980.

Hufton, Olwen. "The Role of Women in the Early Modern Court." *The Court Historian* 5 (2000): 1–13.

Huisman, Philippe, and Marguerite Jallut. *Marie Antoinette. L'impossible bonheur.* 1970.

Isherwood, Robert. *Music in the Service of the King: France in the Seventeenth Century.* Ithaca, 1973.

Jallut, Marguerite. "Château de Versailles: Cabinets intérieurs et petits appartements de Marie-Antoinette." *Gazette des beaux-arts,* 6th period, 63 (1964): 289–354.

———. "Les petits appartements de Marie-Antoinette au temps de la Révolution. Le XIXe siècle et la destruction." *Revue de l'histoire de Versailles et de Seine-et-Oise* 56 (1965–67): 87–97.

Jones, Colin. *The Great Nation: France from Louis XV to Napoleon.* New York, 2003.

Kaiser, Thomas E. "Ambiguous Identities: Marie-Antoinette and the House of Lorraine from the Affair of the Minuet to Lambesc's Charge." In *Marie-Antoinette: Writings on the Body of a Queen,* edited by Dena Goodman, London, 2002. 171–98.

Kantorowicz, E. "Oriens Augusti—Lever du Roi." *Dumbarton Oaks Papers* 17 (1963): 117–77.

Kimball, Fiske. *The Creation of the Rococo Style.* Toronto, 1980 (reprint of *The Creation of the Rococo,* Philadelphia, 1943).

Kisluk-Grosheide, Danielle. "Versailles au Metropolitan Museum de New York." *Versalia* 8 (2005): 66–93.

Labatut, Jean-Pierre. *Les ducs et pairs de France au XVIIe siècle.* Paris, 1972.

Lablaude, Pierre-André. *The Gardens of Versailles.* London, 1995 (French original, 1995).

Labourdette, Jean-François. "Conseils à un Duc de La Trémoille à son entrée dans le monde." *Enquêtes et Documents* (Centre de Recherches sur l'Histoire de la France Atlantique) 2 (1972): 73–184.

Lagny, Jean. "L'hôtel de Saint-Simon à Versailles." *Cahiers Saint-Simon* 12 (1984): 7–15.

Laski, Philip. *The Trial and Execution of Madame du Barry*. London, 1969.

La Tour du Pin [Henriette-Lucie Dillon, marquise de]. *Recollections of the Revolution and the Empire*. Translated by Walter Geer. London, 1921.

Leclercq, D. *Les journées d'octobre et la fin de l'année 1789*. Paris, 1924.

Le Guillou, Jean-Claude. "L'appartement de Madame Sophie au château de Versailles: Formation et métamorphoses, 1774–1790." *Gazette des beaux-arts,* 6th period, 103 (1981), 201–18.

———. "La création des cabinets et des petits appartements de Louis XV au château de Versailles, 1722–1738." *Gazette des Beaux-Arts,* 6th period, 127 (1985): 137–46.

———. "Le château neuf ou enveloppe de Versailles." *Versalia* 8 (2005): 112–33.

———. "Le 'côté du Roi' au temps de Louis XVI." *Versalia* 10 (2007): 80–142.

———. "Les châteaux de Louis XIII à Versailles." *Versalia* 7 (2004): 142–67.

Lemoine, Henri. "Les écuries du roi sous l'ancien régime." *Revue de l'histoire de Versailles et de Seine-et-Oise* (1933): 152–83.

Lemoine, Pierre. "Les logements de Saint-Simon au château de Versailles." *Cahiers Saint-Simon* 12 (1984): 17–30.

Le Monnier, H. Introduction to *Procès-verbaux de l'Académie royale d'architecture 1671–1793,* 2 (1911).

Le Roi, J.-A. *Histoire de Versailles, de ses rues, places et avenues depuis l'origine de cette ville jusqu'à nos jours*. 2 vols. Versailles, 1868.

Le Roy Ladurie, Emmanuel. *Saint-Simon and the Court of Louis XIV*. Translated by Arthur Goldhammer. Chicago and London, 2001 (French original, 1997).

Lever, Évelyne, ed. *Correspondance de Marie-Antoinette (1770–1793)*. Paris, 2005.

Levi, Anthony. *Louis XIV*. London, 2004.

Lévis [Gaston, duc de Lévis]. *Souvenirs-Portraits de Gaston de Lévis*. Edited by J. Dupâquier. Paris, 1993.

Levron, Jacques. *Les courtesans*. Paris, 1960.

———. *Les inconnus de Versailles*. Revised ed. Paris, 1988 (first edition, 1968).

———. *Versailles, ville royale*. Paris, 1964.

Lilti, Antoine. *Le monde des salons. Sociabilité et mondanité à Paris au XVIIIe siècle*. Paris, 2005.

Louis XIV. *Mémoires*. Edited by Jean Longnon. Paris, 2001 (1st edition, 1978).

Louis XV. *Lettres de Louis XV à son petit-fils l'infant Ferdinand de Parme*. Edited by Philippe Amiguet. Paris, 1938.

Luynes, Charles-Philippe, duc de. *Mémoires*. Edited by L. Dussieux and E. Soulié. 17 vols. Paris, 1860–65.

McGowan, Margaret. *The Vision of Rome in Late Renaissance France*. New Haven and London, 2000.

McManners, John. *Church and Society in Eighteenth-Century France.* 2 vols. Oxford, 1998.

Mansel, Philip. *The Court of France, 1789–1830.* Cambridge, 1988.

——. *Dressed to Rule: Royal and Court Costume from Louis XIV to Elizabeth II.* New Haven and London, 2005.

——. *Pillars of Monarchy: An Outline of the Political and Social History of Royal Guards 1400–1984.* London, 1984.

Marais, Mathieu. *Journal et mémoires sur la Régence et le règne de Louis XV (1715–1737).* Edited by M. de Lescure. 2 vols. Paris, 1863.

Maral, Alexandre. *La chapelle royale de Versailles sous Louis XIV.* Sprimont, 2002.

Marie, Alfred. *Naissance de Versailles. Le château—les jardins.* 2 vols. Paris, 1968.

Marie, Alfred, and Jeanne Marie. *Mansart à Versailles.* 2 vols. Paris, 1972.

——. *Versailles au temps de Louis XV 1715–1745.* Paris, 1984.

Maroteaux, V., and J. de Givry. *Versailles. Le grand parc.* 2004.

Massounie, Dominique, *L'architecture des écuries royales du château de Versailles.* Paris, 1998.

Maurepas, Arnaud de, and Antoine Boulant. *Les ministres et les ministères du siècle des Lumières (1715–1789).* Paris, 1996.

Mauricheau-Beaupré, Ch. *Versailles, l'histoire et l'art: Guide officiel.* Paris, 1949.

Maza, Sarah. *Servants and Masters in Eighteenth-Century France: The Uses of Loyalty.* Princeton, 1983.

Melzer, Sara E., and Kathryn Norberg. *From the Royal to the Republican Body: Incorporating the Political in Seventeenth- and Eighteenth-Century France.* Berkeley, 1998.

Mercier, Jean-Sébastien. *Tableau de Paris. Nouvelle édition, corrigée et augmentée.* 8 vols. Amsterdam, 1783.

Mercy [Claude-Florimond, comte de Mercy-Argenteau]. *Correspondance secrète entre Marie-Thérèse et le comte de Mercy-Argenteau, avec les lettres de Marie-Thérèse et Marie-Antoinette.* Edited by A. Arneth and M. A. Geffroy. 3 vols. Paris, 1874.

Meyer, Daniel. "L'ameublement de la chambre de Louis XIV à Versailles de 1701 à nos jours." *Gazette des Beaux-Arts,* 6th period, 113 (1989): 81–104.

——. "Les obsèques de Louis XIV et de Louis XV." *Revue de l'histoire de Versailles et de Seine-et-Oise* 58 (1970): 67–86.

[Michaud]. *Biographie universelle.* Under the direction of M. Michaud. 45 vols. Paris, 1843–65.

Michel, Christian. "Le château de Versailles devant les Lumières." *Eighteenth-Century Life* 17 (1993): 95–101.

Milovanovic, Nicolas. *Du Louvre à Versailles. Lecture des grands décors monarchiques.* Paris, 2005.

Mitford, Nancy. *Madame de Pompadour*. Revised edition. London, 1968 (1st edition, 1954).

Morison, Elizabeth, and Frances Lamont [Charlotte Moberly and Eleanor Jourdain]. *An Adventure*. London, 1911.

Mossiker, Frances. *The Queen's Necklace*, 122. London, 2004 (1st edition, 1961).

[Mouffle d'Angerville]. *La vie privée de Louis XV, ou principaux événements, particularités, et anecdotes de son règne*. London, 1781.

Moussoir, G. "Les Gardes-Françaises à Versailles." *Revue de l'histoire de Versailles et de Seine-et-Oise* 17 (1915): 5–25.

Mukerji, Chandra. *Territorial Ambitions and the Gardens of Versailles*. Cambridge, 1997.

Newton, William R. *La petite cour*. Paris, 2006.

———. *L'espace du roi*. Paris, 2000.

Nivernais, duc de. *Lettres sur l'état de courtesan*. Edited by Lucien Perey. Paris, 1891.

Noël-Waldteufel, Marie-France. "Manger à la cour: alimentation et gastronomie aux XVIIe et XVIIIe siècles." In *Versailles et les tables royales en Europe XVIIème–XIXème siècle*, 69–84. An exhibition catalogue, Musée nationale des châteaux de Versailles et de Trianon. Paris, 1993.

Nolhac, Pierre de, *La création de Versailles*. Paris, 1925.

———. *La résurrection de Versailles*. Paris and Versailles, 2002 (1st edition, 1937).

———. *Versailles et la cour de France. Marie-Antoinette dauphine*. Paris, 1929.

———. *Versailles au XVIIIe siècle*. Paris, 1926.

———. *Versailles. Résidence de Louis XIV*. Paris, 1925.

Norton, Lucy (ed. and trans.), *Saint-Simon at Versailles*. London, 1980.

Oberkirch [Henriette-Louise, baronne d'Oberkirch], *Mémoires de la baronne d'Oberkirch*. Edited by Suzanne Burkard. Paris, 1989 (1st edition, 1970).

Palatine, Princesse [Élisabeth-Charlotte de Bavière, duchesse d'Orléans]. *Lettres de la princesse Palatine 1672–1722*. Edited by Olivier Amiel. Paris, 1985.

Papillon de La Ferté. *Journal des menus plaisirs du Roi, 1756–1780*. Clermont-Ferrand, 2002.

Pardailhé-Galabrun, Annik. *La naissance de l'intime*. Paris, 1988.

Pérouse de Montclos, Jean-Marie. *Versailles*. New York and Paris, 1991.

Perrin, Bernard. "Un Versailles inédit vu par un solliciteur à la Cour du Grand Roi (1699–1704)." *Revue de l'histoire de Versailles et de Seine-et-Oise* 55 (1963–64): 151–206.

Petitfils, Jean-Christian. *Louis XVI*. Paris, 2005.

Picciola, A. *Le comte de Maurepas. Versailles et l'Europe à la fin de l'Ancien Régime*. Paris, 1999.

Pinot-Duclos, Charles. *Considérations sur les moeurs de ce siècle*. Edited by F. C. Green. Cambridge, 1939 (first edition, 1750).

Pitou, Spire. "The Players' Return to Versailles, 1723–1757." *Studies on Voltaire and the Eighteenth Century* 73 (1970): 7–145.

Polignac, Comtesse Diane de. *Mémoires de Madame la Duchesse de Polignac. Avec des particularités sur sa liaison avec Marie-Antoinette, Reine de France.* Paris, Year 5 [=1796].

Popkin, Jeremy D., ed. *The Panorama of Paris: Selections from* Le Tableau de Paris. Philadelphia, 1999.

Price, Munro. *The Fall of the French Monarchy.* London, 2002.

———. "Versailles Revisited: New Work on the Old Regime." *History Journal* 46 (2003): 437–47.

Racinais, Henri. *Un Versailles inconnu. Les petits appartements des Rois Louis XV et Louis XVI.* Paris, 1950.

Ranum, Orest A. *Richelieu and the Councillors of Louis XIII.* Oxford, 1963.

Reyniers, François. "Contribution à l'histoire de l'hôtel de Seignelay à Versailles." *Revue de l'histoire de Versailles et de Seine-et-et-Oise* 69 (1971): 67–115.

Richard, Pascale, and Emmanuel Ducamp. *Versailles: The American Story.* Paris, 1999.

Richelieu [Louis-François-Armand, duc de]. *Mémoires authentiques du Maréchal de Richelieu (1725–1757).* Edited by A. de Boislisle. Paris, 1918.

Rogister, John. "From Louis XIV to Louis XVI: Some Thoughts on the *Petits Appartements.*" *Eighteenth-Century Life* 17 (1993): 146–66.

———. "Le petit groupe et le grand cercle de Madame de Pompadour à la Cour." *Versalia* 7 (2004): 168–78.

Rohe, Daniel, and Daniel Reytier, eds. *Les écuries royales du XVIe au XVIIIe siècle.* Paris, 1998.

Royon, Olivier. "La noblesse de province face à la noblesse de Cour. In *La noblesse de la fin du XVIe au début du XXe siècle, un modèle social?* 217–32. Edited by J. Pontet et al. Anglet, 2002.

Rubin, David Lee, ed. *The Sun King: The Ascendancy of French Culture During the Reign of Louis XIV.* Washington, D.C., 1992.

Rudé, G. *The Crowd in the French Revolution.* Oxford, 1959.

Sabatier, Gérard. "La gloire du roi. Iconographie de Louis XIV de 1661 à 1672." *Histoire, Économie et Société* 19 (2000): 527–60.

———. *Versailles ou la figure du roi.* Paris, 1999.

Saint-Priest, comte de. *Mémoires.* 2 vols. Paris, 1929.

Saint-Simon [Louis de Rouvroy, duc de Saint-Simon]. *Historical Memoirs of the Duc de Saint Simon.* Edited and translated by Lucy Norton. 3 vols. London, 1967, 1968, 1972.

Salmon, Xavier. *Pomp and Power: French Drawings from Versailles.* An exhibition catalogue. London, 2006.

Salmon, Xavier, ed. *Madame de Pompadour et les arts.* An exhibition catalogue, Musée national des châteaux de Versailles et de Trianon. Paris, 2002.

Salvatori, Philippe. *La chasse sous l'Ancien Régime.* Paris, 1996.

Sapori, Michelle. *Rose Bertin. Ministre des modes de Marie-Antoinette.* Paris, 2003.

Saule, Béatrix. *La journée de Louis XIV 16 novembre 1700.* Paris, 1996.

———. "Tables à Versailles 1682–1789." In *Versailles et les tables royales en Europe XVIIème–XIXème siècle,* 40–68. An exhibition catalogue, Musée national des châteaux de Versailles et de Trianon. Paris, 1993.

Schama, Simon. *Citizens.* London, 1989.

Sénelier, Jean. *Le mystère du Petit Trianon. Une vision dans l'espace-temps.* Nice, 1997.

Sévigné, Madame de. *Lettres.* Edited by M. Monmerqué. 12 vols. Paris, 1862–66.

Shennan, J. H. *The Parlement of Paris.* Stroud, 1998 (1st edition, 1968).

Solnon, Jean-François. *La Cour de France.* Paris, 1987.

———. *Versailles.* Monaco, 1997.

Spawforth, A., ed. *The Court and Court Society in Ancient Monarchies.* Cambridge, 2007.

[Starcky, Laure, ed.]. *Louis XVI et Marie-Antoinette à Compiègne.* An exhibition catalogue, Réunion des musées nationaux and musée national du château de Compiègne. Paris, 2006.

Stein, Perry. "Madame de Pompadour and the Harem Imagery at Bellevue." *Gazette des Beaux-Arts,* 6th period, 123 (1994): 29–44.

Stratmann-Döhler, Rosemary. "Les logements des courtesans à Versailles." *Eighteenth-Century Life* 17 (1993): 167–81.

Strong, Roy. *Feast: A History of Grand Eating.* London, 2002.

Taylor, Irene, and Alan Taylor, eds. *The Assassin's Cloak: An Anthology of the World's Greatest Diarists.* Edinburgh, 2003.

Têtart-Vittu, Françoise. "Grandes robes d'étiquette à la cour de Marie-Antoinette." *Versalia* 9 (2006): 142–55.

Thomas, Chantal. *The Wicked Queen: The Origins of the Myth of Marie-Antoinette.* Translated by Julie Rose. New York, 1999 (French original, 1989).

Thompson, Ian. *The Sun King's Garden: Louis XIV, André Le Nôtre and the Creation of the Gardens of Versailles.* London, 2006.

Thompson, J. M. *The French Revolution.* Stroud, 2003 (1st edition, 1943).

Tiberghien, Frédéric. *Versailles. Le chantier de Louis XIV 1662–1715.* Paris, 2002.

Tilly [Alexandre, comte de]. *Mémoires du comte Alexandre de Tilly.* Edited by Christian Melchior-Bonnet. Paris, 1986 (1st edition, 1965).

Tourzel [Louise-Élisabeth-Félicité, duchesse de]. *Mémoires de la duchesse de Tourzel.* Edited by Jean Chalon. Paris, 1969.

Trabouillet, L. *L'état de la France, contenant tous les Princes, Ducs et Pairs, et maréchaux de France, les Évêques, les Juridictions de la Roïaume; les Gouverneurs des provinces; les Chevaliers de trois Ordres du Roy.* 3 vols. Paris, 1699.

Véri [abbé de]. *Journal de l'abbé de Véri.* Edited by Jehan de Witte. 2 vols. Paris, n.d.

Verlet, Pierre. *Le château de Versailles.* Paris, 1985 (1st edition, 1961).

———. *Le mobilier royal français.* 4 vols. 2nd edition. Paris, 1990–99.

Vigarello, Georges. *Concepts of Cleanliness: Changing Attitudes in France Since the Middle Ages.* Translated by J. Birrell. Cambridge, 1988 (French original, 1985).

Visconti, Primo. *Mémoires sur la cour de Louis XIV (1673–1681).* Paris, 1988.

Voltaire. *Le siècle de Louis XIV.* Paris, 1845.

Walpole [Horace Walpole]. *Horace Walpole's Correspondence.* Edited by W. S. Lewis. 48 vols. Oxford and New Haven, 1937–83. See vol. 5, section 7 for Paris journals.

Walton, Guy. *Louis XIV's Versailles.* Chicago, 1986.

Watson, Alan (editor and translator). *The Digest of Justinian.* Philadelphia, 1998.

Weber, Caroline. *Queen of Fashion.* London, 2007.

Wootton, David, ed. *Divine Right and Democracy.* Harmondsworth and New York, 1986.

# INDEX

# Index

# Index

# Index

# Index

# Index

# Index

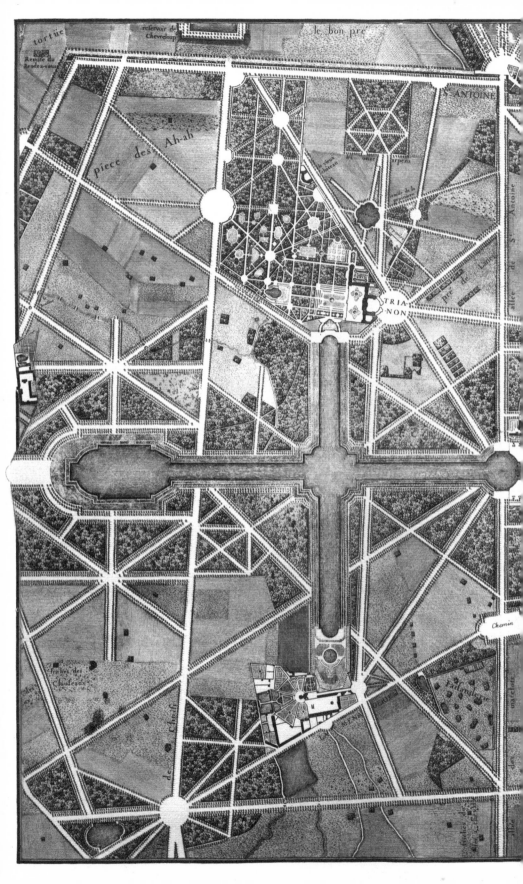